The Chieftains

The Authorized Biography

Also by John Glatt

*Rage & Roll; Bill Graham
and the Selling of Rock
Lost in Hollywood; the
Fast Times and Short Life
of River Phoenix*

The Chieftains

The Authorized Biography

by

John Glatt

St. Martin's Press ✻ New York

ISBN 0-312-16605-2

First published in the United Kingdom by Century Random
House UK Ltd

First U.S. Edition: September 1997

10   9   8   7   6   5   4   3   2   1

For Charles Comer – 'Showbiz is my Life'

Acknowledgements

First and foremost I'd like to thank all The Chieftains, their wives and families for generously allowing me into their lives and the many hours they spent patiently telling me their stories. I am particularly indebted to Paddy and Rita Moloney for placing their trust in me as well as the friendship and goodtimes I had while researching the book with Matt and Geraldine Molloy, Kevin and Joanie Conneff, Martin and Graínne Fay, Derek Bell and Seán and Marie Keane.

I am also grateful to the following for sharing their times and experiences with The Chieftains with me for this book: Bono, John Boorman, Garech Browne, Jackson Browne, Cara Butler, Maurice Cassidy, Danny Cleland, Dan Collins, Charles Comer, Ry Cooder, Eamon de Buitléar, Eamonn Doran, Dr John, Marianne Faithfull, James Galway, Art Garfunkel, Donny Golden, Nicholas Lord Gormonston, Nanci Griffith, Seamus Heaney, Don Henley, Tony Hollingsworth, Anjelica Huston, Christy Hyland, Jimmy Ibbottson, Trevor Jacobs, Colin James, Tom Jones, Michael Kamen, James Keane, Dolores Keane, Sen. Edward Kennedy, Tamara Drew Kinch, Larry Kirwan, Ian Lee, Jo Lustig, Gloria MacGowran, Tony MacMahon, Seán MacReamoinn, Joannie Madden, Mary Ellen at the Fitzpatrick, NYC, Brian Masterson, Dolly MacMahon, Paul McGuinness, Sarah McLachlan, Ronnie McShane, Burgess Meredith, Sandi Miller, Chesley Millikin, Aedin Moloney, John Montague, Helena Mulkerns, Carlos Nunez, Brian O'Neill, Seán Potts, Peadar and Eoghan Ó Riada, Keith Richards, Feargal Sharkey, Jim Sheridan, Pete Smith, Ricky Skaggs, Peter O'Toole, Michael Tubridy, Midge Ure and Gail Zappa.

I am also grateful to Steve Macklam, Sam Feldman, Charles Comer and Sinèad Murphy for their invaluable guidance and encouragement. My agent Peter Miller of PMA and his team of

Acknowledgements

Harrison, Yuri and Jodi all deserve a special mention for their unstinting support. I also owe an enormous debt to my editor Andy McKillop whose insight and advice were crucial to this project and his assistant Jo Tapsell for her patience. My thanks also go to my American editor Jim Fitzgerald and his team Reagan Good, Tara Schimming and Dana Albarella for all their invaluable help.

I would also like to thank: Char Power, Laurette Ziemer, David Hayes, Emily Winterson, Pat Molone, Stephanie Killoran, Dot Murphy, Valerie Reynolds, Christopher Bowen, Denise Childs, Fred and Linda Wehner, Wensley Clarkson, Patricia O'Connell, Laura Kenny, Treasa Ní Earcáin and Kate O'Dwyer of the Irish Traditional Music Archives, Vicky Herman, Kate Sullivan, Danny Trachentenberg, Cari Pokrassa, Lisa Vance Raby, Yasmin Brennan, Daphna Inbar, Roger Hitts, Annette Witheridge, Chris and Susan Comegys, Irene Stephenson of the *Irish Times*, Stuart Krichevsky, Pamela Dorman, Howie Finkelstein, Audrey and Mavis Hirschberg and the Molloydaies – Peter Molloy, Peter Flanagan and Liam Shannon.

Contents

Contents

'These guys are the real deal – They're Seriously Fiery'
Dr John, May 1995

Prologue

At 2:45 p.m. on Wednesday May 17th, 1995 a large coach drew up outside the Intercontinental Hotel in Hamilton Place just off London's Hyde Park. No one waiting in the hotel's smartly furnished lobby would have given a second glance to the six casually dressed, apparently bored, middle-aged men, aimlessly standing around by the front doors. Suddenly a much younger man burst through the doors announcing the arrival of the coach, and the members of the world-renowned traditional Irish musical group The Chieftains slowly shambled out of the hotel to make global television history.

The London Television Centre was a 20-minute drive across the River Thames on the South Bank. For the first time ever, America's top-rated *The Late Show With David Letterman* had moved across the Atlantic to do a week of shows in a bid to boost ratings during the all-important sweeps week. Not even Letterman's predecessor Johnny Carson had pulled off a live show from London and the CBS show's producers had booked a stellar guest list for this Wednesday.

The night would have a definite Irish theme. The legendary actor Peter O'Toole would make a grand entrance on a camel, followed by a one-off performance by The Chieftains with special guests Van Morrison and Sinéad O'Connor.

The organization and planning to get these giants of Irish music together on the same stage had been weeks in the making. The Letterman talent bookers had been trying to get Van Morrison to make a guest appearance for years but to no avail. The enigmatic superstar had finally agreed after hearing that his long-time friends and collaborators The Chieftains were to appear for an unprecedented second time in less than three months.

The plan was to perform Morrison's beautifully lyrical ballad *Have I Told You Lately That I Love You?*, a single from The Chieftains' new hit album *The Long Black Veil*. Sinéad O'Connor, who also appeared on the album, had been added at her own request so she could fulfil a lifelong ambition to sing with Morrison, her childhood hero.

During the short ride to the studio, The Chieftains' leader Paddy Moloney told the rest of the band how a nervous O'Connor had called him at 10:30 that morning about performing a song she'd never sung, in front of a satellite TV audience of millions around the world. Moloney had comforted her like the musical uncle he is to her, and arranged to send over the song's score which he later went through with her over the phone.

Waking up that Wednesday morning Moloney had felt dog tired after completing ten dates of an English tour in as many days. After the final show at Birmingham Town Hall the previous night, Moloney and the rest of the band had impetuously decided to drive the 100 miles down to London in the coach. Celebrating the end of the gruelling tour they drank beers and ate too much of the food prepared by their New Zealand chef Helen. On arrival in London some members of the band went out to a party while Moloney retired to the comfort of his suite at the Tara Hotel in Kensington.

The main tour had finished, but straight after appearing on the *Late Show* The Chieftains would board a flight to Los Angeles. For the next three days they would be fêted by Hollywood. They would play concerts at the premiere of Mel Gibson's new movie *Braveheart*, the two-million-dollar wedding of the Eagles' Don Henley, and film a concert for an upcoming *House of Blues* TV show.

Thirty-two years after forming The Chieftains, Paddy Moloney's international standing had never been higher. The mastermind of The Chieftains had seen his vision of popularizing Irish traditional music come to fruition and that night's Letterman show would rubber-stamp his group's global recognition. The surprisingly small man with a ready smile possessed a calm and tranquillity that betrayed little of the frenetic pace he maintained and the huge pressures he shouldered.

A self-confessed workaholic, there were never enough hours in the day for Moloney. Since the release of *The Long Black Veil*, a musical homage to The Chieftains from rock icons like The Rolling Stones, Sting and Mark Knopfler, Moloney had been in constant demand. In just four months *The Long Black Veil* had gone gold in countries all over the world, making it the band's most successful album to date and lifting them out of cult status into the pop mainstream.

The master of the Irish uilleann (or elbow) pipes now moved effortlessly from playing traditional Celtic music to composing full-orchestral symphonies and film scores to travelling around the world in search of other musical styles and masters to play with. Future projects included a concert with Luciano Pavarotti and scoring a song for the new Disney compilation album *Winnie The Pooh*.

When they arrived at the television studios The Chieftains were hustled into the green room where they were greeted by Van Morrison. Always unpredictable, Morrison seemed unusually cheerful when he greeted Moloney. 'He was in a very funny mood,' said Moloney a few days later. 'But that's Van. You can never predict what will happen, but that's what makes the man tick.'

The 4:00 p.m. soundcheck went off without a hitch. The computer-generated stage plot, drafted by Chieftains' road manager and general chaperone Dan Cleland, was agreed by all camps and Morrison's duet with O'Connor worked wonderfully in rehearsal.

Back in the green room Peter O'Toole arrived and started reminiscing with Moloney about their old days in Dublin. Then the strikingly tall but now frail-looking, white-haired actor told Moloney how he knew the bagpipes and asked to try out his set.

'I was afraid,' said Moloney. 'The reeds are very temperamental and easily destroyed. I think he was hoping he might be able to play it on the Letterman show.'

Instead Moloney rigged up a makeshift set of pipe reeds and O'Toole silenced the green room as he triumphantly piped a tune to a round of applause.

'I wound up in Paddy's dressing room with all the boys and that delightful singer Sinéad,' says Peter O'Toole who is a big fan of The Chieftains' music. 'I had a go on the pipes and of course I was assured by his companions that I was raising a couple of snakes but that was as far as I got.'

The green room had a party atmosphere. At intermittent periods talk show host David Letterman, who was getting pumped up for the show with loud rock music, came running out of his dressing room to welcome guests. Van Morrison was clearly enjoying himself, drinking and cracking jokes with the various Chieftains scattered around the room.

'At one point Van just turned to me and said, "How old are you?," ' remembered Danny Cleland, who was born the year Moloney founded The Chieftains. 'I said, "I'm 32." Van goes, "Jeez, I'd thought you'd be at least 50 by now working for The Chieftains." Paddy just burst out laughing. Van was poking fun at everyone.'

Ninety minutes later the show was well underway. As The Chieftains took their positions on stage for their live performance, during the final break in the show, Van Morrison was poised offstage to walk on with Sinéad O'Connor. Wearing a huge wide-brimmed hat, dark glasses and a black full-length coat, Morrison had artfully asked Letterman to display his upcoming album *Days Like This* instead of *The Long Black Veil*.

'Typical Van,' said Moloney later. 'He got someone to put up his new album and we never got mentioned at all.'

When Letterman introduced the superstar ensemble as 'some of Ireland's greatest musicians' millions of viewers all over the world saw Moloney play the serene introduction to *Have I Told You Lately* on his tin whistle, as Morrison escorted Sinéad O'Connor to the stage.

The first sign that something was not quite right was when Morrison delivered the first line of the song and started laughing, totally throwing his partner.

'Sinéad was quite frightened when she saw him in such form,' said Moloney. 'He was stumbling around a bit.'

Ignoring what they'd rehearsed, Morrison began singing Sinéad's harmony parts and burst into his trademark scatting during The Chieftains' musical interlude as he began trying to conduct them with extravagant waves of his hands. By this time Sinéad was giggling and Moloney, fiddler Seán Keane and flautist Matt Molloy could barely keep straight faces.

In a grand finale Van Morrison lunged towards Sinéad's microphone, missed and almost fell over, prompting the alarmed singer to cry 'Oops!' Throughout it all The Chieftains never missed a beat as they played straight men to Morrison's antics. As the performance finished, a delighted Letterman walked out exclaiming, 'Thank you gentlemen. Lovely. It was beautiful.' Letterman would later call it the best musical performance that he had ever seen on the show.

Back in the green room a happy Van Morrison rushed over to

Moloney and hugged him, saying it was time to make a follow-up album to their hugely successful 1987 collaboration *Irish Heartbeat*.

'We've had some incredible moments over the last seven or eight years,' said a weary Moloney. 'But the last album took two years off my life and I don't know if I could do another one.'

Later, the boyish-looking Chieftain harpist and group comedian, Derek Bell, affectionately known as 'Ding Dong', put the whole thing into his own unique perspective, by saying, 'Well, we played the piece extremely well and nobody disgraced themselves which was a big relief. One realizes that we were on an extremely prestigious thing that millions of people all over the world were watching, probably to their own detriment. I find it quite frightening that we have taken off into such mega-stars.'

PART 1

1

Planting the Seeds

In 1792 the Belfast Harpers Society invited folklore collector Edward Bunting to organize a festival of Irish Music. Fearing that the traditional harp music they loved was dying, the Society turned to Bunting in desperation hoping he could turn the tide. A natural promoter, Bunting decided to stage a play-off between ten of Ireland's best harpers as the festival climax.

The festival was a great success, drawing hundreds of musicians from all over Ireland. Dublin people flocked to an array of concerts and performances and there were also musical workshops where aspiring young harpers could get tips from the masters.

When the competition judges finally announced the result of the harp competition the three grand winners were awarded £10 a year each for life. More importantly though for posterity, Bunting and his staff met with each harper in turn to write down all their music in a collection and preserve it for future generations of Irish musicians.

Two hundred years later Bunting's musical descendant Paddy Moloney would feel compelled to repay the debt by commemorating the bi-centenary of the Festival with a gala concert pairing The Chieftains with the modern Belfast Harp Orchestra.

'It's in memory of Edward Bunting,' explained Moloney at the time. 'He was a great collector of Irish music and he'd known all those rogues of harpers as I like to call them.'

Throughout The Chieftains' 33-year career championing traditional music, Moloney had often visited the rich treasure trove of the Bunting collection for material. Now in a delicious irony The Chieftains would record the very same songs preserved by Edward Bunting in a tribute called *The Celtic Harp* to world acclaim. The Bunting album would bridge two centuries to finally fulfil the

Belfast Harpers Society's prayers by taking Irish music soaring to new heights by winning a Grammy award in Hollywood.

But Irish traditional music is ephemeral and without boundaries. Faithfully passed down orally from generation to generation, the music has provided a stirring backdrop for the history of Ireland. It has given the Irish hope and inspiration through eight centuries of colonization, the 1845 holocaust of famine and continuous poverty and hardship.

During the great wave of emigration that followed the Irish famine of the 1840s, when millions abandoned their homeland, Irish sons and daughters faithfully took their music with them and transplanted it across the world where it took roots and grew. Ironically this was at a time when many Irish people turned their backs on their music and culture. It would be another two decades before musical pioneers like The Clancy Brothers, The Chieftains and The Dubliners would popularize traditional music again in Ireland and take it around the world.

* * *

Paddy Moloney was born on August 1st, 1938 in the north Dublin suburb of Donnycarney. His father John, a sergeant in the Irish Army, was a decent bagpiper and his mother Catherine played accordion and sang.

Tragedy hit the Moloneys a year before Paddy's birth when his eight-year-old brother John was knocked over by a motorbike and sidecar, which went out of control killing him and another boy as they were out walking. It was the first motorbike accident in Ireland and made all the Dublin papers. As a child Paddy found himself constantly in the shadow of his late brother, who was always spoken about in the house as if he was still alive, as he grew up with his two elder sisters, Mary and Esther. A younger sister, Sheila, was born in 1941 as John Moloney was preparing himself to serve in the Second World War.

Right from the cradle Paddy, always known as Pat by the family, found himself surrounded by Irish music. His aunt Elizabeth and her children and their friends would regularly come to the Moloney home for musical evenings. Everyone played an instrument or did a special party piece as entertainment and Paddy was often rocked to sleep by the fire to the radio programmes *The Ballad Makers, Saturday Night* and *Round the Fire.*

Christmas was a magical time in the Moloney household and Paddy's very first memory at the age of three is of his mother packing the brown case, which she still has, to spend the holidays at his grandparents' little farm, high up in the Slieve Bloom Mountains in Ballyfin, Co. Laois.

Paddy remembers, 'I saw my mother put some jelly into the case and when she wasn't looking I dug in and picked open the cardboard box and ate some. I put it back and thought that was the end of it.'

When they arrived at the farm, his grandmother Julia Conroy helped his mother unpack while a guilty Paddy sheepishly looked on.

Recalls Paddy: 'My grandmother suddenly screamed, "My God, Kate, a mouse has got into your case."

'I didn't say anything. I was terrified that they'd catch me. They kept saying, "Oh, it was a mouse all right." They knew darn well who had done it.'

Twice a year, during Easter and the three-month summer holidays, Paddy and his sisters would stay with Granny Conroy and her husband Stephen, who was a concert flautist. Once the children arrived in the country off came their shoes and socks and they would go barefoot everywhere.

The only time they were expected to dress up was for Mass on Sunday and holy days, which were serious formal family occasions. Out came their best clothes, everyone would be scrubbed clean and the smell of boot polish would permeate the farm house as Paddy and his sisters shone their shoes to perfection.

Then the Conroy's old horse Paddy would be brought out to the front of the cottage and harnessed to a large trap. There would be stifled giggles as the children watched their huge Granny struggling to get into the trap which sunk down measurably under her weight. Eventually when everyone was safely packed into the trap, they rode the five miles downhill to the village church and tethered the horse to a big metal ring on a long wall alongside the other horses.

During the summer holidays so many members of the family would stay at the Conroys that three children would often have to cram into the old settle bed with straw mattress. But after a day running around outside, they all slept like logs.

The first time Paddy ever heard the sound of the pipes was from his uncle Stephen, an excellent bagpiper who had won an all-Ireland competition in his youth. He would arrive early and march up and down the kitchen playing beautifully crafted solo pieces which rang out through the cottage. Sometimes, late at night, Uncle Stephen would go out to a small wood behind the cottage and play soothing lullabies to the infant Paddy and send him into a deep sleep.

At weekends the Conroys would host hooleys or parties in which all the children took part. These were informal and friends and neighbours would turn up with flutes, melodeons, the odd fiddle and spoons. They always started at 8:00 in the evening and the music and dancing often went on until 8:00 in the morning with two tea sittings in the middle of the night. If the hooley happened to finish on Sunday morning everyone would rush off and go straight to Mass.

'We'd dance all night,' Paddy recalls. 'And it was wild dancing. Unbelievable. Finally, at 6:00 or 7:00 in the morning there was always old-time waltzes to finish off the dances.'

But on special occasions there would be well organized house dances that everyone heard about in advance by word of mouth. On the appointed night Paddy's seven aunts and uncles and untold numbers of cousins and friends would pile into the cottage for a night of traditional music and dancing. Often so many turned up that the party spilled out into the farmyard.

Although just 60 miles from Dublin, daily life in the Slieve Bloom Mountains was unaffected by the outside world and had remained unchanged for centuries. One of the most popular pastimes was affectionately referred to as 'rambling.' At any time of the day or night a neighbour might arrive at the front door breathlessly exclaiming, 'God save all here,' and just walk in, sit down and join in the stories of what was going on, particularly in the area. Under the unwritten rules of Irish hospitality everyone was always welcome.

Grandfather Conroy often took Paddy off rambling to friends' houses where he played tunes on the flute which the young boy picked up by ear and would put to good use years later. Those days spent with his grandfather were some of the happiest he would ever know and he experienced an inner peace he would never forget.

'These were the best days of my life,' admits Moloney today. 'So simple. Nature. Little places to play. Going down to the little river to wash. Little things like that were so important.'

Paddy and his grandfather regularly visited an eccentric old flute player called Fint Lanham to share tunes. It was well known that Lanham kept his flute in the river weighted down by a large stone, believing it would improve the sound. When Lanham's flute went missing he became convinced that Paddy had stolen it and soon the local Garda sergeant was cycling up the steep hill to the farm on a scorching hot summer's day to investigate. The young boy was terrified that he might go to prison but the highly amused policeman was never in any doubt that this was another of the old man's fantasies. The flute was found behind the Sacred Heart picture hanging on the wall. That was the last time they ever rambled to Lanham's house.

Growing up, Paddy had an inexhaustible curiosity to find out as much as he could about the world. He was lucky to have a willing and exceptional early teacher in his grandmother. Julia Conroy was self-educated and highly respected in the community and known as a great reader. She had a huge collection of books on all subjects and delighted in reading out loud to Paddy and the other neighbouring children.

Although she lived in a remote area high up on a mountain, Julia Conroy had her own distinct worldly philosophy about life. Her views and ideas were an enormous influence on her grandchildren. Indeed, one of the first songs Paddy ever remembers hearing was his grandmother singing her favorite song, *Little Maid from Malabar*, as she sat on top of an old wooden churn during one of the house parties. Half a century later The Chieftains would record it with Ry Cooder on *The Long Black Veil* album after renaming it *The Coast of Malabar* as Paddy feared 'Little Maid' would have a different meaning outside Ireland.

At the age of eight Paddy went to his first wake after the death of a neighbour while he was staying in Co. Laois. 'There was the body laid out on the bed and I was sitting down saying a prayer. Then one of the older mourners kicked me up the arse with his boot and I went flying onto the corpse. That was the sort of irreverent humour they had. I had nightmares for ages. But it was also a wonderful lesson to learn about life and death at such an early age.'

For two weeks every summer Paddy's father John Moloney would turn up in Ballyfin to visit his family during his annual vacation from the army. As money was so tight he used to get up at 5:00 a.m. and cycle the 60 miles to the Slieve Bloom Mountains arriving at 8:00 that night. He was a good father and provider and would often send little parcels containing presents for his children who would always be waiting hopefully at the top of the lane for the postman.

Paddy spent most of his childhood in Donnycarney where the main sources of music were the wireless and an old wind-up HMV gramophone which he still has. As an infant he was allowed to wind up the gramophone when friends and family came around for dances. The Moloney's had a collection of old 78's ranging from piping soloists to John McCormack and pop records of the 1940s as well as old songs like *I'm Looking Over a Four Leaf Clover*.

In those days, although there was little Irish music on the radio, RTE did broadcast an Irish Ballad programme every Saturday night and a half-hour-long live Ceili Band Session on Sunday nights. Although they were on at 9:30 p.m., and Paddy was tucked up in bed upstairs, he and his sister Sheila had no trouble hearing the music through the floor as the radio was always turned up to full volume.

By now Paddy was smitten by traditional music and knew he wanted to be a musician one day. Possessing a rich imagination he often daydreamed about the origins of the music, where it came from and how it found its way to other countries.

'There's an old Irish poem that makes me feel how far back our traditional music goes,' says Moloney. '*Thánaig Long o Valparaiso* ("A ship came from Valparaso and they raised the sails in the bay.") I used to conjure up all these great ideas about where the ship came from and the music it brought such as the ballad *The Coast of Malabar*, and what its connection was with Ireland. It was magical for me.'

Paddy's first musical landmark came when he finally convinced his mother to let him try her single-row melodeon, which was always kept well out of reach on the top of a high dresser in the kitchen. Finally Catherine Moloney gave in to his pleas and her four-year-old son played his first real musical instrument. Just recalling the experience today sends Paddy into ecstatic reminiscences. 'The tune I tried to play was a simple version of *Roll Out the Barrel.* You see, the first four bars could be played on one note, by pulling it in and out. Oh God, the smell of that melodeon was great.'

Catherine immediately recognized her son had a rare musical gift and from then on did everything she could to develop it. That Christmas Eve she took Paddy to see Santa Claus and then bought him a white tin whistle with a shiny red top for one shilling and nine pence in Bolgers in North Earl Street, Dublin. As soon as they got on the bus to go home, he started to teach himself the scale. As they got off, another passenger, unknown to Paddy, said 'Keep at it, son, and you'll soon get the high D.' The passenger was Leo Rowsome, who was later to became Paddy's pipes teacher.

'It was the greatest treasure I ever had,' says Moloney today.

Now that he had power of expressing the music he heard in his head through an instrument, Paddy Moloney would be unstoppable.

* * *

As he became more accomplished on the tin whistle, Paddy began to realize the potential power of his music and how to use it to his best advantage. Having just started at the St Mary's School in the nearby district of Marino, Paddy, who was far smaller than his classmates, found he could easily counter any potential bullying, and ensure popularity at the same time, simply by playing his whistle, giving recitals and acting out songs.

'I was like the pied piper,' he says. 'I used to get all the gang out in the avenue after school. I'd play the whistle and have everyone marching after me in a procession.'

Paddy's school teacher, Brother Seamus McCaffrey, had a love of traditional music and took the promising student under his wing, teaching him the tonic solfa notation system, which he still relies on. Employing the Mary Poppins' method 'Do Re Me Fa So La Ti Do' Paddy could now instantly pick up tunes and write them down even while they were being played.

Musically he was always at or near the top of the class. With his classmates he spent an hour a day on their tonic solfa. When the feared school inspector made his annual visit it would always be young Moloney who was called out to the front of the class to demonstrate tonic solfa to perfection.

Brother McCaffrey, who has since left the brotherhood and got married, encouraged Paddy to join the school band run by Brother Forrestal. And it was when he heard fellow pupil Leon Rowsome playing uilleann pipes Paddy had an epiphany. He knew at once this was the instrument he was born to play.

The uilleann pipes were developed in the 18th century as a more sophisticated indoor version of the old Irish war pipes, once banned by Queen Elizabeth I who saw them as a threat. Worked by a bag filled by a bellows and not a blow pipe, there is a chanter or melody pipe which is fully chromatic and gives a range of two octaves. Regulators and drones can be added to accompany the melody.

Leon's father Leo Rowsome was then known in Ireland as 'The King of the Pipers' and, as well as making uilleann pipes, he led his own quartet of pipers who had a regular half-hour programme on RTE. Once a week after dinner the whole Moloney family would dutifully gather around the radio in the parlour to listen to the Leo Rowsome Pipes Quartet.

By this time Paddy was itching to get his own pipes and per-suaded his mother to take him to see Leo Rowsome, who also lived in Donnycarney, for advice. Rowsome was encouraging but said a practice set cost £5 which was a whole week's Army pay for John Moloney who was constantly struggling to make ends meet.

'I tried everything to get round my father,' recalls Paddy. 'He kept saying "Pat, we just don't have the money." But my mother and father scraped and scrounged and somehow got the money together.'

Catherine Moloney arranged to pay Leo Rowsome for the practice pipes in two installments and enrolled her son for the maestro's Friday evening classes at the School of Music in Chatham Street.

Every Friday evening Catherine took her son to the school where he'd take down a new tune for 15 minutes and then play Rowsome the one he'd learned the week before. The pressure was enormous as Rowsome could only devote half an hour to each student. Many lacked the required dedication and dropped out.

After the lesson Paddy and his mother would either have tea in Bewleys or dash over to the Gaiety Theatre near the school to try to catch their favourite comedians, such as Jimmy O'Dea or Maureen Potter in a variety show. Although money was scarce Catherine would find a shilling each for them to go up in the gods, while Paddy ran on ahead up flights of stairs to get their seats. It was while watching the comedians and other vaudeville acts at the Gaiety that Paddy developed a taste for the theatre and a love of performing. His father constantly took his children to pantos and plays at the Abbey Theatre. Years later, he did the same for his grandchildren.

The first summer Paddy proudly took his new practice pipes to his grandparents he caused a stir as uilleann pipes were rare in that area. His Uncle Stephen was delighted that his nephew was following in his piping footsteps and brought the boy along to meet the fellow members of the Ballyfin Pipe Band to which he belonged. Paddy would spend summer evenings rehearsing with them in a small band hall and became their official mascot.

When they marched up and down the main streets of neighbouring towns, such as Roscrea and Birr, Paddy was their secret fund-raising weapon. He would sit on the huge bass drum in the middle of the square playing his pipes and drawing a huge crowd that threw coins in a hat besides him. His first ever public performances were triumphs and raised record donations.

* * *

In 1947 Leo Rowsome felt Paddy was ready to make his official public debut with 20 other pipers at an open air concert at Phoenix Park – just a few yards away from where The Chieftains would play for Pope John Paul II almost 40 years later in front of an audience of 1.3 million people. A picture taken of the concert shows Rowsome conducting the diminutive Paddy, who's wearing short trousers with his legs dangling two or three inches off the ground.

'I was so proud,' says Paddy. 'This was my first concert and it was such a great feeling. It was so important.'

By now Paddy had become the leading light in the St Mary's School band and was often allowed to conduct. And after a year of piping lessons, Rowsome entered his most promising pupil in a major piping competition in Dublin called the Feis Atha Cliath. Just ten years old, Paddy was entered for the under-14's piping section and was by far the youngest of 20 competitors. He came in fourth and was devastated.

'It was very competitive and the nerves were terrible,' Paddy recalls today. 'It was very important to get up there and compete. I could never accept failure.'

11

Feeling disgusted with himself Paddy redoubled his efforts, putting in even more hours of practising every day. He easily won the competition the next year. Paddy received a standing ovation from the crowd and a delighted Rowsome lifted the little boy onto his shoulders for a triumphant lap of honour around the hall.

Closely watching Paddy's winning performance was another ambitious young Dublin musician and future Chieftain named Seán Potts. A couple of years older, Seán had already heard Paddy's piping and had been highly impressed. As Paddy, the last to perform, mounted the stage, Seán told a friend, 'Here's this little bastard who's going to win. He's fantastic.' After the performance, Seán's friend commented, 'He's been on this Earth before'.

By this time Paddy had become the Dublin College of Music's star pupil, always representing the Piping School in the annual college concert. The piece he always played was *Carolan's Concerto*, which would later become a highlight of The Chieftains' repertoire and help a new generation discover the long forgotten works of the blind 17th century harp player. He had also started writing his own music. At the age of 12, his first proper composition was *The Ivy Waltz*.

After two years of weekly lessons at the School Of Music, Paddy was ready to move on to bigger things. Every Monday night Paddy would visit his neighbour the piper Peadar Flynn at 25 Oak Road, Donnycarney for his regular weekly sessions, which would attract some of Ireland's greatest pipers. Flynn, who had lost a finger during the Irish War of Independence in which he'd served as an officer in the volunteers, had turned his home into a haven for pipers.

At the age of 11 Paddy was introduced to these extraordinary sessions which served as a master class for him. Piping legends such as Séamus Ennis, Willie Clancy, Dan Dowd and Tommy Reck often attended and although still in short trousers Paddy Moloney never shied away from playing in the masters' company and duly impressed them with his style and technique.

'I became the living hope for the pipers. The saviour of the pipes to be,' states Paddy. 'I was one of only a handful of pipers showing any promise. They'd always try to help me out saying, "Try it this way" or "Try these pipes. See what you think of this one." I loved it and those evenings of music changed my life.'

It was at Peadar Flynn's that Paddy picked up much of his music and helped to lay the groundwork for his later career. He learned hundreds of traditional tunes from the greats and, with his photographic memory, once he heard a tune, it would never be forgotten.

Although even then Paddy Moloney stood out among the other young pipers as having the potential for greatness, where was there to go? As the 1950s dawned few people in Dublin had any use for traditional music and commonsense told him he didn't have a chance in hell of ever making a living playing his country's music.

'Playing music was always a hobby to me,' says Paddy. 'Every Friday when my mother brought me to the school of music she always used to say, "Learn music but never forget you have to get a decent job." '

2

Learning the Ropes

In the 1940s and 1950s, traditional music had little following in Ireland, even though popular songs were taught in schools. Surviving in rural pockets dotted around Ireland, traditional music became parochial, varying in accent from one community to the next.

In Dublin it was driven deep underground. Seldom performed in public, traditional music was generally banned in public houses and the only places to hear it were at ceilis, private house parties or sessions like Peadar Flynn's.

'There was no general interest,' remembers veteran radio broadcaster Ciarán Mac Mathúna. 'You had these people who quietly went to one another's houses with fiddles under their coats in case anyone would see them. Those were interesting days.'

The new rock'n'roll music from America was in fashion, and for a young musician to be caught with a tin whistle or fiddle by his school mates laid him open to ridicule. Like a secret society a daring new generation of traditional musicians was struggling against the tide without any encouragement or support.

'Our music was often scorned at as *Culchie* music for tinkers,' remembers future Chieftain Seán Keane, who grew up in Dublin in the 1950s. 'To be seen carrying a fiddle around made you look like a sissy, but to be involved in Irish music was it altogether. You were the odd one out.'

In 1951 the old Pipers' Club in Thomas Street, Dublin, realizing traditional music was close to extinction due to the apathy of the young, took decisive action and formed Comhaltas Ceoltóirí Éireann, with an urgent mission to revive the music. 'The music was brilliant,' remembers Paddy. 'Leo Rowsome used to be the mainstay piper there and he'd play for a whole hour and then there'd be a gathering of other musicians who would play. And it developed and got bigger and eventually grew into this brilliant music festival which attracted musicians from all over Ireland.' Concentrating on young people, it established a regular network of regional and national music festivals and competitions called fleadhanna cheoil, where musicians could spend a weekend meeting each other, competing and playing.

The first fleadh ceoil was held in Mullingar in 1951 and attracted just 200 people, including 13-year-old Paddy Moloney, who was one of a group of 14 Leo Rowsome's students attending this milestone event. Kitted out in matching double breasted flannel suits with long trousers, made by Rowsome's tailor brother, the group traveled down to Mullingar confident of beating all opposition. But disaster struck when Paddy's uncle Jim, who lived in Mullingar, organized a house dance for the visiting musicians.

'What happened to me was terrible,' said Paddy. 'I, of course, sat up playing all night and I went into the competition the next morning with my eyes half closed. I came second. I was disgusted with myself. I only got second out of 26 because I was so tired as I'd only had a couple of hours sleep.

'I made sure I was in good form the next year when I won my first all-Ireland medal.'

Over the next few years the fleadhanna cheoil flourished and provided the fertile breeding ground for many traditional groups who would later find international fame. Finally traditional musicians realized they were not alone and there were many like-minded people sharing their passion. This created a strong common bond between the young musicians who began to meet regularly to socialize and play together.

By this time Moloney had started going with Peadar Flynn to the newly established Pipers' Club in Church Street, which had become one of Dublin's regular venues for traditional music sessions. As word spread about the club, up to a hundred musicians from around Dublin would crowd into the tiny room to perform.

At first heads would turn when a serious-looking small boy in short trousers was led in by his mother. But it wasn't long before the older musicians recognized the musical brilliance and sheer determination of the young Moloney and made him their musical son. Initially Paddy had to be content to just sit and watch the other musicians play, but soon he was allowed to play tin whistle and eventually he began to show his prowess on the uilleann pipes.

The Pipers' Club created a lot of interest among other Dublin artists and writers. Brendan Behan was a regular visitor and some years later Paddy would accompany him on the tin whistle as he sang the Gaelic ballad *Druimfhionn Donn Dilis* to rousing applause. As Moloney became more proficient, he scraped together the money to buy himself a second-hand set of pipes, with the full set of keys and regulators, for £30 – the same set he still uses at concerts today, more than 40 years later.

After a successful army career, John Moloney was offered a commission but that would have meant relocating out of Dublin, so he stayed on as a sergeant in the army until the late 1940s.

'He was an amazing man,' says Paddy. 'A week after he retired out of the army he found a job immediately in the Irish Glass Bottle Company, where he stayed until he was 65 and got his pension. One of the biggest regrets of my life is that I never ever heard him play the bagpipes.'

At the age of 16 in 1954 Moloney left school with an impressive character reference from his teacher Brother S. Ó Slartara, after easily passing his Primary Certificate Examination.

'Patrick Moloney is a boy of excellent ability,' wrote Brother Ó Slartara. 'Most regular, punctual and industrious. He is a self respecting, trustworthy boy and seems to have come from an excellent home. It gives me great pleasure to recommend him for any position to which he is suited.'

On the strength of the reference Paddy began working for Baxendales, Ireland's second biggest suppliers of builders' materials, as a junior accountant and bookkeeper. His wages were 36 shillings a week, out of which he gave his mother 30 shillings, spent two shillings on bus fares and saved the rest. Paddy still has a tiny ledger from his first days at work.

Eager to succeed in his new career, that September Moloney ambitiously enrolled in night school to study accountancy but soon found the studies clashed with his growing musical commitments.

'I was doing grand for the first three months,' says Moloney. 'But then the Christmas disaster set in. There'd be music sessions and parties. The music just totally took over so I never did complete my career as an accountant. Thank God.'

* * *

Although Michael Tubridy was born in the centre of traditional music in the port of Kilrush, Co. Clare, there was nothing in his early childhood to suggest him as a future Chieftain. His parents were farmers. His mother played some concertina, but the only music Michael heard as a young child was a collection of old gramophone records which were mainly traditional.

Michael recalls, 'I grew up in that atmosphere of listening to the music and I learned to like it. There weren't any classes or any sessions in those days.'

There were always instruments such as mouth organs and jew's harps lying around in the Tubridy home and Michael would spend hours every day with the local musicians learning bits and pieces of music and trying out new tunes.

When he was 13 his brother Seán joined the local defence force pipe band and proudly brought his new bagpipes home. Michael loved the pipes and started learning marches at home and, although he was underage, was allowed to join the band when he was 15 as they were short of recruits.

Michael was delighted to discover that some of the older band members played traditional music and naturally gravitated to them. One boy called Micky O'Shea played hornpipes and started teaching traditional tunes to Tubridy who had no instrument to play them on. As practice chanters were so expensive he cleverly adapted an ordinary Clarks' tin whistle by boring a hole in it to give the required high D note. Michael learned fast and within a year he was confidently playing at house dances with other local musicians.

'The main reason for playing the music was dancing,' says Tubridy. 'The two of them went together.'

Leaving home at 17, Tubridy headed to London where he got himself a job as a fitter's mate doing plumbing and pipework all over England. One day Michael was strolling through London's Petticoat Lane Market on a Sunday morning when he passed a stall and noticed a man haggling for an old timber flute. 'He walked off when they couldn't agree a price. I picked it up and I tried to play but I couldn't get anything out of it as I'd never played one before.'

Nevertheless Tubridy bought the flute for just 30 shillings. It was only much later when he was in The Chieftains that he found out it was a Randall & Rose flute from the late 1820s and worth a lot of money.

17

'I've been playing it ever since,' he said.

After a year in England, in summer 1954, Tubridy was accepted for an engineering course at University College, Dublin. He soon fell in with a group of other students who played traditional music and they started going to each other's digs swapping tunes and playing at parties around the university.

Then the softly spoken Tubridy and his friends heard about the Thomas Street Pipers' Club and decided to go. One of the first musicians that Tubridy met was a young piper called Paddy Moloney and a 24-year-old tin whistle player called Seán Potts, whose legendary grandfather John was said to have brought 'the music' of Co. Wexford to Dublin a hundred years earlier.

* * *

As a third generation member of one of Ireland's most celebrated musical families, Seán Potts was literally raised in the music. The Potts' home in the Liberties area of Dublin was always full of musicians and from the time he was a baby, Seán was taken to the Friday night music sessions at his grandfather's house.

'My father John handed down the music he heard from my grandfather to me and in turn I've handed it down to my son,' says Seán.

At the age of four Seán was given a small fiddle by his grandmother but never bothered with it. When he was ten his grandfather gave him a set of uilleann pipes but although he had a few lessons to his great disappointment he could never quite master them.

'The tin whistle seemed to come without any effort at all,' says Potts. 'It just came to me like that without any practice or lessons or anything.'

As a youngster at school just after the Second War, Seán Potts was careful not to tell his school friends he played traditional music.

'I was very shy about it,' he remembers. 'If the tin whistle fell out of my pocket I would be very embarrassed.'

Potts loved meeting musicians who had come up from the country so he could play and learn new tunes. As a teenager he joined the Youth Hostel Organization and ventured out to traditional musical strongholds like Clare and Wexford to explore the music further.

'I went all over the country visiting local musicians of note,' says

Potts. 'We had cheap accommodation and I was seeking the music all the time.'

He also developed a love of ceili dancing and loved to attend the Gaelic League-run Sunday night dances at Dublin's Mansion House. As a regular on the traditional music scene Potts was well aware of the young Paddy Moloney and had seen him many times over the years. However, it wasn't until the mid-1950s, when a flute player from Sligo called John Egan started a rival Pipers' Club in Church Street, that Potts really got to know his future Chieftains colleagues Paddy Moloney and Michael Tubridy.

The big attraction of the new Pipers' Club was its Wednesday sessions that attracted many musicians who happened to be in Dublin on business.

Paddy Moloney: 'I absolutely adored the Church Street nights. I went along there every Wednesday night and I loved listening to the old musicians. They made a special feature of asking me to perform with me being the youngest member of the congregation.'

Seán Potts says he always tried to corner Paddy for a session and, as tin whistle players, the two soon developed an astonishing musical rapport which would become an integral part of the early Chieftains.

'Paddy's piping was brilliant and his tin whistle playing was wonderful,' says Potts. 'We used to play off each other and there was a unique understanding between us from the start. I could feel his music which is a great thing when two people are playing together.'

But the musical rebel in Moloney wasn't content just to play the old style traditional Irish music and was itching to try something new. A natural leader, he began forming a series of groups to experiment with different combinations of instruments to reflect the music he heard in his head.

'I was never happy with the thump, thump, thump and all the instruments playing together in what I called "thrash the beetle",' says Moloney. 'I always felt that there had to be something extra put in it.'

To experiment with his new sound he started a quartet with Michael Tubridy on flute, Anne Walsh on piano and Jack Dervan on fiddle. The group would meet for practice sessions at Paddy's house and play around Dublin. But they also went all over Ireland for shows that often turned into adventures. He also helped form the Shannonside Ceili Band.

'These were great outings,' said Tubridy. 'All right, we used to get about £1 each for the night, but we loved playing together and you'd always have plenty of stories to tell after the ceili.'

One night the Shannonside Ceili Band had a Sunday night gig way out in Upperchurch in Tipperary but Anne Walsh couldn't come. Desperate for a pianist Paddy enlisted the help of his old school friend Leon Rowsome. The brother of one of the band was a grocer and drove everyone to Upperchurch, which was 100 miles from Dublin.

'When we arrived we stopped to ask this woman the way to where we were supposed to be playing,' said Tubridy. 'She looked at us and said, "Oh, you're the band playing at the ceili?" We said we were and she replied, "I don't know whether it'll be on or not because two people died in Upperchurch today." '

The ceili did go on, but unfortunately when they got there, there was no piano. However, as the ceili was to raise funds for the church, the local parish priest had agreed to lend his piano. 'We were curious when we heard an unearthly noise from the road outside,' Paddy laughs in remembering the incident. 'The piano was being pushed up the main street to the hall. By the time it was lifted on to the stage it was horribly out of tune, so Leon spent the night dancing.' After the ceili finished at three in the morning the band members drove off back to Dublin but the van ran out of petrol in Naas outside the city and they had to hitchhike back. Moloney just made it back in time to be behind his desk to start work Monday morning at Baxendales.

As a teenager with boundless energy, Paddy Moloney burned the candle at both ends and although he was out late every night playing music with his various groups he never missed a day's work. But, never seeing the music as anything more than a hobby, he never dreamed that he could ever make it his profession.

Moloney loved to branch out and dabble in different styles. It was the age of skiffle when all it took was a couple of guitars, a washboard and a ukulele to start a group. Paddy was most impressed with Lonnie Donnegan's skiffle hit *Putting on the Agony*, which had stayed at No. 1 for weeks. This led to one of his more memorable early musical experiments in the heavily country-influenced skiffle with his guitar-playing friend Charlie Tindall, who sang Hank Williams' songs and had the distinction of being the only guitarist ever allowed to join the Pipers' Club.

His group The Three Squares caused a minor sensation when they appeared at a Guinness annual concert in the mid-1950s, wearing cowboy hats and striped shirts. To the horror of the purists they played an eclectic mixture of skiffle, country and western and traditional Irish music. As a highlight of the performance Paddy donned a long hillbilly beard for his solo ukulele spot in *Putting on the Agony*.

'I still have my washboard and ukulele I played in the Three Squares,' says Paddy proudly. 'We even had three little red squares painted on the washboard.'

Paddy also played George Formby-type ukulele for a group called The Happy Wanderers, who at one time played five concerts a week for fun. Additionally, Moloney was later the driving force behind the Loch Gamha Ceili Band, which included his friends Éamon de Buitléar, Tony MacMahon, Seán Bracken and the late Paddy Bán Ó Broin.

Every Monday, Moloney would drive out to Bray outside Dublin on his new green motorbike to teach de Buitléar new tunes to play. In exchange for the lessons, de Buitléar used to take Moloney out hunting.

'I was mad about guns at the time,' remembers Paddy. 'We used to go out into the forest shooting wood pigeons. And then we'd play a few tunes.'

Tony MacMahon, who also played accordion, remembers Paddy visiting him one day at his digs at traditional pianist Bridie Lafferty's in Home Farm Road.

'Paddy had his new motorcycle parked outside the door,' says MacMahon. 'It was a lovely country evening and we were talking about things. Eventually I got in Bridie's Citroen, which I hadn't been driving very long, and I unfortunately reversed it all over Paddy's motorcycle. We were all very upset and as you can imagine Paddy didn't like it at all. Luckily, there was very little damage.'

The Loch Gamha Ceili Band used to rehearse in Seán Bracken's house in Marino and went on to achieve some success in Dublin in the late fifties.

'The Loch Gamha was great fun and we'd play in people's houses,' says MacMahon who now directs documentaries for RTE. 'Paddy was always in great humour but he was always very single-minded and very professional. He was a person who was going to go someplace and whatever he did, he did very well and very conscientiously.'

Moloney, who made one of his first radio appearances at the age of fourteen on *Children at the Microphone*, was recorded when RTE radio archivist Ciárán Mac Mathúna happened to record his pipe and piano duet with Anne Walsh, which won that year's prestigious national oireachtas music competition. The listeners loved it so much that Mac Mathúna, who played a key role in popularizing traditional music with his two weekly radio shows, played it for 14 straight weeks.

In about 1956 Moloney decided he was bored with the music competitions and decided to retire at the top and concentrate on performing.

'I didn't totally approve of them,' says Moloney who won a total of four all-Ireland medals as well as numerous regional ones over the years. 'It got to the stage where I felt the judges were mainly schoolteachers and not even pipers. I no longer saw why I should be adjudicated by people who didn't know what they were talking about.'

* * *

In the summer of 1956 Michael Tubridy took Paddy Moloney on a week's cycling tour to Clare so he could show his friend the music scene he grew up in. The holiday, which has gone down in Chieftain mythology as 'The Tour de Clare' got off to an inauspicious start when Tubridy broke a pedal on his bicycle going down a hill outside Ennis, about 110 miles from Dublin.

Moloney: 'Bang. Mick's old war-horse of a bicycle broke and it turned out to be the best day we ever had.'

Convinced the holiday was over, the dejected twosome walked to a nearby house and knocked on the door for help. They were invited in by a farmer who was delighted to see them carrying instruments.

'He was a concertina player and of course Mick's bicycle was forgotten and we all started playing,' says Paddy. 'Then we went over to somebody else's for lunch and there was more music and dancing.'

Meanwhile the farmer had fixed the bicycle and sent the two

youngsters on their way to Milltown Malbay, the hometown of the great piper Willie Clancy. As soon as they arrived they found Clancy in a hotel and announced they were here to play.

'Willie came down with another piper called Martin Talty,' said Paddy. 'We were in the middle of a great old session when someone comes in to tell Martin that his cow has got stuck in a drain. He wouldn't stop playing and said, "leave the bloody cow there, it'll be all right until the morning." '

The session broke up at about five in the morning and Paddy and Tubridy were invited back by banjo player Jimmy Ward to stay in his guest house.

'It was lashing down with rain outside,' said Moloney. 'There were five of us to one room with only two double beds and a single and I wanted to go to the jacks. I couldn't turn on the light so the only thing to do was open up a window because I wasn't about to go out in the yard and get wet. This was way before I ever had a pint of Guinness.'

The next day the two bleary-eyed youngsters left to cycle back to Tulla to play at the fleadh ceoil which was being held that weekend. During one of the sessions Moloney noticed an expensive car pull up and a young man with very long hair and bright piercing eyes getting out accompanied by the beautiful Connemara traditional singer Máire Áine Ní Dhonnachadh.

The young man, who wore a heavy Aran sweater and had an aristocratic air, seemed to like Paddy's piping and applauded enthusiastically after every solo. When Moloney finally put his pipes down to rest The Hon. Garech Browne strolled over and introduced himself. Browne told the piper that he had seen him winning the previous year's oireachtas competition with future Dubliner Barney McKenna and loved his playing.

'I thought he was a girl at first,' laughs Paddy. 'He had long hair, which was very unusual in the 1950s, and a babyface. But then of course I heard him speak and he had a very low voice. It was very strange.'

This fateful meeting with the young heir to the Guinness fortune would change Paddy's life and have a decisive impact on the course of Irish traditional music.

3

High Society

Garech Browne was born in 1939 into a world of riches and luxury, light years away from the Donnycarney army sergeant's son Paddy Moloney. His mother, Oonagh, was one of the celebrated 'Guinness girls' in the 1920s who had later married Lord Oranmore and Browne.

Garech grew up with his brother Tara in the splendour of Castle MacGarrett in the rugged west of Ireland in County Mayo, where 150 servants were employed. As a young boy, he became close friends with many of the servants who took him out on expeditions to meet local musicians and hear music and their old traditions would have a lasting effect on him.

His family moved in the highest circles in Ireland and Cyril Connolly, Lucien Freud, John Huston and Claude Cockburn were frequent visitors to the house, all befriending young Garech and instilling in him a great love of Ireland and the arts.

At 15, Garech, who also uses the Irish version of his name Garech a Brún, was prompted to start investigating Irish music when his French teacher in Paris asked him a question he couldn't answer.

'I decided I wanted to know more about the music so I set out on a voyage of discovery,' explained Browne. 'At that early period I met many musicians including the great pipers Willie Clancy, Seamus Ennis and Leo Rowsome. They were great masters.'

Asked what had inspired his musical seduction, Browne replies simply, 'My ears. That's all I can say in answer to that. Having used my ears, which is what I thought they were for, I made what everybody then thought was a very unwise decision.'

That decision was to walk out of the Le Rosey Swiss boarding school in the middle of term and start visiting Fleadhanna Cheoil, seeking out traditional musicians such as Paddy Moloney. He even had piping lessons from Paddy's teacher Leo Rowsome but, although promising, soon realized he lacked the talent to become a top class piper. Paddy played with him and remembers him having as much promise as many of Leo's pupils.

Each Tuesday evening at 7:00 p.m. Browne religiously listened to Ciárán Mac Mathúna's *The Job of Journey Work*, the Radio Éireann programme which had featured Paddy Moloney and Ann Walsh's popular pipes and piano duet. Like many others in Ireland Browne discovered several regional styles of traditional music through this programme.

From the first days of Irish radio in the 1930s traditional music had always been played live in a Dublin Studio, producing a homogenized version of the music which ignored the regional styles and variations. At the end of the 1940s advances in recording technology finally allowed Radio Éireann to buy good quality mobile recording equipment so traditional musicians could be recorded in their own environment. An early radio pioneer and champion of traditional music was the broadcaster Seán Mac Réamoinn who would be an early supporter of The Chieftains.

In 1955 Mac Mathúna, who had a degree in Irish and worked for the Folklore Commission, succeeded Mac Réamoinn on Radio Éireann. He was given the assignment to travel the length and breadth of Ireland with the newly formed mobile unit to discover and record traditional musicians in their own environment.

'I had a weekly programme called *The Job of Journey Work* where I played recordings that I had made in different areas of Ireland,' said Mac Mathúna. 'There had been a traditional scene of course but people didn't have contact with one another. The music was very much alive but very much hidden in the smaller Irish communities. We were discovering a hidden Ireland.'

Mac Mathúna's radio programme spawned an enthusiastic following of traditional fans and musicians but the purists were worried that national radio exposure could contaminate the music and weaken its local accent.

'The radio certainly would have brought musicians together from different parts of the country who were hearing one another for the first time,' admits Mac Mathúna. 'But it gave them more self-confidence as they heard their music being broadcast on the national airwaves.'

* * *

When Paddy Moloney returned from his week in Clare he went to visit Garech Browne whose Dublin-base was then a small two-bedroom mews flat at 41 Quinn's Lane, just a short walk from St Stephen's Green. With their shared passion for traditional music, the two soon became friends.

'We liked each other instantly,' says Browne. 'We went to a lot of music festivals together in my car, a new Mercedes, talking to people and always discovering some new musician or other.'

Garech Browne brought Paddy to meet his mother Oonagh Lady Oranmore at Luggala, the picturesque country house deep in the Wicklow Mountains which she had been given as a wedding present by her father Ernest Guinness in 1936. He also introduced Paddy into his social set which included his cousin Desmond Guinness, The Knight of Glin, and Lord Nicholas Gormonston.

'We used to have great times,' remembers Paddy. 'The parties that took place in Quinn's Lane were just incredible. The slagging was terrible. We always called Garech "The Quare Fellow" and Gormonston the flasher. The other name I had for him was Gorm-andghastly.'

There was drinking among Garech's crowd but Paddy claims that in those days he mainly drank tea and cold water to keep cool although that didn't stop him from having a great time. The jovial young piper could always be relied on to be the life and soul of any party and was always ready and willing to whip out his tin whistle and entertain.

'We had great musical evenings,' remembers Lord Gormonston. 'Wonderful parties.'

Paddy was a great social success and it wasn't long before he and Browne had become a double-act and, unbeknown to them, acquired the nickname Ballcock and Browne from Garech's friends; an allusion to the first aviators to fly the Atlantic and Moloney's day job selling house fittings.

'You would just go and play,' says Moloney. 'I recall one particular evening with myself and Barney McKenna. I'd never had curry in my life and Garech, who was into Indian food, had two big pots of curry sent over at about two in the morning from Dublin's very first Indian restaurant which had just opened in Leeson Street. That was the first time I'd ever had curry and I thought it was great.'

It was through Garech that Paddy's horizons broadened dramatically as he began meeting both the cream and the underbelly of Dublin society, who all seemed to find their way up the steep wooden stairs to attend the impromptu parties. It was here that Paddy first met the sculptor Edward Delaney who would design the early Chieftains' record covers.

'Garech had everyone,' says Paddy. 'Lords, ladies, dropouts, the lot. People like Horrible Joe, Desmond Mackey, Margaret Barry and Brendan Behan with his parents. He knew all the wonderful characters around town in the late fifties.'

Paddy's life now revolved around music and he formed and played in countless *ad-hoc* musical groups. One pet project at this time had him teamed up again with Seán Potts, future Dubliner Barney McKenna, singer Larry Tracey and the late flute player and step dancer Paidí Bán Ó Broin, who encouraged them to speak Gaelic. Moloney considers this group to be the very first incarnation of The Chieftains.

'I formed this group to develop my musical ideas even further,' he says. 'This built on my earliest experiments with traditional music and was a very important stage of my musical development. Everything that I went on to accomplish later with The Chieftains had its roots here.'

Moloney coached the musicians and organized twice weekly practices at his parents' home in Donnycarney. Later the group went on a playing holiday to a *fleadh* in Lisdoonvarna and Spiddal in Galway where they all shared the same bedroom.

'That was the greatest feast of music and one of the best holidays that I ever had with Paddy,' remembers Potts who was there with his girlfriend and later wife Bernie. 'Unfortunately I ran out of money in Lisdoonvarna and it was killing me that they were going on to Spiddal so we jumped on my motorbike and drove the 150 miles back to Dublin to borrow more money. Then we came straight back and met up with Paddy in Spiddal. He was delighted to see me and we played music all day and all night. It was absolutely brilliant,' said Potts.

One night they were playing in a little country house without electricity high up in the Galway mountains when their Tilley oil lamp went out, leaving them in the dark.

'It was a rare session,' remembers Paddy. 'And the Tilley started to fade a bit. There was a bottle of poteen, the proud drink itself, being passed around, which in those days I wasn't tasting much to my regret. Somebody went along with the bottle and poured some of the poteen on the lamp instead of oil. Whoosh! Off she went, and we continued playing, no problems.'

There were parties every night of the holiday and Moloney, Potts and Tindall would roll home at five or six in the morning, strip off their clothes and go skinny-dipping with the sun coming up in Galway Bay.

Although he was having the time of his life in Dublin with the music and his new social connections, Moloney still saw Baxendales as the sensible career that would make his mother proud and worked hard from 8:30 a.m. to 5:45 p.m. A tireless worker he prided himself on knowing everyone of the 7,000 items that Baxendales sold.

'Baxendales taught me discipline,' says Moloney. 'That was a great lesson for me to learn early on and has helped me in everything I've done since.'

When his friend Éamon de Buitléar began writing a live weekly children's show for Radio Éireann he asked Paddy if he would supply the music. Given total creative freedom, de Buitléar wanted to use the show to expose Irish children to the Irish language and traditional instruments and music.

'I felt that if there was some way you could get the children to be attracted to the music through stories, even unconsciously, they might develop a taste for it later,' says de Buitléar.

The problem was the show aired at 5:00 p.m. when Paddy was supposed to be behind his desk at Baxendales. Ever resourceful, on the morning of the broadcast Paddy would leave his pipes with Éamon, who worked at Hely's Fishing Tackle Shop in nearby Dame Street, and then go on to Baxendales. At about 4:00 p.m. Paddy would suddenly announce he was going out to buy stationery for Baxendales and run out to RTE's Henry Street studios where de Buitléar would be waiting with his pipes.

'We'd just do one run through and then we'd go out live,' explained de Buitléar. 'I had this character called Lúdin Mac Lú who was a leprechaun and his mouse friend Lucín. And whenever the mouse got into a jam the leprechaun would play this magical tune.

'Paddy would have a whole series of whistles laid out on the table in the studio. While I was reading a story Paddy would provide musical accompaniment on his whistles. After the broadcast Paddy would run back to Baxendales holding some pens or something that I had given him to provide an alibi.'

A couple of years later de Buitléar produced a cartoon version of the radio series and double tracking allowed Paddy to play a duet with himself on uilleann pipes and whistles for the soundtrack.

By some small miracle no one from Baxendales ever listened to the radio at 5:00 p.m. and his career there blossomed after he joined the Irish Transport and General Workers' Union. It wasn't long before he became active in a union dispute. 'I used to voice my opinion rather strongly and I became a bit of a nuisance. Then my manager called me into his office and said, "You've been coming up with some inflammatory statements. But that's all going to stop now because we've decided to put you on the management." I thought, "Thank you very much".'

Moloney found the sudden change from worker to management difficult to handle at first.

'It was dreadful having to change my whole attitude towards my fellow "brothers" and go onto the other side,' he said. 'But we still remained friends.'

In his new position Moloney was put in charge of a pool of 30 typists. One morning the young executive's head turned when an attractive new raven-haired clerk called Rita O'Reilly arrived for her first day of work wearing black laced native Indian sandals and a little green skirt.

'She was as proud as punch and I thought, "That one's a dinger."' It was his first meeting with his future wife.

* * *

Rita O'Reilly has the fiery temperament of the long line of quarrymen she is descended from. For generations her family have hewn granite from the Dublin Mountains which has been used in the building of some of the city's most beautiful churches and houses.

Her great-grandfather O'Reilly, who owned quarries in the Wicklow Mountains in the last century, made his own personal protest against the bourgeoisie. A strikingly tall man with long red hair and beard, he couldn't abide the rude Dublin gentry who would arrive at his quarry in their horse and carts and picnic on his land without asking permission.

One day he'd had enough and decided he was going to teach these bad-mannered trespassers a lesson they'd never forget. Stripping naked behind a rock, he came running out towards them screaming. The shocked picnickers fled in such a hurry that they left their food behind. Great-grandfather O'Reilly was delighted and brought the food home to his family and caused a stir as no one in the community had ever seen bananas before.

Rita's own father Faley was the last of the old-time quarrymen. At the age of four, as was custom with the eldest child, Rita was sent to live with her mother Peg's parents in Milltown, then a small village three miles outside Dublin. Her grandfather Paddy O'Neill was a successful businessman and Rita moved into his high class family grocers just over the bridge at Milltown. The building dates from the early 19th century when it originally had a thatched roof. Later in 1840 the roof was removed and an extra storey was added.

Rita was sent to St Mary's School which was just a short walk away from her parents' home. The tiny school was situated in a wild mountain area and only had only four teachers who had a tough time controlling the unruly girls. Rita remembers her classmates doing 'terrible things' and jokes that it was all something like John Boorman's film *Deliverance*. At the age of seven, she left to go to St Anne's, a strict convent school in Milltown, where she stayed on a scholarship until leaving school at sixteen.

The Dublin of Rita's childhood was summer walks into the city with friends and cream buns at Bewley's coffee shop in Grafton Street, where it was left up to the honesty of the customers to tell how many cakes were eaten. Her family loved to sing and at holidays and get-togethers everybody would do their party piece.

Remembers Rita: 'My father sang but my mother said he couldn't. She was a terrible woman for saying things like that because then she put me off singing. I still can't sing but that doesn't stop me.'

At 16 her parents decided that although Rita was getting high marks at school and could have stayed on to go to university, she should leave St Anne's and get a job as money was scarce. Her grandfather knew the manager of Baxendales, a Mr Murphy from Milltown, and persuaded him to give Rita a job in the accounts department.

Rita was very nervous on her first day at work as she was brought into the huge antiquated Victorian-style open plan office, where all the staff sat on big desks opposite one another. She was introduced to a young man named Paddy Moloney and told that he was to be her boss and given her first assignment of answering the telephones.

'I was terrified,' remembers Rita. 'Paddy must have noticed that I was getting my knees in a knot and came down to me. He was very kind and reassuring.

'It's hard to understand now but I had never spoken on the phone in my life. No one had phones, for God's sake. There were few public telephones in those days never mind there being one at home.'

Over the next few months Rita and the other girls spent each afternoon helping Paddy tally up the day's sales for the whole company. Pretty soon 20-year-old Paddy was captivated by Rita's quick intelligence and feistiness and the fact that she didn't think twice about standing up to him.

'We used to get into these dreadful rows in front of everyone,' remembers Moloney. 'They used to call them the four o'clock symphonies.'

Says Rita: 'We used to fight because I wouldn't take any of his bullshit. I would stick Paddy until four o'clock and then I couldn't take his nonsense and we'd start to fight. I'd scream at him and throw things across the desk at him. The whole office knew what was happening.'

In view of their conflict in the office their fellow workers would have been astonished that Paddy and Rita were actually enjoying a secret office romance that was heading to the altar. It began eight months after Rita started at Baxendales and Paddy asked her out for a date. At the time she had no idea he was a musician, as he kept his other career well hidden at the office, and only found out months later after accidentally opening his desk and finding pictures of Paddy with his pipes.

Their first date began as a pretty typical one of going to the cinema, but Rita began to wonder what was going on when Paddy insisted that they go and visit the piper Seamus Ennis who was ill in a TB sanitarium.

'That was an exciting date for a young girl,' Rita remembers, deadpan.

Another time Paddy failed to turn up and meet her at the appointed time on a Sunday evening at their special meeting place under Clery's clock in O'Connell Street. After waiting two hours Rita was about to storm off in a rage when Paddy's mother arrived to say her son couldn't make the date. She explained that he had been offered a concert in Mullingar and couldn't turn it down as it paid £2.

'I was furious,' said Rita. 'I was fiery then and I told her I was furious that Paddy had left me standing for two hours and hadn't had the manners to warn me.

'She looked at me and said, "But he is getting paid £2 for the concert," which was a lot of money then. The next day I walked up to him in Baxendales and said, "Paddy, you stood me up for £2." He just laughed as he normally does.'

As their relationship progressed Paddy introduced Rita to Garech Browne and his musician friends and she became part of their group attending concerts and fleadhanna cheoil. Rita's grandparents were very strict and did not approve of the 17-year-old going out all night to hear music. When Paddy invited her to come to a weekend festival with his friend Garech, Rita's grandmother only reluctantly allowed her to go as Paddy's sisters would be there too.

'My first introduction to Garech was walking through this hotel with Paddy and I saw this apparition,' Rita remembers. 'Now you must picture the long long hair and he didn't have it tied back. Flowing curly hair. And you have to remember that in those days bad language was unheard of and, as my grandfather said, it was only the cornerboys who hung around street corners who used it.

'As we came down this corridor Garech roared, "Well, Moloney, ye fucking bollocks, how the hell are you?" Well he did have a nice accent but I nearly died. I thought what type of friends does Paddy have?'

That night they all danced and played until the sun came up and then Paddy, Rita and his sisters all slept together in someone's minibus while Garech stayed at a hotel.

Garech Browne always delighted in mischief and it soon became his mission to lead the innocent young Rita astray to the consternation of her grandmother. He was most successful when Grandma O'Neill gave her permission to go to another fleadh ceoil on condition she was home by midnight. It was such a good event that no one except Rita wanted to leave. At one in the morning she was still on the dance floor desperately pleading with Garech to drive her home.

'I said, "Garech, I must go home. My grandmother will kill me." And Garech looked at me as if I was making a fuss and told me I was only an hour late. He forgot to add that it was a three hour drive back to Dublin."

By the time Garech had driven them back to Milltown it was 7:00 a.m. and the laundry horn, signalling the start of the day's work, was sounding. As they passed St Anne's School Rita made the mistake of saying she was an ex-pupil. A delighted Garech announced that his friend, the traditional singer Máire Áine Ní Dhonnchadha, taught there. So he stopped the car to run over to her window and dance an impromptu jig to the accompaniment of Paddy's tin whistle.

When they finally crossed the bridge to the shop Rita's furious grandmother was standing outside.

'I was mortified,' says Rita. 'As soon as they saw my grandmother, Paddy Moloney and Garech Browne ran across that bridge and left me to take my punishment. I think I was grounded for a year.'

Almost 40 years later Browne still relishes the incident with glee, saying proudly, 'I've always been a bad influence on everyone and I hope to remain so until the day I die. But I'm also a good influence as Paddy will certainly agree.'

* * *

In 1959 Garech Browne decided to use his influence and money to further the cause of traditional music on record. He formed Claddagh Records from his flat in Quinn's Lane to make an LP of Paddy Moloney's piping teacher Leo Rowsome, but being under 21 and still a minor he couldn't legally become director of a company. His only professional qualification was as a cabbie. He had his own badge, and this allowed him to drive horse-drawn carriages. However, Claddagh incorporated into a company shortly after he came of age and he assumed the position of company chairman.

'I set out to make something happen,' said Browne. 'None of the major record companies believed that two sides of 20 minutes each of pipering was something that anyone would listen to. But we didn't think that this was the case and indeed we were proved right.'

Claddagh's first recording, *Leo Rowsome's The King of the Pipers*, was received very favourably by the critics. Charles Acton of

The Irish Times described it as 'technically excellent' and showing 'uilleann piping of a virtuoso order'.

'This first of Claddagh records is a splendid sample for everyone with any interest in our true national pipes,' wrote Acton.

Traditional musicians soon realized Browne's genuine love of their music and his sincerity in trying to preserve it.

'I mean this was his life,' says Paddy Moloney. 'It was seen as a rich man's hobby but I thought what he was doing was great.'

Browne was delighted with the encouraging response and determined that Claddagh should carry on as his personal crusade to preserve all aspects of Irish, Scots and other traditional arts. For the next Claddagh release Browne persuaded the great Irish poet Patrick Kavanagh to talk to a tape recorder about his life in Dublin and read some of his poetry. The resulting Claddagh record, called *Almost Everything*, has become a lasting memorial to the poet who died in 1967 and remains the only existing recording of him reading his own work.

'Claddagh Records now gives us the opportunity to have the poet in our drawing room,' wrote Anthony Lennon of *The Irish Times*.

But other writers were far less charitable and cruelly accused Browne in print of being a dilettante who got a kick out of mixing with peasants.

'Somebody wrote that Leo's record was a foible and that I was merely slumming it,' said Browne, who was Claddagh's only full-time worker at the beginning. 'There was a lot of prejudice against me by people who had no idea of my motives and what I was trying to accomplish. I started Claddagh Records to make money for the musicians and other people concerned and turn around their image and also that of traditional music.'

* * *

In late 1959 an extraordinary documentary about the Irish War of Independence called *Mise Éire* or *I am Ireland* struck a deep chord in the national conscience. The film's soundtrack used traditional Irish airs played by a full orchestra to wring the utmost emotion from the images on screen. The composer/arranger was a young unknown called Seán Ó Riada who became an overnight sensation in Ireland as his score took on a life of its own, being played continually on the radio and became a best-selling E.P.

Paddy Moloney heard the evocative Ó Riada score with great interest when he saw the film at the Regal Theatre and was impressed by the impact the full orchestra had on the tunes he'd been playing since he was a young child.

'The simplicity got to me immediately,' says Moloney. 'It was a lovely score of traditional airs that were put together and arranged in a most traditional style. *Mise Éire* really brought Seán to the front and quite rightly so.'

The stunning success of *Mise Éire* helped to create a new interest in traditional music as Irish people began to take a new pride in themselves and proudly rediscover their past.

Ceoltóirí Cualann

Sharing the same birthday as Paddy Moloney, Seán Ó Riada was born John Reidy on August 1st, 1931 in Cork City. John and his sister Louise were the only two survivors of the eight children born to John Thomas and Julia Reidy. An accomplished fiddle player from Clare, John Reidy senior was stationed as an army sergeant in Adare, Co. Limerick.

Growing up in Adare the boy showed little interest in the Irish tunes that his mother tried to teach him. Serious about her children's musical education, Julia Reidy found a piano teacher called Mr Metcalf and in return for a free room in her house he agreed to teach John and Louise and save them the journey to Limerick.

After leaving school John was accepted by University College, Cork, to study for a Classics degree but only lasted a year before transferring over to the music department. In 1952 he graduated with an honours degree in music and had developed a keen interest in modern jazz. By this time he was well known in the Cork City music scene, playing with an assortment of jazz groups and dance bands.

While at university he had married a fellow student called Ruth Coghlin and a year after he graduated they moved to Dublin, where Reidy had been appointed assistant director of music at Radio Éireann. Reidy's career at Radio Éireann was short-lived as he hated the bureaucracy and paperwork it demanded and he resigned after less than two years.

Now in his mid-20s Reidy set his sights on a new life in France, bluffing his way into a job for French radio. Moving to Paris with his young wife he spent a year doing freelance work for French radio, immersing himself in the flourishing Paris jazz and Be-Bop scene. While in Paris he became the regular accompanist of Greek singer Juliette Greco and befriended the composer Mikis Theodo-rakis, who would later find international fame with *Zorba the Greek*. But after a year he became disillusioned with Paris and returned to Cork.

Reidy's fortunes changed when he accepted the post of music director at Dublin's prestigious Abbey Theatre which would still allowed him to work for Radio Éireann during the day. It was during this period that Reidy wrote his score for *Mise Éire* changing his life forever. His transformation into Seán Ó Riada was about to begin.

As befitting his new job and status, Ó Riada took the lease on a large Georgian house at Number One Galloping Green, on the road from Dublin to Bray and moved his family to Dublin. Caring little about money, he lived well beyond his means, adopting the persona of a country squire and began to hunt and fish.

One day, soon after moving to Galloping Green, he strolled into Hely's Fishing Tackle shop and was served by Éamon de Buitléar.

'Seán Ó Riada came into Hely's and he was buying a gun to go pheasant shooting,' remembers de Buitléar. 'I recognized his name when he signed it on the application form for a licence. We started chatting and as we were both interested in fishing we decided to go out on a fishing expedition together.'

While they were fishing Ó Riada told the young accordion player that he needed some traditional musicians for a play called *The Golden Folk*, which was being presented as part of the 1959 Abbey Theatre Festival.

'Seán told me that the idea was to have a group of traditional musicians playing throughout the play,' said de Buitléar. 'Now this was unheard of and had never been done.'

The play, by Bryan MacMahon, was about gypsies in Ireland. Reidy's plan was to have traditional musicians playing straw-costumed Wren Boys and actually performing on stage during the wedding scene.

Éamon de Buitléar agreed to help and immediately called his friend Paddy Moloney who met with Reidy at the Abbey Theatre.

Paddy: 'I was immediately struck by John's great charisma. This great way of coming in with a big cigar, which wasn't really him at all. It took me some time to realize that behind it all was this simple, very shy person.'

Moloney agreed to help Reidy with the play and drafted in Seán

Potts, veteran accordion player Sonny Brogan, fiddler John Kelly and flautist Vincent Broderick to play in the production.

The Golden Folk was a big success with the public and critics alike and every night the traditional musicians got a standing ovation. Long after the curtain fell the players would stay behind supping a few drinks and making music and Paddy Moloney remembers these 'little sessions' as being far better than those on-stage.

John Reidy – who now used the Gaelic version of his name Seán Ó Riada – was delighted by the audience's enthusiastic response to the traditional music and realizing it had potential decided to start his own folk orchestra. After inviting Moloney and the other musicians to join he asked the regular Abbey Orchestra violinist Martin Fay.

* * *

Martin Fay was the eighth generation of his family to be born and bred in Dublin. His father Joseph Christopher Fay was an Al Jolson-style song and dance man who performed for his own amusement. His mother Annie had a good collection of Irish records. Much to the young Martin's delight, he was allowed to be the 'winder-upper' of the family's treasured gramophone.

Staunchly working class, the Fays lived in the Cabra district of Dublin. Martin was the youngest of four children, with two older brothers, Joe and Paddy, and an older sister Ann.

Ann Fay was a good pianist and started teaching Martin to play when he was just four. Within a year he had made his show business debut as the 'gimmick' at the local roller skating rink playing one-handed piano. Little Martin lived for roller skating and every Saturday afternoon he'd be first in the queue outside the Cabra School Hall.

When he was six, Martin was taken to see the new Stewart Granger hit film *The Magic Bow* at the Savoy Cinema on O'Connell Street. Granger played the great Italian violin virtuoso Niccolo Paganini in the film about his life, but it was the violin soundtrack, performed by Yehudi Menuhin, that struck a deep chord in the young boy.

'I was just captivated by the fiddle music in that movie,' he remembers. 'I was too young to understand the story but I just loved the sound of the damn thing. I came home and said, "Da,

I've got to learn the violin." And my father, being the guy he was, a fiddle appeared, which must have cost him a week's wages, and I was packed off to the School of Music to start lessons.'

Ann Fay was already at the Municipal School of Music studying piano so he had no trouble getting accepted for the extra music studies, which were outside of his normal education at St Canices and later at O'Connell's Christian Brothers' School.

As a young boy Martin remembers hearing his uncle Andy Kelly, who was a famous mandolin player in traditional circles. But the music didn't impress the young boy any more than the other kinds of music he was hearing at the time.

'I had no interest whatsoever in a future career in Irish music,' said Martin. 'I wouldn't have known it from Arabian music. Classical music was my forte. I wanted to be a soloist in Carnegie Hall.'

By the age of 13, Martin was on course for a career as a classical violinist and dreamed of being another Paganini or Menuhin. But his interest in the violin was looked down on among many of his friends in Cabra.

'That was a bit of a joke in the neighbourhood,' says Fay. 'Yer man's learning the violin. That was a standing joke. Saxophones were hip in those days but not violins.'

Martin loved his Thursday afternoon music class at the Municipal School of Music, where his violin teacher Seán MacKenzie had seen his potential and was taking a special interest. It was MacKenzie who was responsible for Fay's professional debut on the fiddle in the Butlins holiday Camp Orchestra in Mosney in Co. Meath. Although as Martin was only 15 years old and under age at the time he had to lie and pretend he was 17.

'For kids, Butlins at that time was like going to Disneyland now,' says Martin. 'I was playing in the theatre orchestra and that first job went hand in hand with my first pair of long pants. I wore short pants at school but there was no way you could play in Butlins in short pants.'

MacKenzie managed to arrange special dispensation for Martin to be absent from school from May to begin rehearsals for the June to September summer season. Playing in the Butlins' band was great all-round experience for the young violinist who played everything from the popular hits of the day to light classical to opera.

'You name it, I did it,' says Martin. 'I was a good reader and that was saleable. It didn't matter what you put in front of me. Butlins was my first introduction to professional music.'

Come September, and the close of the season, he found himself back at school, and managed to sail through his Intermediate Certificate the following year. Mr MacKenzie was still determined to help Martin with his career and helped him secure the position of stand-in violinist for the Dublin Opera season held at the Gaiety Theatre. Although by day he was still a schoolboy, at night he'd put on his suit to fill in for a sick violinist and delight in performing for the first time with a real orchestra.

As he neared the end of his schooldays, Martin was having to face the fact that all the doors to his becoming a professional classical musician seemed to be closed and music would have to remain a hobby. For in the early 1950s, Dublin was full of mature classical musicians from Italy, Germany and Czechoslovakia who had played in some of Europe's leading orchestras before the war. When it came to a career in classical music, what chance did 'a Joe Soap from Cabra' have of achieving a job in the Irish Symphony orchestra when there were so many older and more experienced virtuosi around?

So having resigned himself to a nine to five regular job, Fay left school at 18 and got himself an office job with a Dublin electronics firm called Unidare.

'I had a nice little number there,' says Martin. 'From now on music was only going to be an interest. I would keep in touch with it but at that time everybody had to get themselves a job.'

As he was preparing to start working at Unidare, fate smiled on Martin a third time in the shape of his old teacher Seán MacKenzie who conjured up another musical lead for the young man. MacKenzie played first violin in the famous Abbey Theatre and managed to secure Martin a place in the six-piece orchestra, playing overtures and intermission music.

'I was working in Unidare nine to five and at night I was playing in the Abbey Theatre,' says Fay. 'Then I went off to the bar and to play snooker. Quite often I would go straight into work without any sleep whatsoever. This went on for 15 years until The Chieftains went professional.'

It was shortly after Martin started that the Abbey Theatre hired Seán Ó Riada as the new music director. Ó Riada first really caught

Martin's attention when he started dropping the odd Irish number into the Abbey intermission music instead of the usual safe repertoire.

'I'd nothing against Irish music but look what was being offered with the ceili bands at the time,' said Fay. 'I had my sights on something else altogether and I'd listen to Irish music just as quickly as I'd listen to Rumanian music or Hungarian music. It was just so repetitive at the time.'

Normally stand-offish and reserved, Martin Fay was quickly charmed by Ó Riada's charisma and somewhat flattered and surprised when the famous composer of *Mise Éire* started taking an interest in him. During performances, when the orchestra had an hour off between the overture and the intermission, Ó Riada and Fay would sit on the Trinity College Wall behind the theatre where they'd chat and trade jokes.

'The man was magic and a musical genius,' Martin says now. 'I got on so well with Seán and he spent so much time with me. That sounds like blowing trumpets, the big man that he was, but he could have been anywhere during that hour. I think he respected me for what I wanted to do, but he was overpowering in the nicest possible way.'

It was the hard-drinking Ó Riada who first introduced the young man to alcohol when one night he took Fay upstairs to the Abbey Theatre bar after the show and insisted on buying him a drink.

Fay remembers it like this: 'He said, "Have something."

'I said, "I don't drink Seán."

' "Oh, you do, have something." '

'So right or wrong he brainwashed me into having a short whiskey and a quick bottle of stout to chase it. Here's a non-drinker and I've started off on whiskey and a bottle of stout as a chaser. I didn't know what he was talking about. I could give lessons on it now but that's besides the point.

'So I knocked this whiskey back and chased it. And that was my introduction to drinking, thanks to Mr Seán Ó Riada. Funny thing, I've never stopped since. He was a good teacher in every respect.'

* * *

As soon as *The Golden Folk* run finished, Seán Ó Riada wasted no time in recruiting traditional musicians for his permanent folk orchestra. Ó Riada told Martin Fay, who had finally agreed to attend the first Sunday rehearsal at Galloping Green, that he envisaged his new group as a 'folksy chamber orchestra playing Irish music'.

'I met Paddy Moloney, Seán Potts and the others on my first visit to Galloping Green,' Fay recalls. 'They were already deep into Irish music which I wasn't. I knew Irish music. I played Irish music but I wasn't patriotic about the thing. I wasn't flying flags. I was heading on the classical way.'

But once he started playing with the traditional musicians, Fay began to realize that there was far more to the music than he'd thought.

The first rehearsal at Galloping Green was attended by Paddy Moloney, on uilleann pipes and tin whistle, Michael Tubridy on flute, Seán Potts on tin whistle, John Kelly playing fiddle, Sonny Brogan and Éamon de Buitléar on accordions and Ronnie McShane on bones. Ó Riada was music director and brought along a bodhrán, or goat skin drum, which was rarely seen in traditional music at that time.

Veteran broadcaster and writer Seán Mac Réamoinn attended that rehearsal.

'I remember well the first evening of music held there,' says Mac Réamoinn. 'What Ó Riada was doing was developing the inner logic of the music and the only parallel I can make is that of jazz where he was giving different instruments their head. They did their break, as it were, but he managed to weld them into a unity. And the sound that emerged, with tunes that many of us knew for a long time, was quite exciting.'

Paddy Moloney was heavily featured by Ó Riada as soloist and his uniquely intricate piping style became a trademark of the group. But the young piper voiced his objections at Ó Riada's plan to use two accordions in Ceoltóirí Cualann.

'I was anti-accordion at the time,' admits Moloney. 'I thought it was a deplorable and vulgar instrument that was often out of tune with itself, unlike the wonderful concertinas and melodeons I had grown up with. Accordions just didn't fit in with the sound I wanted to hear.'

Nevertheless Ó Riada insisted on using accordions and Sonny Brogan made his mark on Ceoltóirí Cualann by introducing a lot of his tunes into its repertoire. Moloney, Brogan and the tobacco-chewing John Kelly also provided Ó Riada with many of the tunes that later became identified with the group.

'Seán was very quick to pick up tunes once he got in on Irish music,' said Moloney. 'That's an old Irish tradition and I think that was his forte.'

In an interview given in 1981, the late John Kelly (who together with Sonny Brogan made up what was known as the Laurel and Hardy of Ceoltóirí Cualann) said that Ó Riada employed great tact in dealing with the traditional musicians, getting them to do exactly what he wanted without ever offending them.

'He never said a harsh word against the musicians no matter how wrong they'd be,' said Kelly in 1981. 'He'd never say, "You-don't know a damn thing about that." He said it in a different way and everyone was happy.'

Ó Riada had the musicians rehearsing every other Saturday night at Galloping Green but it was more like a party than work.

'That was like going to the races,' Kelly went on. 'We used to have a break and a few drinks in the interval and it was great *craic* altogether.'

There was an excitement in the air about forming the group and Seán Potts, then working for the post office, asked Ó Riada whether they would become rich and have a huge following like Elvis Presley. Ó Riada jokingly replied that they'd develop their own following but his main hope was that other groups would copy them and help traditional music.

'Seán was a very very talented man and we all had great respect for him,' says Michael Tubridy today. 'He had a great command of arranging music and people and getting them to do what he wanted them to do.'

Now fully immersing himself in traditional music, Ó Riada started meeting Paddy Moloney every Monday evening in the Trinity Bar in Pearse Street during breaks at the Abbey as he was eager to learn everything he could from the gifted young piper. And over drinks, the university-educated honours' graduate wearing his favourite trilby hat with a feather sticking out of the band, started picking the brains of the traditional self-taught Irish piper; and vice versa.

Ó Riada was fascinated by Moloney's natural musical style and incessantly questioned him about his approach to harmonies and arrangements. But Moloney, who had developed his own unique piping technique naturally could not give the academic any easy answers.

'We'd have a little chat about the music and write out tunes,' remembers Paddy. 'Once we tossed around the tune *The Ship and Full Sail*. He said, "You write it your way with your harmonies and then I'll write it out my way."

'You see Seán had a full Bachelor of Music training and he was way ahead of me in that respect. I'd be putting in harmonies that were not in line with the book. He said, "Paddy, if you did this in a musical exam you'd be knocked out." I said, "I don't care. I like what I'm doing with this tune."

'And he said "fair enough" and he wrote it out and we played it. It was never a case of Seán writing out the tunes, it was improvised. Just like jazz.'

Over the next few months Ó Riada carefully rehearsed the musicians at Galloping Green and readied them for their first public performance.

'Some of the musicians couldn't read music at the time,' said Éamon de Buitléar. 'One time Seán Ó Riada wrote out the following rhythm beat for me on a piece of paper which I placed in front of me on a music stand:

"Ham, butter and eggs
  Ham, butter and eggs
  Ham, butter and rashers and eggs
  Ham, butter and eggs." '

The Sunday night invitation-only sessions soon became an institution, attracting writers, singers, poets and musicians from all over Ireland. The rambling house would be in complete chaos with books and musical scores piled up everywhere. On one occasion Ó Riada was unable to find his ringing telephone as it was buried so deeply under papers.

The guests would be met at the door by Ó Riada with a glass in hand and his wife Ruth would serve up tea and cakes throughout the session. Half-way through Ó Riada might call a temporary halt to the proceedings and adjourn next door to the pub for a few drinks. Then it was back to the house until the wee hours of the morning, playing music and telling stories.

Garech Browne was a regular and used to bring Brendan Behan and his parents, Stephen and Kathleen.

'Galloping Green was a peak,' remembers Browne. 'One night people were dancing so hard that the vibrations shattered one of the windows. I had one of my worst hangovers there. I was drinking Powers Whiskey and that ran out so Seán gave me some brandy. When that ran out he gave me poteen. I didn't feel extraordinary well the next day for some reason.'

At another Sunday rehearsal Ciarán Mac Mathúna was there to record a traditional singer for a Christmas broadcast.

Browne recalls: 'First Sonny Brogan fell into a coal scuttle and then the singer was so drunk two people had to literally hold him up from either side in front of the microphone so he wouldn't fall down. I mean it's extraordinary that he could sing even though he couldn't stand, but he could and he sang perfectly.'

It was in this atmosphere of organized chaos that Ó Riada functioned, seeming to care little about the real world or the practicalities of living in it.

'I remember once he pulled up in front of the Abbey Theatre in a Jaguar to take me to Galloping Green for a rehearsal,' says bones player Ronnie McShane, who worked as props master at the Abbey Theatre. 'He said, "Ronnie, look at this car, it's brilliant. Can you lend me some money to get some petrol?"

'And when we arrived at Galloping Green, Ruth came rushing out to tell him that the electricity had been cut off because the bill hadn't been paid. That was the larger than life man Seán was. Driving a Jag when his electricity's been cut off.'

Ó Riada was earning £11 a week working at the Abbey and very often that was his sole source of income. He always told his wife Ruth that he only made £10 so he could keep the extra £1 for his beloved cigars.

Lack of money meant there were just the bare essentials at Galloping Green as they could afford few pieces of furniture. There were holes all over the wooden floor which he made a point of using as ash trays for his cigars to the great amusement of his friends.

Drink flowed freely through rehearsals and all business was discussed in the nearby pub, although Michael Tubridy never touched a drop of alcohol.

'Those rehearsals were terrific fun,' says Éamon de Buitléar. 'Seán

Ó Riada was very witty and never hauled any musician over the coals although it must have been absolute hell for him at times, for somebody who had such a keen ear for music, to hear some of the things that were happening.'

When Ó Riada finally decided that his 'folk orchestra' was ready to be heard he arranged a prestigious debut concert at the Shelbourne Hotel. But when Seán Mac Réamoinn met Ó Riada the night before, the group was still without a name.

'We had all sorts of ideas for names running around in our heads,' said Mac Réamoinn. 'One of the great roads of ancient Ireland was Cualann Way, which is popularly thought to have gone near the present road by Galloping Green. I said let's call it Ceoltóirí Cualann, which literally means Musicians of Cualann, and he said, "That's it. Great."

'So it was a phony creation, mainly on my part I'm afraid.'

* * *

From the very beginning the purists dismissed Ceoltóirí Cualann as rebels but the public loved them. Ó Riada carefully presented Ceoltóirí Cualann like a classical orchestra and for the first time placed traditional Irish music on a concert platform. His *Mise Éire* fame meant that the early Ceoltóirí Cualann concerts got a lot of attention.

'Seán Ó Riada was experimenting,' explains Ciarán Mac Mathúna. 'He did different arrangements and produced a lot of these slow airs as well as the dance music. He brought in the harpsichord and it related back to an older classical or traditional harp music.'

Dublin society embraced Ceoltóirí Cualann but some group members mutinied when they were asked to perform in black tie at a gala concert organized by the Irish music company Gael Linn at the Gaiety Theatre.

'I said I'll never get into a monkey suit,' said Paddy Moloney. 'I think I was the one who objected greatly and Seán picked me up on it and came out in a green herring jumper so we got our way. We don't like being pushed into anything.'

After the early success of Ceoltóirí Cualann in 1960, Seán Ó Riada decided that the best platform to present his new group would be live radio. So he went to visit his old friend Kevin Roche, then assistant music director of Radio Éireann, with an ambitious proposal for his own show.

'The first I heard of the existence of the group was when Seán came to me and asked me to listen to them with a view to broadcasting,' Roche says today. 'I auditioned Ceoltóirí Cualann and I was absolutely bowled over by what they were doing and I offered them a series straight away.'

Called *Reacaireacht an Riadaigh*, the six show series turned Paddy Moloney, Seán Ó Riada and Martin Fay and the other members of Ceoltóirí Cualann into national radio personalities, creating an unprecedented demand for traditional music.

Once a week the musicians would rehearse at Radio Éireann's studios at the back of the General Post Office in O'Connell Street. Moloney would be the first to arrive. The others would shuffle in one by one, often recovering from the excesses of the night before. Seán Ó Riada would always be late and come running in out of breath from one meeting or another.

Every week the cheerful strains of *The Dingle Regatta*, with Paddy Moloney's lilting, introduced the show and became a firm favourite among its growing audience. But few of them would have realized that Ceoltóirí Cualann's version of the tune, which became the group's signature tune, was totally inaccurate.

Paddy Moloney smiles at the memory: 'I gave that tune to Seán spontaneously at one of the rehearsals but unfortunately I mixed up two tunes and got the second part of it wrong. It didn't matter though because it blended beautifully and became our theme tune that was played at the beginning of every show Ceoltóirí Cualann ever did.'

The veteran accordion player Sonny Brogan liked a drink and often used to arrive at rehearsals a little the worse for wear.

'Once we were sitting in a pub in Grafton Street after a show and we were discussing how Sonny had come into a rehearsal half pissed and messed it up,' remembers Ronnie MacShane. 'One of the other members of the group said to Seán, "This is ridiculous. We'll have to get another box player."

'Now Seán very seldom lost his temper but he did on this occasion and he screamed, "He's worth ten of what you are as a player!" No way. He was very loyal to his people.'

The half-hour radio programmes caught on immediately and over the next few years Ceoltóirí Cualann became very popular.

'Those first radio programmes were great,' remembers Moloney. 'It was a great breakthrough for Irish music. A lot of these shows were very experimental and I remember that Seán would read some very strange poetry. I once said to him, "You could have brought a donkey into the studio going yeehaw and you'd have got away with it."

Ó Riada had no head for business and it was always always left to Paddy Moloney to make sure the group got paid, leading John Kelly to dub the piper The Napoleon of Ceoltóirí Cualann.

In 1961 Paddy Moloney made his first trip abroad when he was invited to attend the Celtic Congress in the north of Brittany. At first Paddy thought he was going to Wales and it took two days before he realized he was going to France. Terribly excited at leaving Ireland for the first time, Paddy brought a Brownie box camera and embarked on what would become a life-long love affair with Brittany. At the festival, where he played, Paddy met the Celtic folklorist Polig Montjarret, who would play a vital part in the Chieftains' later Celtic collaborations, and folk musician Alan Stivel, then in his teens.

'The word Celtic never meant anything to me before 1961,' says Paddy. 'That's when I fell in love with Breton music and I began to realize about the Celtic culture and all the similarities. The Breton music punched me completely with its incredibly melodic form that fitted in perfectly with traditional Irish music. I've never lost hold of it since.'

Back in Dublin, Seán Ó Riada was delighted when Ceoltóirí Cualann was invited to do the music for the film version of *The Playboy of the Western World*. Paddy Moloney remembers how Ó Riada's attempts to impress the film's producers backfired at a business meeting at Galloping Green. Trying to play the part of the affluent and worldly country squire, Ó Riada set the scene by deliberately leaving his open gun lying around next to a few cartridges. To complete the picture two brace of pheasants hung over the table ready for cooking.

While Ó Riada greeted the film producers the band members waited in his cellar so they could be introduced later. Unfortunately the cellar was freezing so they lit a turf fire and burned a chair to keep warm. Upstairs, Ó Riada and the producers started hearing coughing and broke off from their meeting to investigate.

'The chimney was blocked so we were all smothered in smoke,' said Moloney. 'When he brought down the producers, they couldn't see anything because there was so much smoke. Seán would chance his arm at anything. After we did the music for *The Playboy of the Western World* in 1961 with Siobhán McKenna he suddenly decided he was a Hollywood director. I remember him saying, "Paddy, I'm off to Hollywood." And he had a big brown case packed and he was going to Hollywood to do a film. Of course it never happened. He got as far as High Wycombe and he came back with his tail between his legs and that was the end of it.'

At one point Ó Riada decided that Moloney should quit his job at Baxendales and offered to use his influence to get him a job in the Radio Éireann Light Orchestra, playing pipes, whistle and flute.

'He sat me down in Galloping Green and said, "Paddy, it's like this. You'll be paid £17.50 a week and you'll have a pension." He even went through all the great benefits without ever mentioning the disadvantages.

'I said, "Hang on Seán. I'm not a sight reader. When it comes to putting a big score in front of me I might get embarrassed." He never saw that. Didn't want to know about it. He was going to get me into the Light Orchestra and that was that.'

Ceoltóirí Cualann's music director and its main soloist often argued musical points during rehearsals and there was a certain tension between them after Paddy stopped his Monday night meetings with Ó Riada. Éamon de Buitléar believes that the growing 'jealousy and competition' between the two created a healthy musical dynamic in the group.

'Seán could see Paddy's talents and kept featuring his uilleann pipes at the forefront of Ceoltóirí Cualann,' explained de Buitléar. 'And Paddy has a head like a computer. We'd all be writing down complicated notes to remind us where we would come in a particular piece but Paddy could memorize it and never had to write anything down.

'So if anything went wrong Paddy would always know what was going on and so all the other musicians would be watching Paddy for their cues.'

Moloney admits he was cocky in those days but says he and Ó Riada were closer than many people supposed.

'I had my own ideas,' he states. 'And I always argued back. Maybe that's a big disadvantage. I think I did rub people up the wrong way. But it was never meant personally but always musically.'

Many people were suspicious of the university-educated Ó Riada and felt he was merely exploiting the traditional musicians to his own advantage to build a career on their talents. The *Irish Times* journalist Charles Acton wrote a whole page of scathing criticism of Ó Riada which caused a sensation. Ó Riada replied to Acton in print, but popular opinion was on the side of the famous composer of the *Mise Éire* film score.

5

The Birth of The Chieftains

In the early 1960s more venues for traditional music, folk and ballad-singing were opening in Dublin. Musicians paired off together in numerous combinations to take advantage of the situation.

'That was the start of the exploitation of traditional musicians,' said Seán Potts, who by now was married with a young son, Seán Óg (now an accomplished piper), and daughters to support.

'We were brought into these places to play and boost the sales of drink. That's what we were there for. Now the money was very poor and in order to make a decent few bob we had to do a couple a week.'

At the centre of the Dublin music scene was O'Donoghue's in Merrion Row, within striking distance of the Shelbourne Hotel. O'Donoghue's was the only pub in Dublin to allow traditional music and it soon became a vital meeting and networking place for players who wanted to be in the know. It was in the back area of O'Donoghue's that Ronnie Drew and Paddy Moloney's good friend Barney McKenna held court long before they formed The Dubliners.

'It was a great spark,' remembers future Chieftain Seán Keane, then an ambitious 16-year-old fiddler and O'Donoghue's regular who was playing with his brother James in the up-and-coming Castle Ceili Band.

'It was amazing the way the whole scene revolved around a dozen musicians at that time.'

A young flute player from Sligo called Matt Molloy, who had just come to Dublin to work for Aer Lingus, met Paddy Moloney and teamed up with him to play regularly at The Old Sheiling Hotel in Raheny. The converted manor house was owned by entrepreneur Bill Fuller who, apart from making a fortune in gold mines in Nevada, sold legendary rock promoter Bill Graham the Fillmore

West in San Francisco. Fuller hired a traditional singer called Dolly MacMahon to run ballad nights at the Old Sheiling and she insisted that traditional music be part of the bill.

'Myself and Paddy used to do the traditional spot,' said Molloy. 'Ballads were the gods so we used to do the first ten minutes before the ballad singers like Paddy Reilly would come on.'

Molloy, who started off at one night a week with Moloney, was soon playing six nights a week earning £4 or £5 a night paid under the table with no questions asked. Smart musicians would play at least four or five regular spots each night, criss-crossing Dublin from venue to venue to make the next gig on time. They were always paid in cash and very often the money they earned would be drunk away by the next morning.

Seán Keane's brother James, who played on the same midnight bills at the Grafton Cinema as Martin Fay and Paddy Moloney, once notched up an incredible 13 gigs in one night.

'That was the activity in the 60s,' said James. 'I wanted to be playing 24 hours a day and I didn't give a damn where. Those were unbelievable times. I was making a lot of money and having the time of my life.'

Another popular traditional music venue was a high class restaurant called the Metropole Lounge where the Gael Linn Cabaret, featuring Paddy Moloney, Martin Fay, Seán Potts and Brendan Ó Duill, played in the Green Room.

'There was so much demand for traditional music,' remembers Seán Potts. 'You have to realize how mercenary we all were. We suddenly realized we could make money and instead of being artists we became real art dealers.'

Paddy Moloney was playing with so many bands that even he was finding it hard to keep count of the various activities he was involved in. One of his most successful collaborations came in 1962 when he teamed up with future Dubliner Barney McKenna and spoons player Mary Jordan as the only traditional players in a musical review at the Old Gate Theatre.

'We all did a solo spot and then at the end we would all join in a big bash singing all of these old Dublin ballads and things,' remembers Paddy. 'It was the first concert ever of its kind with traditional music and the three-week run sold out completely. In fact, it was after this that the Dubliners was formed.'

Martin Fay was now earning more playing fiddle than he was

for his day job as a purchasing officer for Unidare. 'It was supposed to be my sideline as I was only making £9 a week. Money wasn't the thing. You had to get yourself a job so you could retire in style when you were 65. That was the norm. You did what your father did. Our horizons were limited but we were satisfied.'

*   *   *

Another vital factor in the rebirth of traditional music came ironically from across the Atlantic. In 1959 The Clancy Brothers from Co. Tipperary had gone to New York and found themselves at the epicentre of the folk music explosion of the early 1960s.

Radio Éireann's Ciarán Mac Mathúna spent time in New York in 1962 to record a special radio series on the new crop of Irish musicians in America.

Mac Mathúna: 'The Clancy's got together singing in Greenwich Village for bottles of beer. Then they became friendly with Bob Dylan and suddenly became an important part of that folk song revival.'

Within a year, The Clancy Brothers had become folk superstars, graduating out of the club scene and playing prestigious venues such as Carnegie Hall and selling out coast-to-coast tours. When they returned home they were tremendously popular with their brand of Irish ballads.

'I think there were many people who were listening to groups like The Clancy Brothers and others, as popular music and not as traditional,' said Mac Mathúna. 'Suddenly they became very interested and started to go to the places that were the source of this music. A lot of people discovered the real traditional thing in its own environment by first hearing the Clancy's in the big halls.'

*   *   *

In 1962 Garech Browne decided to make a third Claddagh record and asked Paddy Moloney to form a group especially for the recording. He sat down with Moloney at his flat in Quinn's Lane to discuss giving him free rein in selecting the music and asked him to suggest musicians. Moloney, delighted at being given the opportunity to express his musical ideas, immediately selected

Michael Tubridy and Seán Potts. He then brought in Martin Fay for his sympathetic treatment of slow airs.

'This was a fantastic chance Garech had given me,' said Paddy. 'And I knew exactly what I wanted to achieve. I said to myself I want to mix this in such a way so it won't just be reels, jigs and hornpipes. I wanted to create a different flavour of music with songs and airs.

'Some of my ideas of blending tin whistle harmonies had been with me since my childhood. They were in my heart and what I wanted to play. The first album came about as a collection of various music from my get-togethers at Garech's home, festivals and musical gatherings such as at the quartets, duets and ceili bands I had been involved in during the 1950s. It was music that I always wanted to put out on an album.'

For the next six months Paddy organized regular rehearsals after work in Rita's and her grandfather's house in Milltown, the birthplace of The Chieftains. He carefully wrote out the arrangements for forty minutes of music and rehearsed the musicians so they would be note perfect for the studio recording.

Garech Browne was a regular visitor to the rehearsals, sometimes bringing his friend Lord Kilbracken, who was christened 'Rasputin' by Rita's grandfather on account of his long scraggly hair and beard.

'The rehearsals used to turn out to be sessions of music,' remembers Paddy. 'I used to bring in bottles of Guinness and we'd have a few jars. Garech was around and enjoying it.'

Rita's Pappa, as her grandfather was fondly known, was always trying to get the musicians out to the pub during practice nights. By about 10:40 p.m. he would become so impatient he would come into the practice room with his flashlight and, pretending that he couldn't see the time, shine it on the old wall clock to remind everyone the pub would soon be calling last call.

'You had to finish in time before the pubs would close and get a pint on the way home,' remembers Seán Potts. 'That was the way we did things.'

Paddy was anxious to find a good bodhrán player and it was Browne who suggested using Davy Fallon, an elderly bodhrán player and farmer he knew who lived in the wilds of the country in Castletown Geoghan in County Westmeath. Fallon, well into his seventies at the time, was one of the great bodhrán players and

Garech drove Paddy down to meet him on a freezing November evening. On the way Browne explained how Fallon's wife hated the bodhrán with a passion and banned it from the farmhouse. She actively discouraged Fallon from playing it, saying that he was making a fool of himself playing an old drum. So he had to hide his treasured bodhrán in the rafters in the barn.

'We took the evening off and drove down in an MG sports car belonging to a lady friend of Garech's,' Moloney recalls. 'After stopping off for some drinks along the way we finally found his house but Garech hadn't got the guts to knock at the door so he had our friend Horrible Joe go in and knock. Davy came out and then said he'd have to go in and talk to his wife before he could go. After about 20 minutes he came out again and we went out to the barn to find his bodhrán but we had to go to a neighbour's house to hear him play so his wife wouldn't find out.'

Davy Fallon used one of the old-style goat skin bodhráns with tambourine jingles around it and Paddy had to convince him to tape up the jingles so only the drum could be heard.

'Davy was a lovely charming man,' says Moloney. 'He played with his big stumps of farmers' fingers – he was one of the old style players. I remember hearing him for the first time and thinking, "My God he's a great player," and whooooaaaa, it turned into a session.

'While I was playing away with Davy I remember that all of a sudden this glass was stuck into my mouth and a huge gulp of brandy was poured down my throat. I nearly exploded. I'd never tasted brandy before in my life. The strongest thing I'd had up to then was a glass of wine. And of course, guess who put the glass of brandy down me. It was Garech. He got me up to every devilment you could believe.'

Finally Moloney was satisfied the group were ready for recording and Garech hired out the Peter Hunt Studios in Dublin for five evenings, so they could start after finishing work.

'It was totally mad,' remembers Paddy. 'We'd start at 7 o'clock and finish at 10:00. Sometimes I had to work late in Baxendales until 8 o'clock and then I'd go off playing. Somehow we got the programme done in five evenings and I still have all the arrangements I did for the music. Everything had to be done properly.'

Garech introduced his beautiful Jamaican girlfriend Tessa Welborn to the band at one of the evening recording sessions.

'We were blasting away in the studio doing the album,' remembers Moloney. 'And suddenly Tessa, who is Jamaican and absolutely gorgeous, came into the studio with Garech. We were all astonished. We hadn't seen anybody like her in our lives.'

Tessa, who was frequently with Browne during the production of the record, saw at first hand the passion and the pride that the young millionaire had for his new discoveries.

'It was his baby,' Tessa, who is still good friends with Garech and Paddy, says today. 'He was creating something and he knew exactly what he was doing although many people at the time thought he didn't.' Garech had given the initiative to these mostly young musicians that he found 'and he realized that he was putting together something that was going to be the essence of old Irish music.'

As producer, Paddy Moloney was striving for perfection and had his musicians do take after take until he was satisfied.

'It was terribly nerve-wracking,' remembers Seán Potts. 'We'd do three hours a night in the studio and there was a lot of pressure for us.'

After the sessions were completed Moloney's group were still without a name and it took weeks of scratching heads before they hit on the right one.

'We wanted a modern sounding name because we were doing a modern sounding production,' said Garech Browne. 'Paddy had originally thought they should be called *The Quare Fellows* after Brendan Behan's play but it was the poet John Montague, a director of Claddagh, who originally suggested the name *The Chieftains*, which was taken from a book of his called *Death of a Chieftain*.'

Browne went to great pains designing the record cover and drafted in his friend, the artist Eddie Delaney who produced an abstract painting of Chieftains.

'Garech was very proud of the sleeve,' says Tessa Welborn. 'He's meticulous about getting everything brilliantly done and he'll spend weeks getting a paragraph right. He works at style.'

Browne also asked the veteran broadcaster Seán Mac Réamoinn, whom he'd met at O'Donoghue's Pub, to pen the sleeve notes. To introduce The Chieftains and their music, Mac Réamoinn quoted from the first ever recorded Chieftains' track '*Sé Fáth Mo Bhuartha*:

'There's music there
And all kinds of Sweetness
In the piper's greeting
At the end of the day.'

The Chieftains was launched in 1963 at a no-expense-spared party in Haddington House in Dún Laoghaire hosted by Garech Browne. Tessa Welborn had especially invited her Chinese actress friend Tsi Chin, who was in Dublin doing a film, as celebrity guest of honour to attract press coverage.

'Garech had all the waitresses dressed up like ladies at Wilton's in white aprons,' said Tessa, who spent two days typing up with two fingers a report of the reception for Browne. 'I mean no one had even heard of The Chieftains at the time but it made all the papers the next day.'

It was a great party and Seán Mac Réamoinn fell fast asleep during the festivities resulting in someone placing a bunch of lilies in his hand as a practical joke.

'It was a typical Irish carry-on,' remembers Moloney. 'There was story-telling and jokes and humour and it was brilliant.'

Tessa Welborn remembers asking Paddy Moloney about the differences between the uilleann pipes and the Scottish bagpipes that have to be blown.

'Well the Irish aren't silly,' Moloney told Tessa, giving the Graves musical dictionary definition. 'They designed them especially so you can play with one hand while holding a drink with the other.'

Seán Ó Riada reviewed *The Chieftains* in *Hibernia* magazine. 'The record is, generally speaking, splendid,' he began. 'However, perhaps a more detailed criticism would be of interest and possible use, not only for the prospective buyer, but also to the musicians generally.'

Complete with bar charts to illustrate his finer points he used words like 'clumsy' and 'unpleasant,' noting that Moloney's playing of the slow air *Cailin na Gruaige Doinne* 'is excellent but more attention to phrasing is needed in the group playing'.

Finishing his review Ó Riada wrote condescendingly: 'To sum up, then, a most enjoyable record and if I have enumerated some few blemishes as they appear to me it is only because I hope Paddy's next record will be even better and that this is but the first of a series.'

Paddy Moloney read Ó Riada's review with astonishment.

'I was annoyed at first, having done similar spontaneous harmonies and phrasing of tunes in Ceoltóirí Cualann,' said Moloney. 'I thought, "Why the hell did he do it?" I found it all rather fascinating but I didn't bother to reply to it.'

6

Reaping the Harvest

When Paddy Moloney and Rita decided to get married during the rehearsals for *The Chieftains*, it was left up to the groom to take care of arrangements, with dire results. What was to be the Dublin musical wedding of the year, almost didn't take place after Moloney asked Ronnie McShane to arrange special transport to drive the bride from her parents' home into Milltown for the ceremony.

The good-hearted Abbey Theatre props man decided to find something befitting the occasion and called his contacts in the movie business.

'I knew a fellow in a company in Baggot Street that used to hire out old cars for films,' says McShane. 'I said I wanted a nice big decent car for a mate of mine who's getting married.'

To McShane's delight he was given the same 1920s green Dodge car that James Cagney had brought over to Dublin when he starred in the 1959 film *Shake Hands with the Devil*. Paddy was also excited when he heard they were getting James Cagney's car for the wedding and decided not to tell Rita so it would be a special surprise.

On their wedding morning, McShane had the old Dodge sent up to the hills to collect Rita and bring her to the ceremony. But neither Paddy or McShane had reckoned on the reaction of the young bride who was expecting a sleek black limousine, more in keeping with the occasion. For as soon as Rita saw the dusty veteran car pull up outside she burst into tears.

'It was a desperate-looking car,' says Rita, still upset by the memory. 'It was a mushroom colour and I wanted black so I refused to get in it. It was shit.'

Rita's parents tried everything to get their daughter to drive to the church in the Dodge but she refused to budge.

'I just wouldn't go in that car,' says Rita. 'I told my father, "You can go by yourself down to the church and tell them that I'm not getting in."

When Rita's mother arrived at the church 20 minutes after the ceremony should have begun, the concerned bridegroom rushed up to see what had happened. Paddy was shocked when he heard about Rita's refusal to ride in the Dodge but decided to leave it up to Faley O' Reilly to persuade his daughter to come.

As Paddy and the other guests anxiously awaited Rita's arrival, Seán Ó Riada walked in half an hour late carrying his wedding present of a huge rug. As Paddy wanted Ó Riada to play the organ for the ceremony he had previously paid off the regular church organist to take the day off.

'All the trickery I had to go through,' remembers Moloney. 'The organist didn't want to take my money but I said, "Look, the great composer Seán Ó Riada's coming from Cork. Seán, of course, arrived late and it was lucky that Rita was late or he wouldn't have played."

Although 20 minutes late, Rita finally agreed to drive to the church in the Dodge. There were sighs of relief from Paddy and the rest of the guests when the bride, dressed in a white veil, was escorted into the church by her father to the rousing strains of the organ. But the groom did a double-take when he realized that as a joke Ó Riada was playing a tune called *Cailíní in Fhactory* (*The Girls of the Factory*), instead of the customary *Wedding March*.

'I was the only one who recognized what he was playing,' says Paddy. 'The terrible man just looked at me and winked.'

The ceremony went off without a hitch, but when the wedding party assembled to pose for pictures no one could believe the sorry state of the official photographer laid on by Ronnie McShane.

'He arrived by motorbike and he had a huge rip in the back of his trousers,' remembers Rita. 'Everytime he wanted to take a photograph and turned around, his arse was hanging out. This was not the stylish wedding I'd always dreamed of.'

Later at the reception at the Salthill Hotel in Booterstown, McShane redeemed himself. Paddy was concerned as his family and Rita's were not socializing and sitting at opposite sides of the hall. But McShane, being the natural humorist sprang into action.

'I was trying to get both families together,' he said. 'I was saying silly things like, "Paddy tells me that Rita's aunt used to do your washing." '

As the reception progressed relations between the families thawed. There was plenty of food and champagne and Paddy Moloney led all the musicians in a rousing session of music and dancing.

After the reception Moloney was saying good-bye to his tearful mother, and borrowing change for the taxi, when Dubliner Barney McKenna staggered up with his banjo, saying he thought the wedding was at ten that night.

'Poor Barney was half-sloshed,' says Moloney. 'He kept trying to get us to go back in for a few more tunes saying he thought it was going to be an old-style wedding.'

Covered in confetti, the happy newly weds drove to Dublin Airport where they boarded a plane to London en route to their Spanish honeymoon.

* * *

Back in Milltown Paddy and Rita settled into domestic life in her grandfather's grocer's shop. The young couple had wanted Pappa to sell the shop and come and live with them in a semi-detached house nearby but the old man did not want to move. So, Milltown became their home for many years to come.

'Music started to take over my life then,' says Moloney. 'Everything was revolving around it.'

After the release of *The Chieftains*, Moloney, Martin Fay, Seán Potts and Michael Tubridy embarked on a new series of Ceoltóirí Cualann radio shows called *Fleadh Cheoil an Radio* (Festival of the Radio). The shows were proving so popular that Radio Éireann had ordered 22 for 1964.

One of the high points of the show was a weekly competition to find the best players of the various instruments among the radio audience. At the end of the season Ó Riada and two other judges would select the grand winner. In late 1964 the fiddle competition was won by a very tall, good-looking 17-year-fiddler called Seán Keane. Seán Ó Riada was so impressed by the teenager's style of playing that he invited him to join Ceoltóirí Cualann.

'I remember Ó Riada bringing in Seán Keane to meet the group,' says Éamon de Buitléar. 'There were two fiddlers in Ceoltóirí Cualann at that time, Martin Fay and John Kelly, but Seán had impressed everyone with his great talent.

'At that time Seán was a tall slender young fellow with lovely blond hair and I can remember Ó Riada going round boasting, "I have a fiddle player now who looks like a Greek god and plays like an angel." '

* * *

Seán Keane was born on July 12th, 1946 in Dublin and, from his earliest days, was weaned on traditional music. His parents, Mary and Patrick, both played fiddle and the Keane home was well known as an open house for musicians coming up from the country for football matches or on business.

When he was five, Seán and his brother James, who was 18 months younger, were sent to dancing classes but Seán soon got fed up and decided he wanted to learn the pipes. Seán had fallen under the spell after he first heard them played by his uncle Peter Hanley, who was a Dublin fireman.

'When he came to visit he would take out the pipes and you could hear this hum of the drones,' remembers Seán. 'This was such a peaceful sound when we were up in bed and I'd go to sleep as a young child listening to this music.'

At the age of five Seán decided to learn the fiddle, as his fingers were too small to span the pipe's fingering, and when he was six, he was sent to a violin teacher called John Fox. After a few years learning the fiddle Seán was showing great promise and was accepted by the Dublin College of Music to study classical music with violin teacher Clara Green.

As children, Seán and James were taken to the Sunday night variety concerts at the Father Mathew Hall where they had singers, comedians and a token traditional musician at the end.

'We'd go along specifically to hear those musicians,' says Seán. 'It was the only music you'd hear in the week.'

Paddy Moloney remembers seeing nine-year-old Seán and his brother James, who was now playing accordion, arrive at the Pipers' Club in Thomas Street with their father and playing with them. 'They'd sit up and play there. I thought, "God, great musicians. They're going to be great." '

Seán studied classical music up to the seventh grade when he was seduced by the strains of traditional music and started calling in at O'Donoghue's Pub and various Irish music clubs on his way back from music class.

'That ended the serious music for me,' says Seán. 'It was the early Sixties and the folk scene, as they called it then, was tremendously vibrant and it was really the thing to do. The place to be.'

Seán was lucky that his teacher at the School of Music, Clara Greene, did not look down on traditional music like so many other classical musicians and even encouraged him to make the change.

'The classical training helped me a lot,' said Seán. 'There were people who were rigid that a classical player can't be a traditional player or vice versa. But I think it's up to the extent of your musicianship. Obviously I was meant to be a traditional player.'

At the age of 14, Seán started playing fiddle in different bands around Dublin as well as the Castle Ceili Band, which he had formed with his brother, James, who played the accordion, and their friend Mick O'Connor. (In fact, James was to become several times all-Ireland Champion accordionist.) 'The Castle Ceili Band brought a new element into ceili bands,' says Seán. 'We revved it up a bit and there was a lot of precision in the performance.' The Castle Ceili Band started playing small Gaelic League halls in and around Dublin for about 25 shillings a night.

'We'd play all night,' says Seán. 'And then maybe a bag of chips on the way home. You did it for the love of the thing.' Some nights the band would travel out to far-away places like Lixnaw in Kerry, about 200 miles from Dublin, to play at a Ceili Inn for just 30 shillings and then drive back bleary-eyed arriving just in time for work the next morning.

'They were really great fun days,' says Seán. 'The festivals would be weekend jobs. Oh yeah Jesus, from morning, noon and night we'd be boozing and playing until you'd squeezed the last note out of the fiddle and the last drop out of the bottle. Oh, you'd want to be in the full of your health now. I wouldn't do it now, I can tell you.'

Seán left school at the age of 16 and signed on as an apprentice boiler maker, drifting through various jobs until he ended up working for the post office.

'I couldn't wait to get out of school,' remembers Seán. 'I never wanted to admit it, but it was always in the back of my mind, that music was going to be it for me. At that time you were encouraged to get a real job like everybody else. Don't do anything freakish like depending for your livelihood on playing the fiddle. It was serious stuff.'

A year later Seán entered the fiddle competition for *Fleadh Ceoil an Radio* and his whole life changed when Seán Ó Riada invited him to join the famous Ceoltóirí Cualann where Paddy Moloney and Martin Fay were already members.

'This was the big time,' says Seán. 'I couldn't believe it and of course I jumped at it straight away. I think I can remember almost every minute of the five years I was in the group.' Seán's experience at Ceoltóirí Cualann was to be different from anything he had played before. 'Under Seán's [O'Riada] direction [Ceoltóirí Cualann] had a totally different approach to the playing and presentation of music people had been used to,' remembers Seán. 'Up to this, groups such as Céilí bands had played in unison to the accompaniment of piano and drums. Indeed, down through the years I was a member of the Castle Céilí Band, and we travelled the length and breadth of Ireland playing at dances.'

Now a member of Ceoltóirí Cualann, Seán found himself part of the Dublin music set where he met Garech Browne.

'Garech would have a party at the drop of a hat,' says Seán. 'They were fantastic. All-night jobs of course and meeting fascinating characters. The parties were never-ending and there was food and drink and music and talk. It was just endless fun.'

Then in 1964 Seán met the lady who was to become his wife. Marie Conneally also came from a very musical background. She was brought up with her cousins Paddy, John, George and Michael Byrt, and she was also familiar with the local musicians and members of the Kilfenora Céilí Band who often played at her house. 'Marie has been a constant source of encouragement to me,' says Seán. 'It could not have been easy rearing a family for five or six months of the year single-handedly.' Seán and Marie have three children: Darach, the youngest at 19, plays the piano, uilleann pipes and tin whistle; Páraic plays the fiddle and is in a rock band called 'The Lemmings'; and Déirdre, who gave up the fiddle in order to secure her B.Sc. from Trinity College, Dublin, is married to Alex Tracy and is busy bringing up her daughter Molly. 'Molly, at 13 months, is inclined to wriggle her butt when she hears music. So the music goes on,' laughs Seán.

7

The Sixties

In early 1964 The Chieftains performed for the first time in public at a dinner reception following the RTE Golden Harp Competition at the Gresham Hotel. They were such a big hit with the audience that Ulster Television immediately booked the new group to appear on a television show in Belfast.

'It was almost cancelled,' remembers Paddy. 'Garech arrived far too late to get us there in time, and so we had to stop for lunch. And for some that meant a liquid lunch! But young Andy Cockhart, who is now a director of Ulster Television, was most understanding, and agreed to tape the show anyway, even though we were five hours late.'

But they played without bodhrán player Davy Fallon, who couldn't take time off from his farm to come to Belfast. Realizing he couldn't rely on the elderly musician, Paddy Moloney recruited a new bodhrán player in 1966 called Peader Mercier.

* * *

Although Paddy Moloney and the other Chieftains were now celebrities in Dublin from their radio and television appearances and concerts, they still kept their day jobs and treated the music as an increasingly well-paid hobby. Still at Baxendales, Paddy had a promising career and was already carving out a reputation as a cost-cutting executive.

'I was coming up with new ideas,' says Moloney. 'Unfortunately that meant doing away with staff. We never actually sacked anybody, we just never replaced them. Eventually I was in charge of doing taxes and preparing the wages, which was good experience for later.'

Paddy, who became a father in 1964 when Rita gave birth to their son Aonghus, was also discovering a wider, more glamorous new world through his friend Garech Browne, who was enthusiastically embracing the 1960s' revolution in music, fashion and the arts. Garech entertained lavishly at his house Woodtown Manor and had the run of his mother's beautiful Wicklow lodge, Luggala.

When the new rock élite like The Rolling Stones came to Luggala to rub shoulders with the likes of Peter O'Toole, Seán Connery, Richard Harris and Brendan Behan, The Chieftains were often there, too, and whenever they played, they and their music made a lasting impression.

Marianne Faithfull remembers bringing Mick Jagger over to one of Garech's parties in Woodtown in 1964 where she first saw Paddy Moloney play. 'It was almost like something out of the Middle Ages,' she says. 'Garech's parties were out of another time. It was how you would imagine Ireland hundreds of years ago with poets, musicians, children, dogs and horses and carriages. It was just amazing.

'I remember hearing Paddy play the penny whistle first and he was so funny and delightful. We became friends immediately.'

Mick Jagger was also an instant convert to The Chieftains and took their first record back to London and played it for the other Rolling Stones who were duly impressed.

'Since the first time I heard The Chieftains I've never travelled without them,' Keith Richards told the author.

Browne's introduction of The Chieftains to his influential friends was slowly paying off for the group who were achieving cult status among musicians. Paddy Moloney was staggered when he walked into a party at the London flat of the late Rolling Stones' guitarist Brian Jones to find *The Chieftains* playing.

'I couldn't believe that the Rolling Stones were playing The Chieftains,' remembers Moloney. 'Brilliant.'

Irish film star Peter O'Toole was also an early fan of the group and regularly invited them to play at his parties.

'Paddy would pop out and come over with his boys,' remembers O'Toole. 'We'd just have quiet fun and enjoy ourselves. In those days it was skiffle or rock bands with electric guitars or something. What I do know is that it wasn't the uilleann pipes. It wasn't the rage. It was just something beautiful and very nice to listen to.'

Always down-to-earth without any pretentions, Moloney easily adapted into show business circles and became one of the most sought-after guests on the Dublin party scene.

'We suddenly found ourselves in the world of these big film stars,' says Moloney. 'I remember Peter O'Toole, who was filming in Dublin, sending a big limo to collect us so we could play at his party. I was playing *Roisín Dubh* on the tin whistle and somebody made a noise. Peter just took off his boot and hurled it over their heads, wham. Straight through the kitchen window. That shut them up.'

Searching to remember the incident more than 30 years later, Peter O'Toole says laconically, 'Well it doesn't surprise me. Things were often thrown.'

However, the actor does fondly remember one particular night when The Chieftains were over at his house in Dublin playing music. 'We were having a quiet little session. Paddy was playing the pipes and we were dancing and jumping around and the phone rang. "Would I go to a gypsy party?" So I thought, "A gypsy party". I said, "Well, that sounds interesting." Well, I said, "I've got some musicians with me." "Oh that should be all right." '

'So Paddy and I and his boys set off for the gypsy party and we got to a rather posh suburb of Dublin and rang the door bell.'

To their astonishment, the door was opened by the then famous Irish talk show host and compere of the English version of *This is Your Life*, Eamonn Andrews.

'He was a tall chap with a hanky around his head, an earring and a charcoal moustache,' remembers O'Toole. Not quite what I thought this was to be about. I mean they were playing that kind of gypsy.

'So in we went, Paddy and I and the pipes and the drum and the fiddles and whatever. And of course they were more interested in what was going on other than the music. They were fox trotting in the kitchen. And then when things got a bit rowdy we were thrown out.'

Each October at Middlemas, Browne threw a lavish party in the huge country-style kitchen at Luggala which his mother had built him as a present. Garech invited all the leading traditional musicians who would descend on Luggala to play together in musical sessions that are still talked about in awe. Browne would lay on barrels of Guinness and plain stout and servants would wheel in huge silver platters of pigs' feet, hams, cabbage and potatoes.

'There was no such thing as knives or cutlery,' remembers Moloney. 'You'd use your fingers in the old style.'

As the party got wilder and wilder Paddy joined the other musicians in a rousing selection of jigs and reels to get everyone up dancing on the stone floor in the huge kitchen with its open fireplace.

'I'll never forget Lord John Kilbracken was at one of the parties with his girlfriend who had very long hair,' laughs Moloney. 'Her hair kept going into the stout and she kept swinging it around in time with the music and splashing everybody. And we'd play and sing. Wild times.'

One of the most memorable Luggala parties was thrown by Garech's mother Lady Oranmore after the release of the first Chieftains' album. Princess Grace was the guest of honour at the charity fund-raising picnic held on the great lawn where other parties included Mick Jagger and other members of the Rolling Stones.

'It was just a big picnic,' recalls Moloney. 'The Chieftains played and Dolly McMahon sang followed by Leo Rowsome on pipes. It was fantastic.'

Garech's parties could go on for days with the guests grabbing a few hours of sleep before carrying on where they left off the night before. The joke among Garech's friends was that if you visited Luggala you would get 'Luggalad', meaning Browne would hold you for days as friendly hostage enjoying hospitality. Actor John Hurt became a Luggala regular after meeting Garech Browne in 1964 and still is to this day.

'People came here for one night and they'd stay for five,' said Hurt, who received his education in traditional music from Garech Browne. 'There'd be playing every night and out of those five nights extraordinary things would happen. Garech is a genuine patron of the arts and he's provided a haven and a really creative area for great musicians, poets and the arts.'

Hurt remembers seeing Paddy and friends playing at both Woodtown Manor and Luggala in the early days before they became well known.

'They'd roll up and just get the instruments out and play,' says Hurt. 'And it was wonderful music. In those days everyone had a jar and nobody thought about alcoholism or anything like that.

And it was the way it was. We were strong and if we got to bed by 5:00 a.m. we were lucky.'

Paddy Moloney still fondly remembers sitting around the open fireplace at Garech's Luggala kitchen at 7:00 a.m. in the morning after a memorable party with the legendary piper Séamus Ennis and his father Jimmy.

'We spat out the fire,' said Paddy. 'Telling stories and sitting around playing. The last logs were just cinders lining the fireplace and Garech, Jimmy, Séamus and myself were telling stories and it was great.'

* * *

In 1968 Garech persuaded Paddy to leave the security of Baxendales and join Claddagh full time as managing director at £17 a week. It was a difficult decision to leave his promising career at Baxendales after 12 years service with a wife and two young children to support and plunge into the uncertainty of the music business.

'It meant a big change in our whole family life,' says Moloney. 'My mother was really upset and she often asked Rita when was I ever going to get a decent job. However, the penny finally dropped many years later when she saw me in cap and gown to receive my honorary doctorate from Trinity College.'

Paddy plunged enthusiastically into his new job, working from a tiny office in Garech's Woodtown house, and began trying to turn around the fortunes of the company which had an annual turnover of just £668.

'Garech had put his money into a hobby: making albums,' explained Moloney. 'I had to make it a viable commercial concern.'

At the beginning, the majority of Claddagh's business was done in Garech's bathroom during lengthy meetings while the company chairman took his morning bath.

'We'd be talking away for hours,' recalls Paddy. 'Garech would get in his bath and we'd start planning what we were going to do and how we were going to do it. As far as I was concerned in the early days, Claddagh had two boardrooms; Garech's bathroom and the Stag's Head Pub around the corner from where I finally set up an office in Dame Street.'

Paddy soon proved his value as managing director, driving hard bargains for Claddagh and building up a reputation as a hustler. If

Garech Browne was Claddagh's smooth-talking velvet glove, then Paddy Moloney was the iron fist that got the job done.

Moloney spent two weeks of every month away on business, much of it in London where Claddagh had a makeshift office at the Shepherd's Market home of Lady Tiger Cowley, who was one of Garech's many girlfriends.

In 1969 Paddy undertook a three-week solo engagement in a Bronx club owned by millionaire businessman Bill Fuller, with the express purpose of promoting Claddagh albums and The Chieftains.

'I used to be away from home an awful lot,' remembers Moloney. 'I was busy establishing The Chieftains and the record company as an international label. In some ways music is my vocation and it automatically fell onto my family as well.'

Paddy's daughter Aedín, who was born in 1967, grew up during her father's years at Claddagh, and was brought up with The Chieftains.

'Probably my earliest memory of The Chieftains was having an absent father,' remembers Aedín. 'Like it was mummy who dealt with everything and who gave me a slap on the arse when I was bold. Daddy was always out working. He was away or whatever.'

Rita Moloney says family life was very difficult during the early days at Claddagh and she saw far less of her husband than she did years later when The Chieftains became globe-trotting superstars.

'It was his addiction,' says Rita. 'And very difficult for us. We just never saw him.'

Naturally hands-on, Moloney involved himself in every aspect of Claddagh and one of his innovations was persuading Irish book shops to stock records, something which had never been done before. Every Christmas Eve Paddy made it a point to personally deliver Claddagh records to restock the shelves for last-minute buyers.

It was during his first few months at Claddagh that Moloney ran head-on into a conflict of interests which seriously threatened the future of The Chieftains. As a sideline, Paddy Moloney, Seán Potts and Martin Fay all played for the Gael Linn Cabaret and when the question of a contract came up Moloney refused to sign as he worked for the competing Claddagh Records. As a result, Potts and Fay walked out on The Chieftains feeling they could make more money with Gael Linn.

'It was a fairly lucrative contract Gael Linn were offering us,' says Potts. 'At that stage I was married and on a mortgage and I was out to make money. It went against Paddy's principles to sign and in retrospect he was right.'

Looking back, Moloney says he was devastated at losing two Chieftain members.

'That was an awful blow to me,' remembers Moloney. 'I was in an awful state but I wasn't going to let it beat me. The whole strength of The Chieftains was Claddagh Records and then this happens. I should have pushed harder for Seán to stay but I didn't want to lose his friendship.'

Desperate to keep The Chieftains afloat Moloney asked Seán Ó Riada if he could recruit Seán Keane into the group. Initially Ó Riada refused and it was only after Moloney reminded him how he had allowed Peader Mercier to join Ceoltóirí Cualann that he grudgingly agreed.

For the next year The Chieftains soldiered on as a quartet consisting of Moloney, Michael Tubridy, Peader Mercier and Seán Keane, who made his debut at the 1968 Edinburgh Festival, where they played for a week on the same bill as the popular Scottish duo The Corries.

'We had huge success that year as a quartet,' says Moloney. 'That's when things started to take off in an even bigger way for The Chieftains.'

Three weeks before the Edinburgh Festival, Rolling Stone Mick Jagger and Marianne Faithfull traveled 140 miles to Castletown, Co. Kildare just to hear The Chieftains perform at an open air concert. Sitting behind a bush to stay anonymous the superstar couple loved the concert and later attended a banquet in Desmond Guinness' Leixlip Castle. During the meal Jagger rose from his seat to enthusiastically announce, 'Paddy Moloney's going to give us a tune.'

'Mick was very friendly with the Guinness patron at the time,' says Seán Keane. 'We met him a couple of times on his Georgian estate at Castletown.'

Marianne Faithfull remembers Paddy and Garech as being an 'enchanting combination'.

'Paddy was so funny and delightful,' says Marianne. 'He used to tell Mick and me about his mission to spread traditional music through the world and we thought he was wonderful.'

71

In the four years since its release *The Chieftains* record had achieved underground cult status in England after BBC Radio One's highly influential DJ John Peel began to play tracks on his Sunday show *Top Gear* and became a staunch supporter of the group.

'We were the "in" music at that time,' remembers Moloney. 'People like the Beatles and the Rolling Stones were listening to us and spreading the word. It was starting to happen for us and our record started selling in the hundreds.'

When John Peel asked The Chieftains to fill in at the last minute for the English rock band Curved Air, who were unable to play at a three-day festival in Wexford, they were unsure of whether they would be accepted by the new hippie audience. Finally they agreed and found themselves opening for the popular folk-rock group Matthew's Southern Comfort.

Remembers Tubridy: 'We realized this could be a total disaster and we might be booed off the stage, but we said we'd try it and take it one tune at a time. When we went on stage and we saw this audience we didn't know what to think. They were all over the place in the hippie gear of the day and we were dressed respectably, but we just ignored them and played a tune. At first they were very noisy and hardly anyone was listening but we played another one and slowly they began to take notice and sit up and listen. By the time we had finished our set we had them all with us and they were shouting for more so we did an encore.

'I just can't describe what it felt like. We just couldn't believe what had happened because they were a totally alien audience who didn't know anything about traditional music.'

The highly respected English music paper *Melody Maker* profiled The Chieftains for the first time in its Focus on Folk column, noting that the members prefer to remain 'calm amateurs rather than turning professionals'.

'Smart suits, white shirts, sombre ties, short hair, quiet courtesy. Some combination,' read the profile headlined 'Tanks a lot Chieftains.'

Showing a natural flair for publicity and complete mastery of the sound-bite, before it was even invented, Paddy Moloney told *Melody Maker* that there were at least four of five groups already copying The Chieftains in Ireland.

'I think it's flattery,' said The Chieftains' leader. 'I'm delighted to see it happen. Everything we do is our own idea. We haven't copied anyone else's ideas.'

Moloney also attacked Irish showbands, saying 'It can be the most brutal sound' while applauding underground rock music for its honesty and passion.

'I don't give a damn about their long hair,' said Moloney. 'I agree with this pop thing. They are so sincere about their music.'

The national press was also beginning to wake up to The Chieftains and in a rousing concert review *Daily Mail* writer Ken Thompson called them: 'The most in-demand group of traditional musicians in Ireland.'

Describing Paddy Moloney as 'a little laughing fellow who looks as though he would be at ease jockeying home a winner at The Curragh,' Thompson speculated about whether Chieftains' music would ever find success in the mass music audience.

'In the fickle area of overnight smash-hits and lifelong misses,' wrote Thompson. 'It's difficult to say whether the sound of The Chieftains will reach across the Irish Sea to the ear of those Tin Pan Alley cats who exist by anticipating and at times by fashioning trends in pop.'

*   *   *

In late 1968 Paddy Moloney urged Garech Browne to capitalize on the growing popularity of The Chieftains and they started to plan a new record. Their decision happened to coincide with Seán Potts and Martin Fay completing their one-year contract with Gael Linn.

'Things didn't work out well for them and I wanted them back,' says Moloney. 'So I got Garech to do the dirty work and ask them to rejoin The Chieftains and they did. So now I had two fiddlers.'

In April 1969 Paddy Moloney and the reconstituted Chieftains flew to Edinburgh for a weekend to record *Chieftains 2* at the Craighall Studios. Moloney made the decision to record outside Ireland as the studio technology was far superior and they could record on four track stereo. The second Chieftains' record was far more ambitious than the first with lusher, more textured arrangements from Paddy Moloney.

'I saw fuller horizons and more expansion,' explained Moloney. 'I was starting to develop a flow and at last was beginning to be able to do the more adventurous pieces of music I'd always wanted to do. It was a big improvement.'

Moloney was also able to introduce The Chieftains' first recorded work by Carolan, which was an 18th-century song called *Planxty George Brabazon*, which he discovered in the O'Sullivan Collection of Carolan that his sister Esther had given him in 1959 for his 21st birthday.

But the real breakthrough track of the record was *The Foxhunt* which pointed the way to Moloney's future folk orchestrated works with The Chieftains. In an exciting musical canvas of the chase, Moloney used his Chieftains' palette to recreate the sounds of the hunting horns, galloping horses and the barking of dogs.

'A lot of the purists weren't so sure about *The Foxhunt*,' says Moloney. 'They said it was going away from the tradition whereas Seán Ó Riada thought it was brilliant.'

Michael Tubridy's concertina-playing aunt, Mrs Crotty, whom Moloney first met on his cycling holiday to Clare, is immortalized in *Chieftains 2* with the reel named after her.

The Chieftains began recording on a Saturday morning and were finished by Sunday night when everyone, except for Paddy, who stayed behind to mix the album, flew back to Dublin to be back at work on Monday. When Moloney finally returned and listened to the acetates of *Chieftains 2*, he was terribly disappointed. 'The whole thing sounded terrible and I hated it. There was no presence at all in the recording, it sounded flat and dull, as if we were playing behind a blanket, and I was just devastated when I heard it.'

As Claddagh Records were distributed by EMI, Moloney appealed for help to the head of EMI in Ireland whose name was Harry Christmas. Christmas has been introduced to Paddy by their mutual friend Pat Pretty, and was sympathetic and offered to call up Abbey Road studios in London and try to get studio time to cut a new acetate. A couple of days later he called back with the news that the Beatles had agreed to let Moloney have half a day in the studio they had rented for six months to record the *Abbey Road* album.

'The Beatles knew all about The Chieftains' music and liked it,' says Moloney. 'They were off the day I was in there, but Paul McCartney came rambling in to see how I was doing and all of a sudden he was talking to me about music. Then John Lennon and Yoko Ono strolled through the studio.'

Moloney's new acetate was a success giving the perfectionist the exact sound he wanted and *Chieftains 2* was released to rave reviews on both sides of the Irish Sea.

'The Chieftains' Music is no rough hewn rural craft,' wrote *The Times'* music critic Karl Dallas. 'At the centre of it all sits Paddy Moloney, a tiny puck-faced man whose fingers on the pipes seem to acquire an independent existence, skittering over the keys like five-legged sea creatures, creating a music that appeals to the head as well as the heart.'

* * *

In March 1970 Ó Riada's classical work *Hercules Dux Ferrares* was finally published, more than a decade after it had been written, by Garech Browne's new Woodtown Music Publications. Claddagh's new publishing arm had been set up by Paddy Moloney who had engineered its acceptance into the Performing Rights Society. At a reception to launch the publication at the Old Hibernian Hotel in Dublin, Ó Riada surprised everyone by publicly announcing that he'd disbanded Ceoltóirí Cualann in a radio interview with RTE's Liam Nolan.

'Regarding what The Chieftains are doing I can't feel anything but sympathy,' said Ó Riada. 'The Chieftains are a subsection of my own group and undoubtedly they would not have come into existence except for the existence of Ceoltóirí Cualann. Therefore I can't very well, just as a father can't repudiate his own son, I can't repudiate what they're doing. In fact I admire what they're doing but it has tremendous limitations. They are limited to doing this kind of thing.

'I can't see any future for The Chieftains, which is why I have disbanded Ceoltóirí Cualann, the parent group. I feel that part of my life is over and I would like to try something new.'

No one was more shocked at the announcement and the attack on The Chieftains than Paddy Moloney who was with Ó Riada during the reception at the Old Hibernian.

'I felt it was jealousy among musicians,' says Moloney. 'Fair enough. I'm often that way myself. I mean jealousy among pipers is livid. It's terrible. It's part of our tradition and I think Seán had that part of the tradition in him as well.'

Late that night Paddy Moloney called up Ó Riada at the

Shelbourne Hotel to ask him retract his statement and continue on with Ceoltóirí Cualann.

'Ruth answered the phone and said Seán didn't want to talk,' remembers Moloney. 'I don't think the rest of the band knew what he had done at that time. He was broken up and Ruth came back on the phone and said, "Look, Seán just doesn't see any point. He has nothing else he wants to do. Nothing else to offer."

'So I said that we could find something else for him to offer. But he had made up his mind and that was that.'

The poet John Montague, who was close to both of them, says by then Ó Riada was a deeply troubled man and a chronic alcoholic.

'He was a very dangerous drinker,' says Montague, who was also a director of Claddagh records. 'He didn't get hangovers and only occasionally towards the end did he seem befuddled.'

Years of alcoholism had transformed the former rosy-cheeked Ó Riada, who had once looked far younger than his years, into a grey-haired old man who looked at least 60. Montague believes that Ó Riada's real tragedy was that he was never accepted as a classical composer with his works seldom being performed.

'He burned out,' says Montague. 'What do you do if you are a composer and your works are only performed once and respectfully buried. Frustration's not the word for it.'

John Montague says that the real reason for Ó Riada disbanding Ceoltóirí Cualann was that he was physically too weak to take them on the road anymore.

'He had abandoned the whole idea and disbanded Ceoltóirí Cualann,' says Montague, 'His relationship with Paddy was very complicated and at the time it was quite taut as can be expected between somebody who is the director and somebody who is the chief soloist. I don't know how conductors and their stars get along but I'm sure they have to agree to.'

During his final years Seán Ó Riada always stayed with Garech Browne when he came to Dublin for a concert or to do a television show with Ceoltóirí Cualann.

'Seán was a wonderful mixture,' says Garech. 'There were moments when he was very introverted and very quiet. There were moments when he loved the *craic*. He found it difficult to refuse the booze and I suppose that if we'd known more about it in that time we wouldn't have let him go that far. But then everybody drank and nobody talked about it.'

Soon after the announcement, Montague was at a party at Garech's Browne's Woodtown house with Moloney and Ó Riada, who were now back on good terms.

'The joint was jumping,' said Montague. 'Paddy had been playing something beautiful on the tin whistle and the pipes and Seán clapped him on the back and said, "Paddy, you're the best musicianer in Ireland." I thought that was crucial because the word musicianer means all-round. The man with the music. He may not be the greatest tin whistler or the greatest piper but Paddy was certainly the man with the music. It seemed to me that night that Seán was passing on the reins to Paddy.'

*   *   *

In the summer of 1971 Paddy Moloney and Seán Ó Riada collaborated together for the last time on the Claddagh Record that became *Ó Riada's Farewell*. Recorded at Luggala on Garech's Browne's antique upright harpsichord, Ó Riada, who was to die a few months later, poured his heart and guts into the 14 pieces of traditional music.

There was a strange eerie atmosphere at the recording session and on his way to lunch Paddy was walking past the long Georgian windows in Garech's dining room when to his amazement he saw a worried-looking Rita pass by.

'I thought it was strange,' says Paddy. 'I knew she was three miles away in Garech's cottage and she didn't drive or walk in those days. I became more and more worried during lunch and afterwards I thought I'd better telephone her. I asked her how she was and she told me that she wasn't too well. I said I know because I'd seen her go past the window here. She said, "That's very funny because I was out hanging clothes and I fell and hit my head badly and was unconscious for two minutes." I felt a chill rush through me because it was exactly the same time that I'd seen her walk by.'

After the recording session Moloney drove Ó Riada back to Dublin in Garech's car and while they were waiting for the train back to Cork they started talking.

'I knew there was something wrong with him,' says Moloney. 'He had cirrhosis of the liver and his rosy red cheeks were deathly white and he was like an old man although he was only 40. He started giving me a fatherly talk and told me that he thought the two Chieftains' albums showed great promise and asked me if I would carry on.

'I said, "Seán of course I will. I'm only starting and there's an awful lot more that I have to contribute." '

Realizing that Ó Riada was close to the end, Paddy spent two weeks in London mixing Ó Riada's session. Unfortunately Garech's ancient harpsichord had a missing 'A' note and Moloney and recording engineer Ioan Allen painstakingly had to find a good 'A' and then they spent hours carefully splicing it into the quarter-inch tape.

'Seán wanted to do it on Garech's harpsichord and quite right too,' says Moloney. 'If you listen to the album you'll hear the difference of an old instrument which has guts.'

The final editing was completed in September, just a couple of weeks before Ó Riada's illness had prompted Garech and Paddy to arrange to fly him to Kings Cross Hospital to see a specialist.

'I left the tracks in the same order that we recorded them,' said Moloney. 'It was played to him a couple of days before he died and he gave a sign that he approved.'

Ó Riada died on October 3rd, 1971 and three days later he was buried at the little church in Cúil Aodha to the moving strains of *Mo Ghile Mear.*

8

Taking Off

By 1970 electric folk rock was big business with groups like Fairport Convention, Steeleye Span, The Incredible String Band and Pentangle taking traditional folk music and revving it up for the modern generation. When Fairport Convention came to play the National Stadium in Dublin in March, The Chieftains were the obvious choice to share the bill with them. It was their biggest concert to date but The Chieftains didn't change their acoustic set in the slightest when they opened for the high decibel English folk-rock band. Playing an uncompromising mixture of traditional jigs, reels and hornpipes, The Chieftains easily won over the enthusiastic young audience who were soon on their feet dancing.

'I'd heard all these bands like Fairport Convention and Steeleye Span,' says Paddy Moloney. 'To me it was rock going folk and I didn't think it had the full strength of traditional folk music.'

During that period The Chieftains were swamped with offers to go full time professional and make a hard-driving album of Celtic rock with electric guitars, bass and drums like Jig a Jig, who had reached Number 1 in the European charts with a rock version of an Irish reel.

'I certainly wasn't interested in becoming one of those kinds of bands,' Moloney says. 'I wanted to follow the lines of the true tradition.'

On the strength of their performance that night, The Chieftains without any supporting act sold out the National Stadium a month later, with a show booked and promoted by the well-known entrepreneur Jim Aiken.

In August The Chieftains played the Cambridge Folk Festival and made a deep impression with the appreciative audience who gave them a standing ovation. A group picture taken at the festival shows them looking very collegiate dressed in white shirts and dark trousers with Martin Fay holding his trademark cigarette.

As The Chieftains' career took off there were more and more offers of work in England and Ireland and Moloney's toughest job was persuading the other band members to take time off work. Mick Tubridy, now a partner in his engineering firm, was having a particularly difficult time committing himself to The Chieftains and decided to quit: 'My company got this big job building the new passenger terminal at Dublin Airport and I was working nights and weekends. I was in charge of the project and I felt I just couldn't carry on with The Chieftains.

'I tried to get out and I told Paddy I was leaving but he kept stringing me along saying, "Will you come and do the next gig?" He took it one gig at a time and that went on until the project finished in 1972 and I had more time so I stayed. Paddy's a very good manager and there's no way the group would have stayed together if it hadn't been for him.'

Once, while Moloney was still working at Baxendales, the only way he could play an out of town concert was to take sick leave from work. Much to his surprise, a photograph of the concert appeared in the *Independent* the next day. 'Lucky for me, nobody seemed to notice.' His entrée to the film world came in 1969 when film director John Huston came to Ireland to make a movie called *Sinful Davey*, starring a young English actor called John Hurt. Much of the filming was done in the Wicklow Mountains and Luggala and The Chieftains, together with a group of visiting Russian dancers, were hired by Huston to entertain at the wrap party.

During The Chieftains performance Huston's teenaged daughter Anjelica made her first guest appearance with the group dancing a jig in her long leather boots.

Anjelica: 'I was taking Irish dancing at the time so I performed a jig while they were playing. After that Paddy used to come to my father's house in Galway and he would always play for us. I'll always remember him playing a song that I particularly loved called Eileen Aroon. It was magic.'

During the summer months, Garech rented Paddy out a small cottage at Luggala across the lake from the main house as a summer retreat. The lovely old cottage had once been owned by a rabbit trapper and was now officially known as the Trapper's Cottage.

'That's how Paddy got the nickname of The Trapper,' says Browne. 'What, or who, he trapped I wouldn't like to think.'

Paddy's daughter Aedín spent much of her early childhood in the Trapper's Cottage where she and her brother Aonghus weaved a whole imaginary land around a series of stunning rocks.

'It was a fantastic place to grow up in,' she remembers. 'It's very dramatic and very wild with a lake and cliffs. I remember when I was a little girl Mick Jagger came to tea one day with Bianca. That whole 60s' rock 'n' roll set used to come to Ireland and stay with Garech. It was like a Woodstock retreat for them.'

Paddy Moloney says the whole 'sex, drugs and rock 'n' roll' 1960s' lifestyle went straight past him.

'Maybe I was innocent but I never noticed any drugs,' he says. 'It was more fun and games and I suppose there was sex going on but it didn't bother me and there was nothing too vulgar. I found it very innocent and very exciting in those days.'

* * *

In the two years since the release of *Chieftains 2*, the group had carved a solid reputation as the finest and most exciting exponents of Irish traditional music. In early 1971 it was decided to make a third Chieftains album to capitalize on the group's growing popularity. From his Claddagh work Paddy Moloney had made many contacts in the recording industry and always took a keen professional note of how the bigger record companies operated.

'I was getting more sophisticated recording-wise,' said Moloney. 'Different new techniques like the Dolby System were coming into being and I wanted *Chieftains 3* to be recorded state of the art and we used eight tracks instead of just two- or four-track as we had before.'

Booking studio time at London's Air Studios, Moloney hired Ioan Allen, who'd helped Ray Dolby perfect his Dolby System (and is now a top executive of Dolby's US company), as his engineer. Moloney also recruited the services of a professional lilter called Pat Kilduff especially for a track called *The Hunter's Purse*. At that time Kilduff was totally innocent of the ways of the world and had never ventured out of Athlone in Co. West Meath, where he was born.

'He was extremely nervous when I brought him to Dublin for

the session,' remembers Moloney, who told Kilduff to stay put in his Morans Hotel room until he went to the airport the next morning. 'Pat came down for a bottle of stout and met the great traditional fiddler Seán Maguire in the bar. The two of them got stuck in and sat up all night lilting and playing music.'

When Moloney came to collect him the following morning he found the lilter hung over and petrified about the prospect of flying.

'Pat sat beside me and held onto my arm for the duration of the flight because he was so scared,' says Moloney. 'The minute we hit the runway and the plane had stopped Pat burst out of his seat screaming, "Where's the toilet?" He'd been too scared to go while the plane had been in the air.'

During their time in London, the naïve lilter was treated to a guided tour of some of the sleazier parts of the city by the more worldly members of The Chieftains.

'The boys gave him a terrible time,' says Moloney. 'They took him up around the pornographic bookshops in Soho and he just didn't know what had hit him. It was a terrible shock and such madness. We knocked great fun out of it.'

Chieftains 3 was recorded in just a few days but Moloney stayed on in London afterwards to mix *Ó Riada's Farewell* with Ioan Allen. The new album demonstrated further expansion for The Chieftains and featured an early Chieftains' version of *Carolan's Concerto*.

'That was my party piece when I was ten,' says Moloney. 'Leo Rowsome taught it to me first when there were few people playing O'Carolan's music.'

A Trip to Sligo was composed by Moloney after The Chieftains had played an open air music festival in Sligo a few months earlier with Fairport Convention. Each member of the band had his own instrumental melody in the piece which marked a new progressive departure for the group.

For the first time ever *Chieftains 3* had a photograph of The Chieftains instead of the usual Eddie Delaney work. The cover photograph by fashion photographer Claude Virgin was taken in among stone nude statues in the National Gallery in Dublin, and finally gave The Chieftains a visual identity with the record-buying public. Taking infinite care with the cover, as always Garech Browne had his friend, the Scottish folklorist Hamish Henderson, pen the liner notes which announced the record as 'something of an event for the aficionado'.

To promote the new record The Chieftains went on a whirlwind trip to America for the first time in 1972 to play just one concert at the Irish Arts Theater in New York and do some radio interviews.

'It was crazy,' remembers Seán Keane, who had just joined the post office as a telegraph engineer. 'We went over on a Saturday and came back on the Monday. That was my first vision of New York and I couldn't believe it. It was the greatest city and I loved the vibrance of the place bursting with this Irish atmosphere.'

Paddy Moloney was less happy. He refused to stay at the tatty Tenth Avenue hotel the promoters had booked for the group because it had cockroaches. He successfully demanded a move to the first-class Algonquin on West 44th Street, which had originally been promised to them by the promoters.

'It was dreadful,' said Moloney. 'I said, "Look, we're going home tomorrow if you don't put us into the Algonquin." They just didn't want to spend the extra money. Eventually they gave in and we got into the Algonquin.'

Michael Tubridy recalls The Chieftains' first walk down Fifth Avenue when they found themselves in the middle of a dramatic police chase.

'We couldn't resist walking down Fifth Avenue because you always hear about it,' said Tubridy. 'The next thing, we suddenly hear all these sirens and a police car screeches to a halt. Then, to our amazement, a policeman came riding down the road on a horse, pulled up beside us and tied the reins around a pole. He then pulled out a gun and went running across the road in front of us.

' "God," I said, "Jeez, this is really like the wild West." '

While the other Chieftains were sightseeing, Moloney was meeting record company chiefs who were interested in signing the group in the United States. Dealing in the cut-throat American music industry for the first time, Moloney insisted that any deal would have to include the complete Claddagh back catalogue, however uncommercial it might be.

'I could easily have sold The Chieftains at that time,' recalls Moloney. 'If I'd been on my own I would have said "to hell with it", but the principle was that if they took The Chieftains they had to take the spoken-word records and everything. To be honest it didn't bother me. I liked what I was doing.'

Among the audience at the Irish Arts Center to see The Chieftains were John Lennon and Yoko Ono, who had just moved to New

York. Their first ever American concert was a big success garnering rave reviews in the New York Irish Press and they were welcomed by the Irish community as musical heroes. But a day later they were back in Dublin at their mundane jobs as if it had all been a dream.

'It was ridiculous,' says Seán Keane. 'I was up a telegraph pole hanging lines the day after I got back from New York but my head was in another place.'

Back in Dublin, the television director Alan Tongue invited The Chieftains to Belfast to perform *Carolan's Concerto* with the BBC's Northern Ireland Orchestra on a special St Patrick's Day broadcast. Tongue wanted the orchestra's schoolboyish-looking harp player Derek Bell to portray Carolan and be surrounded by The Chieftains with the orchestra behind.

'That's when we first met Derek,' remembers Michael Tubridy. 'At rehearsal we were struck by the fact that he was dressed totally unlike somebody in a big orchestra. We were impressed immensely that his sole was flapping and wasn't held onto his shoe and he had a big hole in the front of his jumper. But he took to us straight away and the fact that he was playing Carolan music and seemed to like it meant we got on well with him.'

After the evening rehearsal, The Chieftains had their first taste of the bitterness bred by the troubles in Ireland when the BBC called a taxi to take them back to their hotel. In the early 1970s the taxis were either Catholic and Protestant and the BBC used the latter as a matter of course.

'We all piled into the taxi,' Tubridy said. 'At first the driver was very quiet but then we started speaking to him and we discovered that he was afraid for his life. He thought that he had picked up a group of Fenians from the South and he was going to get a bullet in the back of his head. Then we started debating with him. "By God we're not like that, we're just musicians." '

Things were far more relaxed when they arrived back at the hotel. They invited the cab driver in for a drink and spent several hours debating Ireland politics over pints of Guinness.

'He thought that everybody in the South had a gun and was prepared to shoot anybody in the North if they got the chance,' says Tubridy. 'That incident left a lasting impression on me.'

The live television show the following day was a great success. Derek's harp perfectly complimented The Chieftains and Paddy knew immediately that this was the missing part of the musical jigsaw he had been searching for so long. Although he was certainly impressed by Derek, he was also a little puzzled by the brilliant harper's rather odd behaviour.

'Derek's an awful rogue,' says Moloney. 'We were chatting to people in the orchestra who told us how he used to get up to all kinds of tricks with the orchestra. One of his favourites was to have a copy of *Playboy* spread out over his music stand. Of course everybody could see the picture of the naked woman but the music director just couldn't understand why the other musicians were constantly walking past Derek. In the end he discovered what was going on but Derek was never reprimanded. It was all taken in good faith. You can get away with those things when you're a genius.'

* * *

Derek Bell was born in Belfast to a successful banker William Bell and his wife Shelagh. Legend had it that when Shelagh's grandfather played the Scottish bagpipes at sea, seals would jump into the boat in delight. Growing up in the early 1920s during the Irish Civil War, William had been taught to play Irish traditional tunes on the fiddle by a game keeper and later played second violin for an amateur orchestra.

When Derek was two years old a doctor misdiagnosed an infant ailment, telling his parents that their son was going blind. While commiserating that nothing could be done to save the little boy's sight he advised them to buy musical toys as therapy to develop Derek's sense of hearing.

'I suppose that's how I first got interested in music,' says Derek, who had nothing but a bad case of short-sightedness. 'It didn't take me long before I started messing around with real instruments.'

Just after his fifth birthday his mother died leaving his father to bring up Derek and his sister Déirdre. At the age of nine Derek easily picked up the piano when he started lessons and was recognized as a child prodigy at the Cabin Hill Preparatory School in Belfast, which he attended. At the age of eleven, Derek composed his first piano concerto and decided he was ready to embark on a career in music.

'I was very brash in those days,' admits Derek, who was now at boarding school. 'I wrote to the BBC and told them I had written a Concerto and that they ought to get Yehudi Menuhin and a school friend of mine to play it on a broadcast.'

The BBC were so impressed with the audacity of young Derek's letter that they invited him into the studio the following week to play one of his piano compositions. That night, after lights out at school, Derek composed a couple of short pieces which he duly performed for the BBC the next week.

'The musical powers to be were very impressed and asked me to come in and do a broadcast,' says Bell. 'From then on I was a regular on a programme called *Children's Hour* and they'd always be calling me up and asking me to compose little pieces if they ever had a few minutes to spare.'

When Derek's music teacher found out his star pupil had written a Concerto he encouraged him to start learning about the other instruments and bought him a decrepit old oboe to play in the school orchestra, which he soon mastered. At the age of 15 Derek told his father that he wanted to become a professional musician.

'He was not happy,' says Derek. 'He thought it was too precarious and he said I could only do it if I could get a musical scholarship to pay for my training which would prove that I had promise.'

A year later, the ambitious teenager managed to win a coveted scholarship in composition to London's prestigious Royal College of Music. William Bell was so impressed with his son that he built him his own practice studio in the house and sent him to London to begin his studies.

Over the next few years Derek studied music in London before eventually travelling to Colorado to study the piano with Madam Rosina Lhévinne, and to Georgia and Salzburg to study the harp with Artiss de Volt. In his 20s and 30s Derek carved out an impressive career as a soloist appearing with an array of symphony orchestras including the Berlin, Moscow, Budapest, Pittsburgh, Liverpool, Dublin and London ones. Incredibly, Derek was almost 30 and managing the Belfast Symphony Orchestra before he first picked up the harp.

Derek recalls: 'There were complaints from the harpists that the orchestra's harps had never been tuned and it was impossible to bring them up to pitch for concerts. As an oboe player, the Arts Council decided I should be able to tune the things and I found that I could using a fork to get the proper note.

'After a few months of doing this I said, "This is silly, I might as well play the bloody thing" so I went down to Dublin and got myself a tutor in the form of Sheila Garchet-Cuthbert and then Gwendolen Mason in London.'

In 1965 the Head of BBC Music Dr Boucher hired Derek as principal harp player with an extra bonus for playing second oboe. But it was another seven years before Derek was invited to play harp with The Chieftains for the St Patrick's Day Special.

'I didn't know much about The Chieftains at that time,' recalls Derek. 'The whole orchestra crowded round Paddy to see that funny thing he was playing.'

After the television show Derek Bell and The Chieftains went back to Alan Tongue's house where they discussed music with Paddy inviting the harpist to come and appear with the group when they next played Dublin.

'I had always wanted a harp in The Chieftains but I'd never found the right person,' says Moloney. 'When we met Derek I finally heard the full strength of the music that had been in my head for so long.'

9

Going Down the Road

In addition to steering The Chieftains and running Claddagh, Paddy Moloney was also producing all the albums for the growing record company. He played on and produced an album by his old friend Dolly MacMahon called *Dolly*, which featured the moving *Love is Teasin'*, which Marianne Faithfull would later perform so effectively on *The Long Black Veil*.

He also produced an album called *The Liffey Banks* by Seán Potts' legendary fiddler uncle Tommy Potts. *The Liffey Banks* has become a traditional classic and is revered by many of today's top Irish musicians. Tommy Potts was an innovative musical genius whose music mixed the freewheeling improvisations of jazz with traditional Irish music for the first time.

'I always saw Tommy Potts as the Paganini of traditional Irish music,' Moloney says. 'He was way ahead and the purists and the regular musicians of his generation frowned on him. I thought he was out of this world.'

It took months of coaxing to persuade Potts to agree to make a record and Moloney had to go and collect him for the drive down to Luggala for the recording session.

Recalls Moloney, 'We had to stop at every pub on the way and have a brandy and port because he was a very very nervous man. Actually he had a nervous complaint and he'd often just come in and sit beside me in the office and just cry for hours. I'd say, "Take it easy Tommy." '

Potts died in 1988 but *The Liffey Banks* remains an indispensable album for today's new generation of Irish musicians.

'I keep on buying *The Liffey Banks*,' says popular young uilleann piper Ronan Browne. 'I always have a copy somewhere, the car or the home. I'll meet somebody and they'll be asking about Irish music and I say, "take [*The Liffey Banks*] and if that interests you, the rest of Irish music will fascinate you too." '

During his seven years at Claddagh, Paddy Moloney, along with his good friend Garech Browne, produced a total of 45 albums of traditional music, poetry and classical music by artists whose work would have been lost forever without Claddagh.

'I would spend months maybe making one album just to get it right,' Moloney says. 'They are very special albums by very special people. It was something I wanted to do that was very important and Garech backed me all the way.'

With the release of each new Claddagh record Garech and Paddy would throw a lavish launch party for the press, sending out printed invitations with Claddagh's new logo. Rita was now helping out at Claddagh's new office in Dame Street with public relations, organizing some of the parties, which always had an open bar and plenty of fine food.

'Our press receptions were the talk of the country,' says Moloney. 'Nobody in Ireland had them in those days and Garech would pick up every Tom, Dick and Harry along the way and say, "Come to the party." We'd spend so much money on the launches that it would take years to see any profits on the record.'

Moloney's careful attention to the press soon paid off with enthusiastic stories on The Chieftains popping up in key influential publications like the music trades' *Variety* and *Billboard* and the English music bible *Melody Maker*. In a full-page feature in *Melody Maker*, writer Patrick Carroll paid homage to The Chieftains who were described as 'one of the world's most influential semi-pro groups'. Carroll continued: 'They have gained more influential popularity through pure excellence and originality, using absolutely no kind of gimmickry or personality mongering, than almost any group of musicians (outside the strictly classical) that one can name.'

Carroll also observed that he'd 'seen more people amazed by the first Chieftains album on first hearing than any other LP bar the first Robert Johnson'.

Garech Browne was now disappearing abroad for months at a time so Moloney was given a free hand running Claddagh, except when it came to designing the record covers. The covers were the Claddagh chairman's pride and joy and he demanded that they be perfect. Unfortunately his globetrotting meant everything had to be done over the telephone.

'It used to drive me mad,' said Moloney. 'I'd be talking to Garech in Bombay about colours and shades and he'd tell me to make the decision. When he came home and saw the sleeves they were never quite right.'

In early 1972 Paddy Moloney got a call from ex-Beatle Paul McCartney, asking him to come to Stockport in the north of England to record some backing tracks for a new album he was producing for his brother Mike McGear's solo album.

'I was delighted when Paul called,' Moloney says. 'The Beatles had just broken up and this was before Wings. I found it fascinating to work with him as I'd never seen recording equipment like that before. We certainly had nothing like that in Ireland. Paul was a genius at working it. He knew how to twiddle the knobs.'

After the session Linda McCartney asked Paddy to pose for a photograph with his uilleann pipes.

'I remember sitting down and trying to concentrate on playing the pipes while she was taking my portrait. Linda went wild with the camera and took hundreds of shots.'

Soon after the session The Knight of Glin, Desmond Fitzgerald, invited Paddy to his wedding at London's exclusive Claridges Hotel. It was the social event of the season as Fitzgerald's friends numbered the rock 'n' aristocracy of the time and the crème de la crème of society. The entertainment was provided by the Beach Boys and Paddy Moloney, who had adopted a hipper image by growing fashionably long sideburns was one of the first out on the dance floor.

'I decided I wanted to do a bit of swinging,' laughs Moloney. 'I brought out the tin whistle for an Irish dance and took up the Countess of Meath and we sort of started dancing. Unfortunately she lost balance as I wasn't able to control her and we both fell into the crowd. Very funny.'

By this time all the members of The Chieftains were in their mid-to-late 30s, with the exception of Peadar Mercier who was almost 60 and tended not to socialize with others on the road. But the rest of the band were having the time of their lives enjoying a second childhood.

'I did have a wild life in my own way,' recalls Moloney. 'We were young and new to it all and therefore we looked on it in a boyish fashion, although we were all married and supposed to be mature.'

Rita Moloney was highly disapproving of The Chieftains' behaviour in those days.

'Paddy was not mature,' she says matter of factly. 'He behaved like a teenager during his 30s.'

The Chieftains were delighted when they were invited by Paddy's old friend Polig Montjarret to play at the 1972 Lorient Festival in Brittany that August. Using his influence with Ireland's Chief Justice Cearbhall Ó Dálaigh, a member of the cultural affairs committee and a future president of Ireland, Moloney managed to get Seán Potts and Seán Keane special dispensations for unpaid leave from their jobs at the post office so their pensions wouldn't be affected. Derek Bell was also invited to accompany The Chieftains on the trip and turned up with his harp under a blanket.

The Chieftains were booked to play three concerts a night at different venues but still found the energy to stay up all night playing music in their hotel bar. One particular night, Moloney and Potts and the rest of the band were so deeply into the music that the hotel owner, who wanted to go to bed, told them to drink what they wanted on the honour system and write it down on a piece of paper.

When they finally finished playing at seven o'clock the next morning they remembered it was the birthday of a folk club owner they knew on the nearby Île de Groix, and decided to surprise him with a huge bottle of his champagne.

Says Moloney: 'We crept into his bedroom and he was asleep with his girlfriend so we started to play him a tune. We opened up the champagne and we all had a glass. A great time. We finally went to bed at noon and slept for the rest of the day and did a concert that night.'

After that, the girlfriend then hired The Chieftains to play at the club owner's private birthday party on Île de Groix, just off the coast of Lorient, and the group were to receive £350 for their appearance.

'We thought we were going to have the greatest night of our lives,' recalls Paddy. 'It was to be highlight of the trip.'

But The Chieftains' dreams of staying in luxury soon evaporated when they were told that the only available accommodation after the party was a Second World War army bunker, facing straight onto the Atlantic. The concrete bunker, now only used by the local boy scouts as a camp, was damp and freezing.

'As luck would have it there were seven beds in the bunker with old bed clothes,' remembers Michael Tubridy. 'The beds were all up against each other so you had to walk over them if you weren't in the one nearest the door.'

Paddy, who would later become infamous for changing hotel rooms if there was slightest thing wrong, made certain to damp-proof his bunk.

'I was very finicky,' he admitted. 'Because my mother had me that way for years about beds. She always used to tell me, "Make sure you don't sleep in a damp bed." So I got out and put plastic sheeting over the bunk and used a rubber band to secure it. I love all these little things you know.'

After much complaining The Chieftains, including Derek cradling his harp, were finally tucked up in their bunks and the lights went off. Not surprisingly no one could get to sleep and one by one each Chieftain announced that he needed to use the toilet.

'And what did Derek do,' laughs Paddy. 'He started playing Handel's Water Music on his harp and kept on doing it as a running joke all night long. Nobody got to sleep for hours.'

At 8:00 the next morning they were awoken by their host whistling Handel's Water Music as he arrived with a bucket of water for them to wash with. Every Chieftain breathed a heavy sigh of relief as he boarded the ferry back to the comforts of Lorient.

From then on Derek became the unofficial seventh member of the Chieftains, appearing with the group whenever he could get time off from the BBC Orchestra.

'I started to write him into all The Chieftains' arrangements,' says Moloney. 'I would introduce him as our special guest and he would come down and sit on the stage for the whole evening and just play four Carolan pieces. He just sort of drifted in.'

When the group toured America for the first time in 1974 Derek Bell was forced into deciding whether to stay with the security of the BBC orchestra or leave to becoming a fully fledged Chieftain with all its uncertainties.

'That was a problem,' remembers Derek. 'My father on his death bed a few years earlier had made me swear that I'd never leave the BBC because that was family security. He wouldn't have died happy if he thought that I was thinking of leaving.'

Things came to a head when Derek asked the Head of Music at the BBC permission for time off to go to America with The Chieftains. 'He told me, "Derek, I'm very very fond of you, and we've done a lot of good work together, but I must tell you straight within these four walls that I have no time for that Paddy Moloney. It's like this, if you want to play in a good orchestra as the company's head harper, and do all those lovely symphony concerts and broadcasts, stay with us. But if you really feel you want to run around with a tatty folk group you'll have to resign."

'So I wrote out my resignation and I've been running around with a tatty folk group ever since.'

Derek's influence on the evolving sound of The Chieftains can easily be heard on *Chieftains 4*, the first album he appears on. His exquisite harp playing introduces the second track of Carolan's *Morgan Magan* and adds a new dimension to their music.

Recorded in London in a single weekend in early 1974, *Chieftains 4* contains Moloney's moving version of Seán Ó Riada's *Women of Ireland*, The Chieftains' heartfelt tribute to the dead composer.

'I wanted a piece to commemorate Seán,' says Moloney. 'I had in fact wanted to play *Women of Ireland* at his funeral but that wasn't to be. I went down to see Ruth Ó Riada and she agreed to let me use it. She wasn't mad about me using that tune but I said wait until you see how it will turn out. Because I could hear it in my mind.'

Chieftains 4 contains Paddy's most ambitious composition to date, *The Battle of Aughrim*. For inspiration Moloney visited the battle site in Galway and let his imagination take over.

'The whole picture of the battle started to evolve in my mind like a vision,' he explained. 'I just walked down along the field beside the old church where the battle took place and I could see these big armies and how things went and didn't go. I could see the bloody fields and all the great patriots lying dead. I could see it all. And then it all started to come together for me.'

During his trip to Galway Moloney caught the flu and back in Dublin the following Saturday morning he was lying in bed running a high fever.

'I had some hot whiskies and somehow the whole Battle of Aughrim fell into place for me,' he says. 'I had a format in my mind and then I started to write it all down.

'I only used Chieftain instruments. No keyboards. No orchestras.

Just harp, bodhrán, whistles, flutes, fiddles, pipes, drones and bones. There's the rattle of bones in the middle of that piece which to me was when the battle was lost and the bodies were lying around.

'The piece then goes into a lament but I finish on a march. Okay we've lost this one, but as they say in Ireland, "Beg Lá eile ag an bPaorach" ("There will be another day"). That was how I envisaged the whole thing. That was the way the Irish thought in those days.

'I often feel I belonged there. I love the simplicity of those days. It was not like today's world. I feel that I belonged in the 18th century where things happened at a slower pace. Things meant more and people had a greater appreciation of what happened. It wasn't just a flash in the pan, here today gone tomorrow. Things that happened were talked about for a whole year. So you know it meant something. And that's why there was better music composed in those days.'

Chieftains 4 also included *Morning Dew*, part of which Moloney later used as the train sequence for his first film score, *Ireland Moving*, with his tin whistle magically weaving in and out of the rock steady bodhrán playing of Potts and Mercier. Years later Moloney would again use the tune as The Chieftains' rousing introduction to *Wabash Cannonball*, which they would record with country star Ricky Skaggs to become a highlight of their stage show.

If *Chieftains 4* took the group to a new musical level, the sleeve notes also broke new ground by achieving the distinction of being partly written by film star Peter Sellers, an unashamed fan. Paddy Moloney had been introduced to Peter Sellers and fellow Goon Spike Milligan in the early 1970s by Desmond Guinness's then-wife, Mariga. It was a memorable evening of music and Sellers conjured it up in his sleeve notes for the album.

'One evening that will always linger in my memory – me and my mate Spike Milligan, who, although born in India is more Irish than they are themselves, were having a jar at that huge place of a house in Kildare, where I was living in a corner of at the time. I had been telling The Milligan about my friend Paddy Moloney – "He's like one of the little folk – a lovely, lively leprechaun, with an enormous musical talent, and a sense of humour to match." The Milligan was in one of his Irish musical moods, with tipple in hand, to steady him.

'In comes Paddy, and within seconds they were in love (in the nicest possible way of course). Out comes Paddy's whistle, and he blew magic into the room. Jigs, airs, reels – "I'll never forget his foot banging up and down, and him all the while playing up a storm," says Milligan. Then, an air that haunts you, and the tears begin. Oh God – it's beautiful.

'The party ended early – about 3:30 a.m. I still have some of it on a tape recorder. This is one of the reasons why Irish music will always have a special place in my heart. Whenever I listen to this Chieftains LP it unlocks a door in my mind, and the memory comes flooding back. Paddy, please keep making records like this for folk like me and The Milligan, and the millions.'

Garech Browne says the rousing endorsement from Peter Sellers was part of a careful strategy of marketing The Chieftains at the time.

'We wanted people to ask the question, "Why is Peter Sellers interested in Irish music?" ' he explained. 'So you made a talking point of it. We wanted to show that it was not something provincial.'

Four years later Moloney asked Peter Sellers if he would photograph The Chieftains for a future album cover. The troubled comedian, who was an excellent photographer, instantly agreed, suggesting they did it in the Orangery at Holland Park in London.

'We had our air tickets and everything,' says Moloney. 'The day before we were supposed to fly to London, Peter sent a message of apology that he couldn't do it and said he'd pay all our expenses. When we got to London we read in the papers that he'd got married that day to his last wife Lynne Frederick.'

Chieftains 4, complete with a striking abstract indigo cover by Edward Delaney, was released to great fanfare that summer. The reviews were excellent with *Hibernia* magazine singling out Derek Bell for special attention.

'There is something for everyone on this new album,' Fanny Feehan wrote in *Hibernia*. 'The addition of Derek Bell on harp to the line-up gives them an exciting new dimension.'

In March 1974 *Melody Maker*, reported that The Chieftains had attained 'an almost cult-like following in England' and declared that the group had now crossed over into popular music.

'It is impossible to explain the incredible prestige of The Chieftains purely in terms of the traditional music they play,' noted music writer Colin Irwin in the double page spread. 'What makes them different from any of the impromptu bands of Irish musicians you can hear sawing away any Sunday lunch time in the Brighton Irish Centre is the care with which their music is selected, arranged and put together under the mischievous eye of Paddy Moloney.

'With his long hair and burgeoning sideburns, piper and tin whistle player Paddy is closer to anyone's idea of a pop musician than any other Chieftain. And the pop scene is starting to become aware of him.'

This feature marked the first time that all Chieftains had been interviewed in a major publication and new member Derek Bell explained that he felt perfectly at home playing traditional music 'despite the frowns and disapproval of those who think it's beneath the dignity of a serious musician'.

Bodhrán player Peader Mercier frankly admitted having no musical talent, declaring that he felt he played 'second fiddle' in The Chieftains.

'But to play second fiddle well is an achievement,' said Mercier. 'It does something for your character and your temperament.'

The new Chieftains' album received good airplay on Radio Éireann and on English folk radio programmes, but more importantly it was also enthusiastically picked up by the highly influential American college radio stations. So when The Chieftains arrived in the States for their first major tour in the autumn of 1974 they found themselves a popular underground music band.

Moloney had to deal with the tough American promoters in the various cities The Chieftains played, including the legendary Bill Graham who promoted a show at the Orpheum Theater in Boston. Moloney always insisted on getting half the money up front in cash and half during the interval.

'I was always very strict and I have my own little rules,' he says. 'I was very particular about how we were treated and if people didn't treat us properly I didn't want to know them. Money or no money. I learned the hard way that you had to watch your step on contracts and who was promoting what and how.'

For the final stage of what Moloney termed 'a world tour', The Chieftains arrived in San Francisco, and were introduced to The Grateful Dead's Jerry Garcia by Chessley Millikan who had organised the tour and previously played him some of their records. The legendary guitarist had loved The Chieftains so much that he invited them to open for his own bluegrass group Old And In The Way, who were playing a show at the Boarding House to be recorded for a live album. Garcia also arranged a radio show with the legendary Tom Donaghue.

'Jerry sent a limo for us and we did the show, which was San Francisco's top-rated radio programme,' says Moloney. 'Jerry interviewed us and we talked and played tunes and discussed the music. Later in the week we opened for Jerry's bluegrass band and it was a wonderful evening of music.'

A couple of days later The Chieftains played an open air evening concert in Los Angeles where an Aran-sweatered Paddy Moloney performed under an American flag hanging from a tree.

'There was quite a large Irish contingent in both Los Angeles and San Francisco and they were very popular,' remembers Chessley Millikan. 'Wherever they went they got good reviews and picked up a big following.'

As well as the Grateful Dead, Millikan also introduced The Chieftains to top rock stars like Jackson Browne and Don Henley of the Eagles, who would both later collaborate with the group. During their visit Paddy Moloney made friends with a group of local musicians who were so moved when they heard The Chieftains play that they had an epiphany, deciding to move to Ireland where they formed the band Pumpkinhead.

'The Chieftains were trailblazers,' said Pumpkinhead singer San Francisco-native Sandi Miller, who still lives in Dublin. 'We were heavily into Irish traditional music and The Chieftains made it very accessible to people who'd never heard it. They just grab you and through The Chieftains we decided to come to Ireland and investigate other music.'

For his first tour of America Derek brought his harp, minus its flight case, but with the rug that covers it when it's not in use, causing constant problems as airlines insisted the instrument required its own seat.

'Derek was very upset about it,' says Moloney. 'We had so many arguments over that harp and rug. But when we told them we couldn't afford another seat they always let us on.'

At the end of the tour The Chieftains caught a plane from San Francisco to Kennedy Airport, New York, where they transferred to Aer Lingus for the flight to Dublin. Weary from almost a day's travelling The Chieftains landed at Dublin Airport at 9:00 on a Monday morning and, with the exception of Moloney, went straight to work.

'We were chancing it a lot,' says Seán Keane. 'It was a total novelty at that time and although I didn't want to admit it, I could feel The Chieftains scratching away to go full time. It was just a matter of time before it broke through.'

* * *

Back in Dublin Paddy Moloney was busy putting the finishing touches to a new album with Seán Potts called *Tin Whistles*. Recorded in a weekend in London, the record captured the wonderful musical chemistry between the two and one of the highlights is the almost free jazz improvisations of their version of *Julia Delaney*, which Seán had learned from his uncle Tommy Potts.

To launch the record Claddagh threw one of its patented open bar press receptions at the new offices in Dame Street. During the Friday afternoon party Moloney got a phone call while he was giving an interview to Dublin music journalist Tony Wilson.

Remembers Moloney: 'There was a voice on the other end saying, "Hello, I'm Stanley Kubrick and I'd like to use your music in a film I'm making." To be honest I'd never heard of Stanley Kubrick and didn't have a clue who he was. Right then and there I was just concerned with the press reception. I said, "That's great Mr Kubrick, I'm afraid I can't talk to you now. Could you ring me back on Monday?"

'I put down the phone and said, "Jesus, Tony, who the hell was that. Somebody called Kubrick or something." Tony Wilson almost fainted. "Paddy, don't you know who that was? That's the Stanley Kubrick who did *2001* and *Clockwork Orange*." I said that was great but I still wasn't truly convinced.'

The following Tuesday the director, who wanted to use *Mná na hÉireann*, from *Chieftains 4*, as part of the soundtrack for his new film *Barry Lyndon*, called back and hammered out a deal over the phone.

A few days later Moloney visited Kubrick at his lavish estate in Elstree, on the outskirts of London, to view rushes from the film and discuss the projected score. At their meeting Paddy took out his tin whistle to play some of the additional music that he had in mind, but Kubrick seemed unimpressed.

The director looked Moloney straight in the face and said: 'Come on, Paddy, that's something you hear on a Saturday night in an Irish pub when everybody's plastered. That's not what I want.'

Moloney felt his heart sink but then the director burst into fits of laughter and said he loved the tune and in the end asked him to do 25 minutes of music instead of the original five.

'He's quite a character, that Stanley Kubrick,' says Paddy. 'But then I'm a bit mad myself.'

10

Storming the Albert Hall

Ironically, it was Paddy Moloney's ambitious attempts to give Claddagh Records international stature that would lead to The Chieftains doing a lease deal with a bigger company and launch them into the big time. In February 1975 the Irish record industry broke new ground by taking a stand at the music industry's prestigious MIDEM Trade Show in Cannes. The Claddagh delegation, comprising Moloney and public relations lady Pat Pretty, helped to man the stand at the week-long fair. Paddy was a hive of activity, networking and making new contacts to further Claddagh and The Chieftains. But with so many different stands at the fair Moloney determined to make the Irish one stand out from the rest.

'I decided to play the bloody pipes to attract attention,' he says. 'After lunch everyone would be in great form and I used to play every day at 4:00 p.m. They used to call it the 4 o'clock symphony and everyone on the other stands were waiting for it. I made more contacts and did more for Irish industry with those pipes than you can imagine.'

One particular fan of Moloney's 4 o'clock symphonies was Jo Lustig, a high-power American manager whose folk rock stable included an array of successful acts like Julie Felix, Fairport Convention, Steeleye Span and Pentangle. Lustig had first seen The Chieftains play at the Cambridge Folk Festival a couple of years earlier and been impressed but at MIDEM he decided to move in and sign them up.

'I thought they were marvellous,' remembers Lustig. 'They weren't professional at the time but I saw their potential.'

Every day at MIDEM, Lustig pressured Moloney to let him take over The Chieftains' management but the ever careful Paddy refused to commit himself.

Paddy Moloney: 'He was on at me continually, "Come on, I want to get you. I want you." I wouldn't make up my mind. I just wasn't sure and we left it at that for the while.'

But it was not all business at MIDEM for Moloney, who was given the run of Garech's mother Lady Oranmore's luxury villa in nearby Antibes, complete with a Vietnamese chef. One of the highlights of that year's MIDEM was the party she threw for the Irish contingent with the only music provided by Paddy Moloney's tin whistle.

'I kept the whole bloody party going,' says Moloney. 'I got everyone on their feet dancing and it was a real hooley.'

Among the guests were film stars Richard Burton and Charlotte Rampling and her fiancé composer Michel Jarre.

'Charlotte was my favourite actress at the time,' says Paddy. 'We were in the kitchen together and I decided I wanted to dance so I got hold of Charlotte and we swung out on the floor. There was a photograph taken of me with this long, tall woman swinging like mad with me. It was so funny but her fiancé Michel was not too pleased and let me know about it. It was all a bit of fun.'

A few weeks later Lady Oranmore sent the photograph of the two dancing to Garech, who put it in his visitors' book. Many years later Rita came across the picture in Garech's book and Moloney had to explain to his wife what he was doing in a compromising position with the sex symbol.

'I caught him out good and proper,' laughs Rita. 'And did he blush.'

* * *

Back in Dublin Jo Lustig stepped up his campaign to sign up The Chieftains and even went to Luggala with Paddy Moloney on a freezing winter's day to discuss a record leasing deal for The Chieftains with Garech Browne. Moloney, who loved driving a tough deal himself, was highly impressed with Lustig, who was considered one of the shrewdest promoters in a business of sharpies. After years of dealing with small-time promoters Moloney had long paid his dues and was determined to move into the big time.

'Lustig is a really tough promoter and he's got the contacts,' said Moloney at the time. 'It's best to go in with a big promoter – the hard knockers as they say – they get on with the business.'

But Moloney had the other Chieftains to think about and would not commit himself unless they all agreed. Becoming increasingly frustrated with Moloney's stalling, the brash American took matters into his own hands and without any prior consultation booked The Chieftains for a London concert on St Patrick's Day. Determined to show that he meant business, he booked them into the prestigious Royal Albert Hall, although they had never played anything bigger than a club in London.

'I called around all the main London venues and was amazed to discover that they were all available,' said Lustig. 'St Patrick's Day in London was a far lesser occasion than I was used to in New York. I'm an optimistic guy. I thought if everything is available I'm going to try the Albert Hall. It was open so I went ahead and booked it.'

Brimming with confidence Lustig immediately got on the phone to Moloney to tell him the good news.

'He said, "Paddy, I've got you a contract. A big contract," ' remembers Moloney. 'I said, "It sounds great Jo, where is it?" When he told me it was the Albert Hall I thought he was crazy. I said "Jo, we're not ready for such a big concert." '

The following day the tenacious Lustig called Moloney back and somehow managed to talk him into playing the Albert Hall with the proviso that if he sold out the 6,000-seat venue the band would go full time with him as manager taking a fee of 25 per cent.

'It could have been a disaster,' says Moloney. 'I said, "Jo, if this doesn't work I'm going to have your head." I knew that after 15 years hard work this could destroy the band if we flopped.'

The rest of The Chieftains could not believe they had really been booked to play a world-class venue like the Albert Hall and refused to take it seriously.

'We thought the whole thing was crazy and just a silly bet,' remembers Michael Tubridy. 'We never thought that the question of us going professional would even arise as we never expected to sell out the Albert Hall in a million years.'

Even Jo Lustig had real doubts about whether he could actually pull it off and sell out the Albert Hall in three weeks as his research revealed that the London Irish, which he believed was The Chieftains' base audience, preferred to celebrate St Patrick's Night in clubs rather than large concert halls.

'I panicked,' admitted Lustig. 'I thought here I am with the Albert Hall, now I've got to fill the seats. It was a huge gamble.'

Lustig promoted the show very heavily using newspapers and radio and also decided to use it as a showcase for record companies with a view to securing a major international record deal for The Chieftains. His campaign soon gathered momentum and captured the public's imagination. Within two weeks Lustig had done the seemingly impossible and sold out the Royal Albert Hall. But the biggest surprise of all was that half the ticket buyers were English.

Melody Maker captured the drama of the occasion when they ran a full-page preview with the banner headline *Chieftains on Trial* the day before the show.

'I can see what could go wrong,' Moloney told Karl Dallas, who was writing for *Melody Maker*. 'I do think it will be a trial piece for us. I'm not worried about it, really if it doesn't work, we'll still go on.'

Asked how he planned to handle the concert, Moloney replied, 'It's very important that the audience is kept happy and totally involved with the music. We're not the sort of group with anything else to offer except the bare music, the bare sound. No glitter.'

Introducing The Chieftains, the softly spoken DJ John Peel, told the Albert Hall audience, 'When they play a sad song it will bring a lump to your throat, and when they play a bright dance you'll have difficulty keeping in your seat.'

But it was to the sound of deafening applause that the seven Chieftains took the stage at the Royal Albert Hall on March 17th, 1975 for the next two and a half hours which would change their lives forever.

'I was very nervous,' remembers Moloney. 'It was like going into a football stadium and listening to the crowd roaring as the teams come onto the pitch. I'll never forget that moment when we walked on the stage and saw the huge crowd. It was brilliant. We were playing for two and a half hours. Solid music. Seven of us. No singing. No dancing just music. And the crowd loved us.'

Martin Fay remembers walking onto the stage, looking up, and feeling the incredible vastness of the Albert Hall.

'We were like ball bearings on the stage,' he remembers saying at the time. 'It was a fantastically big place. My wife Gráinne took pictures and when I saw them we were just little dots on the stage in comparison to the size of the place.'

After just a couple of numbers The Chieftains had the audience in the palm of their hands and by the end of their second set they left the stage to the sound of 6,000 fans screaming for an encore.

'Potts and myself just grabbed each other with tears in our eyes,' remembers Moloney. 'And then we were going back onto the ramp to the stage for yet another encore. It was a great breakthrough for Irish music.'

'It was the greatest thrill of my life,' says Potts. 'To hear 6,000 people applauding a couple of reels and jigs was amazing because basically that's what we were doing. It was absolutely wonderful. I've never experienced anything like it and I think the same thing applied to every member of the band. I saw people crying with emotion.'

After the final encore each Chieftain rushed to find the nearest telephone to report the great news to expectant families back in Ireland. But the triumphant concert had left The Chieftains emotionally drained and there was little celebrating afterwards as they went back to their hotel rooms to savour their triumph.

The next day the critics declared the concert a sensation and a banner headline in the following week's concert review in *Melody Maker* proclaimed *Breathtaking Chieftains.*

Reviewer Steve Lake described The Chieftains as 'A goddamn joy and absolutely essential listening for anyone who feels that acoustic instruments are redundant in the space age. Perfect aural therapy for the heavy metal casualty.'

Marianne Faithfull was at the Royal Albert Hall and noticed a new seriousness in The Chieftains' music from the old days at Luggala.

'It was classical music,' remembers Marianne. 'I think Paddy wanted to make it more solemn as a way of distancing himself from the scene at Garech's where it was all joking and laughing and drinking. And in a way Paddy was playing a part. It was much more serious now.'

Chieftain Seán Keane summed up the band's feelings after its Royal Albert Hall triumph, saying, 'We all knew that there was something different going on. There was a change. We were turning a corner and we were onto a new road.'

* * *

After the Albert Hall, The Chieftains had to face the fact that Lustig had won his bet and Paddy had to think seriously about going fully professional. All the Chieftains, except for Derek, were married with children and there was a lot of fear about the risks involved. Paddy Moloney remembers many an emotional group meeting when he tried to persuade Michael Tubridy, Seán Potts and Seán Keane, who were still unsure, to take the plunge.

'I had a very tough job when I asked them to pull up the stakes. They were afraid and I felt that I had the responsibility on my shoulders. There was a lot of aggro because half the band were not inclined to leave their jobs. I wasn't thinking of six members of The Chieftains, I was trying to consider the 27 mouths to feed. It was a big family. There were children involved and it was a big decision.'

Martin Fay was extremely concerned about gambling his family's stability on the uncertainty of a career in show business. 'I was into my 30s at the time and you don't just pack up a respectable pensionable job to go off on this fly-by-night escapade. Music was a very precarious occupation. What happens if it doesn't work out?

'And that's when this whiz kid manager Jo Lustig starts saying he knows what will be good for the band and what he could do for us. I was promised nine years wages in three years, and being interested in mathematics, that made sense to me. If that was the case I was prepared to work my three years and I didn't care.'

Seán Keane's wife Marie was totally against her husband leaving his job with the post office and joining The Chieftains and urged him to refuse.

'It was a hell of a decision to make and Marie was stunned by the whole thing,' Keane says. 'She didn't want me to do it but I went against her. Once I'd made my mind up she was more than supportive. She said, "If this is what you want go for it." '

In June, The Chieftains and Jo Lustig called a press conference at a London hotel to announce the new deal. But there was a last-minute hitch when Moloney and Lustig retired to private room upstairs to hammer out a minor contractual clause. The guests began to wonder what was happening when they could hear raised voices from behind closed doors. Finally an anxious-looking Moloney and Lustig came down and announced that the deal was off.

'I was going through a real trauma with Jo Lustig,' remembers Moloney. 'There were screaming phone calls. I was riding between what the band wanted and the contract. It wasn't a question of them trusting Jo Lustig, they trusted my judgment.'

But within days tempers had cooled and The Chieftains signed a three-year contract with Jo Lustig with various members negotiating leaves of absences from work in case things didn't work out. The members all agreed that going professional would be a three-year experiment to see if The Chieftains could succeed in the shark-infested waters of big-time show business.

At the time Seán Potts made his position with The Chieftains clear in an interview he gave to the American magazine *Ais Eirí.*

'If I see that in the next two or three years that the commercial interest has really taken over (and) pushed us into a situation which I personally do not agree with, I'll leave. I'll go back as a solo soul player and back to my old drab job in the government. I know that as long as I live in Ireland if *one* person at least said "Jesus, Seán, play that for me again," that's all I want.'

PART 2

11

The Year of The Chieftains

In the audience to witness The Chieftains' sensational concert at the Albert Hall had been Island Records' boss Chris Blackwell, who had been personally invited by Jo Lustig. As The Chieftains' new manager, Lustig was determined to secure an international record deal to take the band to new heights. Blackwell, who had largely built the Island label on reggae, after discovering Bob Marley and the Wailers in the early 1970s, saw The Chieftains' potential and signed them to a long-term American deal. Additionally, Lustig and Paddy Moloney also negotiated generous contracts with Polydor for Europe and the Australian Festival Records label.

'It was time to move on from Claddagh,' explained Moloney. 'We now had to make a living as full-time musicians and if we were to make it on a global basis we had to go to a bigger company.'

Realizing his debt to Garech Browne, Moloney negotiated a leasing deal with Claddagh, giving his old company royalties and limited artistic control for the next four Chieftain albums. But the Guinness heir's pride was hurt and he did not take The Chieftains' departure kindly.

'It was like his favourite toy had been taken away from him,' remembers Moloney. 'There was an uneasiness between us for some time because Garech just wouldn't accept that we couldn't continue with Claddagh if we wanted world-wide success. It was no sell-out and Claddagh was still going to be making something from The Chieftains, although not as much as before.'

With hindsight, Browne now admits that it was a wise move for The Chieftains at the time but even after 20 years the wounds have still not completely healed.

'It may have been the best thing for The Chieftains but from Claddagh's point of view it was the worst thing that ever happened to us,' explains Browne. 'And in the sense that I had set out to make something happen, Claddagh was just the vehicle for their success. But I realized that if The Chieftains were going to be bigger than Claddagh then they would have to fly free.'

The record deal with Island depended on The Chieftains delivering a new album within three months of signing, and Moloney was under the gun when he went into London's Sound Techniques Studio in July. He was also well aware of the vital importance of *Chieftains 5* in consolidating their new career and proving that they were not just a live band and could sell records.

'I had to come up with some good ones for this one,' says Moloney. 'Some of the stuff was really progressive and I was trying to get everyone more relaxed in the studio so they could do their own thing.'

Although Moloney was the undisputed leader of The Chieftains, he actively encouraged the other members of the group to be creative, and finally succeeded in this some years later on *Chieftains 7*. Seán Potts recalls the enthusiasm they all felt about this: 'We all got into that aspect of doing arrangements and compositions which we'd never done before. It was a very exciting period for the band and we felt we were breaking new ground.'

Chieftains 5 begins dramatically with Derek Bell introducing the medieval Irish timpán to The Chieftains' sound for the first time in a piece called *Timpán Reel*. A form of hammer dulcimer, the ancient timpán is first mentioned in the fourth-century book of Leinster where there are references to troops of timpán players leading the armies to war.

As his set piece for *Chieftains 5* Paddy Moloney composed a moving tone poem about the seasons called *Samhradh, Samhradh* or *Summertime, Summertime*, part of which was inspired by a memorable picnic lunch that Paddy and Derek had with Mariga Guinness and the Earl of Antrim in the glens of Antrim.

'We all went out to a bog to cut turf,' remembers Moloney. 'There were 20 of us and we brought a huge lunch. Derek came with his harp covered in a blanket and I had the whistles and pipes. It was a beautiful day and we were all drinking wine. After lunch Mariga took a photograph of us all lying up on the bog stretched out with the harp standing on its own. I remember there was a beautiful breeze blowing through the harp strings and I knew the sound it made would be great for *Summertime, Summertime*. My idea was to get out of the winter into the spring and then into the summer. To me the sound of the swirling wind blowing through the harp strings was the sound of Jack Frost. The sound of winter.'

Moloney also reached back into his early childhood at his grandparents in Co. Laois, to find the regenerative sounds of spring.

'I used the visions that I had down at my Grandmother's place at Easter. It would be cold and wet but Spring was in the air. My imagination would run wild and I'd imagine coming back in the summer and seeing little trees coming up and knowing one day they'd be fully grown.

'And then I had the whole piece building up into a full-lashed crescendo for the summertime with meadows and birds and bees. The whole works. Then I finish with autumn as the music starts to trickle away with the leaves falling. We're back to where we started. It's sad and it's time to go back to school.'

Chieftains 5 also featured Breton music for the first time in the group's repertoire. The Breton piece, *Ceol Bhriotánach*, contained tunes Moloney had picked up while he was at the Lorient Festival a couple of years earlier.

'We were probably the first Irish band ever to record traditional Breton music,' boasts Moloney. 'It was music that I loved.'

The recording session took just a week and Moloney had the final mix completed well on schedule for the Island Records' deadline. The only thing missing was the record cover which required Garech Browne approval. Unfortunately, Browne was out in Korea visiting a girlfriend and seemed in no hurry to sign off on the cover art after it was air expressed to him.

'It was absolute hell,' remembers Moloney. 'Garech was pussy-footing around and we were desperate. I kept asking Garech for sleeve notes and nothing was happening.'

Finally, the day before the Monday deadline for Island Records, Paddy and Rita confronted Garech at Luggala.

Rita: 'I'll never forget the way Garech said to me, "Well it's too late now!"

'I said, "Garech, Paddy's livelihood's at stake here. If we don't have an album tomorrow we have no deal with Island and Paddy has no job. He has nothing." '

Shrugging his shoulders Browne went off to London promising that the liner notes would be written in time but as the night wore on Paddy and Rita became more and more worried. In desperation they called their friend Welsh playwright Alun Owen and told him their plight. Owen, who had penned some of the liner notes on *Chieftains 4*, was highly sympathetic when he heard the story.

'We were nearly crying when we told him the saga,' remembers Rita. 'We were so upset.'

Owen agreed to write the liner notes there and then and have them ready by the following morning. The only thing he asked was for Paddy to buy him a bottle of whiskey for late-night inspiration.

'He saved the day,' said Moloney. 'We stayed up with him until three in the morning while he wrote the notes and, thanks to Alun, we got them to Island on time.'

Island Records were ecstatic at signing The Chieftains and held a press conference to pledge 'a money-no-object campaign to turn them into worldwide superstars'.

Moloney, who that summer had also found time to score the music for a new National Theatre production of *Playboy of the Western World*, could now breathe a sigh of relief but he was not out of the woods yet. In September Jo Lustig announced that he had arranged to film The Chieftains' second Albert Hall appearance in October without first consulting the band. Moloney was furious and ordered Lustig to cancel the deal but the new manager then raised the stakes.

'He told me that everything was off and he wouldn't manage us if I didn't sign,' remembers Paddy. 'He knew he had me over the coals. Most of the band had quit their jobs and we'd put all our eggs into one basket. And then to be told that if I didn't sign this contract there would be terrible trouble.

'I really felt that every time I made a move that looked successful, somebody knocked me down. I had weeks of torment, staying up all night thinking things over. Luckily the other people in the band never knew what I went through.'

Reluctantly Moloney signed the contract for The Chieftains to be filmed at the Royal Albert Hall. The completed movie, which was made by a relative of Garech's, was a disaster and shelved after just one public showing. It resurfaced a couple of years ago and is now a much sought-after collectable for Chieftain fans.

* * *

The build-up to The Chieftains' second solo appearance at the Royal Albert Hall, which kicked off their first full-scale UK tour, was tremendous. The trend-setting *Melody Maker* enthused about The Chieftains almost every week, tagging them THE group to watch in 1975. And when The Chieftains played the Montreux Music Festival in July, *Melody Maker*'s Chris Welch was in the front row to applaud.

'The Chieftains made much of contemporary rock music sound a shallow fraud when they took the stage,' he wrote. 'They contained more real power than a dozen electric bands. It was my first exposure to the traditional Irish music that is their forte, and it was like being confronted with a life source, a purity that has not been allowed to degenerate, nor has been robbed or made sterile like many other ethnic music forms.'

Chieftains' manager Jo Lustig even arranged for *Melody Maker* to sponsor the group's second Royal Albert Hall complete with a Chieftains' trivia competition offering readers the chance to win a private box to see the group in style.

The Chieftains admired Lustig's brash style and felt that he was really taking them places. They were particularly impressed with the entrée he was providing into the rock world by taking them to the right parties and introducing them to celebrities who were already admirers of the group. It was a time of outrageous adrogyny with Elton John and David Bowie dictating the new fashions. The ultra hip London record executives and media types were more used to their stars wearing platform shoes, bellbottoms and glitter than the sombre suits, cardigans and ties favoured by The Chieftains.

Paddy Moloney was literally launched into the colourful world of the 1970's superstars when he participated in a fancy dress charity event called Circassia with the likes of Eric Clapton, Seán Connery, John Huston, Shirley MacLaine, Mick Jagger and Burgess Meredith, which was being filmed at a large estate in Co. Kildare, owned by his dear friend Kevin McClory who was the producer of the first Bond films. Also at the party was the writer Christy Brown, author of *My Left Foot*, later made into an Oscar-winning film.

'I remember the first time I met Eric Clapton, I didn't know who he was,' said Moloney. 'I'd gone out of the party and security was so strict they wouldn't let me back in to rehearse. I started talking to this guy who had a stubble of a beard, who was also having difficulty getting back in, saying I thought it was terrible. He agreed with me and then I asked him who he was and he said, "Oh, I'm the electrician." It was only later I found out that it was Eric Clapton.'

At the beginning of the circus film Paddy had to fly over a mock town square in a full-size balloon playing his tin whistle. As the film starts the balloon slowly descends into the square full of punch-drinking celebrities.

'I was like the pied piper,' says Moloney. 'I was in no danger as there were ropes tied onto the balloon so it wasn't about to fly away. After it landed I had to get out to be welcomed by John Huston who shook my hand and said, "Hello Paddy, how are you?" '

Never publicly released, Circassia intriguingly featured Seán Connery as the Hunchback of Notre Dame and Mick Jagger as a circus clown. It did, however, win an award at a film festival held on the island of St Thomas.

On October 8th The Chieftains kicked off what was billed as a world tour with their second sell-out concert at the Royal Albert Hall in six months. The group's new found popularity was undeniable and 1,500 people had to be turned away at the door, with the box office reporting that they could easily have played a second show.

Playing new material from *Chieftains 5*, which had already sold an impressive 12,000 copies in Britain in its first week of release, The Chieftains turned the Royal Albert Hall into a big hooley and there was dancing in the aisles for their encore of *Kerry Slides*. Even a St John's Ambulance Brigade female helper, who was on duty for the show, threw caution to the wind and started jigging along a back aisle.

'Inhibitions were collapsing in a similar fashion all over the hall as The Chieftains swept into their second encore,' reported *Melody Maker*'s Colin Irwin. 'Dancers filled the aisles and one fleet-footed young lady went into a delightful dance on the stage in front of the beaming members of the group.'

The following week's *Melody Maker* carried the front page headline 'Chieftains Triumph!' with Irwin's glowing review inside declaring that The Chieftains' second Royal Albert Hall appearance 'easily matched the greatness of their first'.

As The Chieftains' publicity machine gained momentum, manager Lustig moved into hyperdrive arranging interviews and fielding world-wide offers for the group. Lucrative offers were coming in daily for the group who were about to leave for a major American tour in November followed by concerts in Australia and New Zealand before Christmas.

'This response indicates they are reaching markets that they may never have had before,' boasted Lustig at the time.

The day after the Albert Hall concert Lustig accompanied Moloney to rock star Mike Oldfield's house to record uilleann pipe backing tracks for his new album *Ommadawn*, the follow-up to his immensely successful *Tubular Bells*. Moloney and Lustig were flown in a private plane to a tiny airport outside Gloucester, near the Welsh border. Waiting to meet them was a chauffeur-driven Range Rover which took them up a mountain to Oldfield's sprawling Tudor estate.

'There were all manner of microphones, wires, guitars and things everywhere,' remembers Moloney. 'Mike came down and introduced himself and then offered me some Irish whiskey, which he thought was very appropriate. I don't like drinking if I'm working, but I had a sip. Then he just started playing me this tune on the guitar and I said maybe I could play it on the pipes. He said great and had me do it again and again. Then suddenly he said, "That's it. It's done." He'd been recording it without me even knowing so we went down to his local to celebrate.'

After getting to bed at midnight Moloney was up early to fly to Southampton to join the other band members for that night's show. The UK tour was a huge success with Moloney travelling up to each venue ahead of time to promote the concert and inspect the hall for sound. The tour finished on October 26th with a triumphant Manchester show.

'It was a great night for the Irish,' reported the *Daily Mail*. 'Their most genuine and long-established folk music heroes completed their take-over of Britain. Happily on last night's showing, there seems no danger of them forgetting where their roots lie.'

* * *

Back in Dublin The Chieftains were happy to return to their normal lives and prepare for their biggest American tour yet at the end of November. Moloney was pottering around in his Milltown home when he received a call from Stanley Kubrick pleading for more Chieftains' music for *Barry Lyndon*. Moloney rang around the other band members who refused to spend precious time away from their families for a London recording session.

'We'd just spent three weeks in England and we were just about to embark on three weeks in America,' says Moloney. 'It was our first major trip going full-time professional and it was a huge culture shock for the band to be away from their families for so long. They said, "Paddy, we don't care who he is, we're not going." '

When Moloney called Kubrick back with the news the film director was livid.

'He thought we were crazy because this was a big film,' remembers Moloney. 'He said, "Paddy, this film will make you famous. It will do a lot for you." I said, "I know it is, Stanley, but the band are the band and I know how they think and feel." '

In desperation Kubrick offered all the group and their families a free vacation in London in return for recording the extra music. After a quick call round the band members Moloney telephoned Kubrick to accept.

Arriving in London The Chieftains' wives and children had their first taste of the high life when they were met at the airport by a stretch limousine, which remained at their disposal throughout their stay. They were put up in a luxury hotel and a sightseeing tour was arranged when the group went into the studio to record *Over the Hills and Far Away*.

The highlight of the trip was a special Halloween fireworks party hosted by the director and his wife at their Elstree Village home. Driving through two gates, The Chieftains' party couldn't believe the opulence of the house estate.

'He put on a massive fireworks display for us in his back garden,' says Moloney. 'All the children had the time of their lives. It was just a wonderful family occasion and I remember roasting potatoes in the fire, which was great. Little things like that are marvellous.'

Ironically, the extra Chieftain track recorded in London never made the final edit of Barry Lyndon as the scene it was to accompany was cut out of the film in the end.

* * *

A couple of weeks before The Chieftains left for their first full-scale US tour, Paddy Moloney gave an in-depth interview to *The Irish Times* about his plan to change American misconceptions about

Ireland and its music. He told writer Niall Stokes that The Chieftains were committed to eradicating the old 'Mother Machree' image of Ireland forever.

'People still think of the country in terms of "Did your Mother come from Ireland?" he explained. 'And we're doing a lot to counteract that because we project a totally different image of Ireland. Traditional Irish music is the greatest music in the world, it could have a very big influence on music internationally if it got a proper airing.'

Jo Lustig, a native of Brooklyn who had lived in England for 17 years, had made the conquest of America The Chieftains' number one priority. He decided to steer clear of using the Irish promoters, who had arranged the group's previous tours, and booked them through the regular rock promoters in each city.

'I wanted to cross them over,' explained Lustig.' So I went to people who normally didn't promote ethnic concerts.'

Realizing that an effective publicity campaign would be crucial, Lustig hired the services of a larger-than-life public relations man from Liverpool called Charles Comer, whose syrupy thick scouse accent and charming personality proved highly effective with journalists. Manhattan-based Comer, who had first come over the America for the first Beatles tour in 1964, immediately went into action laying the groundwork for the tour. Touting The Chieftains as 'the next big thing', Comer used his contacts to generate articles in *The New York Times*, *Village Voice*, and the *Daily News*. Charlie continues to spread the word about The Chieftains, and Paddy and the band regard his efforts over the years as among the most important contributions to their success.

Advance publicity and a single advertisement in the *Irish Echo* helped sell out a solo Chieftains concert at New York's prestigious Avery Fisher Hall in Lincoln Center. Then Lustig cleverly booked the group to open for David Bromberg for two shows at Greenwich Village's legendary folk club, The Bottom Line.

Said Lustig: 'I knew the guy that ran The Bottom Line so I asked him to let The Chieftains go on as an opening act. Because I wanted to place this other audience. It was very funny because it was a very trendy audience and they were all smoking pot. Seán Keane kept asking what that funny smell was coming from the audience.'

The New York Times' pop music critic John Rockwell reviewed the show at The Bottom Line.

'They're about the most unlikely candidates for big-time pop music stardom that have come along in quite some time,' noted Rockwell. 'Their performance late Monday night at The Bottom Line (where they were opening for a properly deferential David Bromberg) was a most pleasing affair.'

Introducing The Chieftains in its New Acts column, *Variety* said that they had The Bottom Line audience eating out of the palms of their hands.

'This gig, before a hip audience, most of whom are not familiar with The Chieftains, shows that they can have wider appeal,' wrote *Variety*. 'Their standing ovation at set's end is deserved.'

At the other end of the New York media spectrum, the radically left-wing *Village Voice* questioned The Chieftains on the troubles in Ireland and then criticized them when they refused to be drawn. In an article headlined 'Chieftains: A Terrible Beauty is Embalmed,' *Voice* columnist Geoffrey Stokes admitted to doing 'Sevens and threes up the aisles with a perfect stranger' at the Avery Fisher concert but in the next line wrote their music lacked tension. Stokes cynically observed that before the Avery Fisher show 'the dominant tone in conversations was passionately political'.

'The Chieftains not only ignore that conflict; they negate it,' wrote Stokes. 'Participating in it only as anthropologists rather than believers.'

Carefully explaining the Chieftains' apolitical stand of the time, Paddy Moloney pointed out that traditional music knew no religious barriers. 'One great thing is that at our concerts we do have Protestants and Catholics. There's no religious or political barrier. In fact the best receptions we've had for our music are in the North.'

In another New York interview Derek Bell, the only Protestant in The Chieftains, described how he once gave a friend a Chieftains album and was told, 'Oh, that's Catholic music.'

'No, it wasn't a joke,' Bell told journalist Nancy Lyon. 'He definitely felt that anyone who played a harp instead of a flute was Catholic. You'd never get that sort of provincial attitude in the South. I've come up against it many times and have to correct people on it. I point out that the source of our music has nothing whatsoever to do with any of the churches. They know nothing about the source of the music. They just think, why is this fellow from the North down in Dublin playing music with these people when he should be marching on the 12th.'

Leaving New York, The Chieftains cut a swathe through North America playing to ecstatic audiences in Toronto, Washington D.C., Boston, Chicago, Los Angeles and San Francisco. Wherever they went they collected great reviews and were acclaimed as a breath of fresh air in the stale world of pop music. This was the tour that laid the foundations for an on-going success in the States by providing a loyal core audience of Chieftains' fans.

'Our music was new in America,' explains Paddy Moloney. 'They had heard the odd album being played on the radio and the word was beginning to spread. People came on spec to see who we were and listen to our music. They were impressed by our performance and thank god they came back again and again.'

True to his word, Jo Lustig cut excellent concert deals and the musicians found themselves earning far more money than they had ever done before.

'I was making three times what I made working for the post office,' says Seán Potts. 'My wife could go and spend as much as she wanted. There was no curtailment.'

To make the tour as cost effective as possible Lustig had The Chieftains working almost every day while they were on the road. And in every city they would be entertained as conquering heroes by the local Hibernian groups.

'We met a different set of people in every place we played,' says Tubridy. 'They made a terrible fuss over us and were terribly sociable.'

By the end of the American tour the pressures of working flat out for almost a year were taking their toll on the group. Tensions were running high and there were frequent arguments.

'There was an awful lot of pressure on The Chieftains in those days,' explained Seán Potts. 'There's a terrible tension on the road but it's the same in all groups. Once you go away for any longer than a week the nerves go. I suppose it's living and talking to the same people day in and day out.'

To maintain group sanity, Moloney persuaded Lustig to cut the world tour short and reschedule the Australian and New Zealand dates for the following year. Explaining the decision back in Ireland, Moloney told *The Irish Times*, 'We were getting along great but by the end of the tour we returned to Ireland exhausted.'

As The Chieftains rested up in Dublin they could finally savour their well-earned victory. After 15 years' hard work they had the world at their feet and to top off an incredible year *Melody Maker* readers voted them the overall Group of the Year in its year-end poll, beating such superstar bands as The Rolling Stones and Led Zeppelin. In the citation for the coveted award The Chieftains were applauded 'for making unfashionable music fashionable'.

12

Hail to The Chieftains

If 1975 had been a defining year for The Chieftains, the prospects at the dawn of the new year were even rosier. *Barry Lyndon* was released at the beginning of January and Paddy Moloney's moving music, which would later win an Oscar, was singled out for special mention by film critics and fans alike.

Declared the movie trade publication *Variety* on its front page: 'What *The Third Man* did for Anton Karas and his zither, Stanley Kubrick's upcoming *Barry Lyndon* might do for The Chieftains.'

The blockbuster movie, which starred Ryan O'Neal as Thackeray's 18th century Irish hero, opened up a huge new untapped audience for Chieftain music everywhere it played.

'That was a great booster for us,' remembers Moloney. 'People were talking about the film and word about us was beginning to spread.'

Rock star Jackson Browne saw *Barry Lyndon* in Los Angeles and was deeply affected by The Chieftains' score.

'I heard the music and it was beautiful,' said Browne, who would soon begin an on-going collaboration with the group. 'It was really stunning.'

Four months later, when The Chieftains played Los Angeles, Jackson Browne took his friend Don Henley of the chart-topping rock band The Eagles to see them.

'They were great,' remembers Browne. 'My first musical influences are really folk music and it was interesting to see this highly developed sense of authentic folk music because it was so orchestral. It had an orchestral quality because of the size of the band and this feeling they had for the music.'

Henley was also smitten with The Chieftains and immediately went out and bought some of their albums.

'I was beginning to develop an interest in ethnic and traditional music and I loved The Chieftains' music,' said Henley. 'My mother is of Irish descent; her maiden name was McWhorter.'

In the first week of January The Chieftains flew to New York to headline an all-star Irish programme at Carnegie Hall including their old friend Peter O'Toole, actress Siobhán McKenna and singer Mary O'Hara. During the trip they were awarded the accolade of a profile in *Time* magazine under the headline 'Piping Hot and Cool'.

'They are, in short, about as average a bunch as any country can produce and not the usual candidates for pop stardom,' said *Time* who had sent a reporter to Dublin a few months earlier to interview Paddy Moloney at The Shelbourne. 'But when they sit down together to play they are something else again.'

Describing The Chieftains on stage as looking like 'a group of old friends taking some Saturday night relaxation in a Dublin Pub', *Time* felt the group's biggest selling point was their 'sheer, unabashed virtuosity'.

'They wander out haphazardly in sweaters, odd jackets and tweed pants, sit in a big semicircle, tap their feet and boast to the audience that Irish music is "the best in the world". They know that their act lacks polish, and they do not care a whit. Their music is what counts. Anything else would be show business. The pop world may just not have seen The Chieftains' like before,' concluded the article.

Rolling Stone magazine gave its seal of approval to The Chieftains with an excellent review for *Chieftains 5*.

'Once in a while there is an album that really holds together, like this one,' Charles Perry wrote. 'Like the austere landscape on the inside spread, the music here is a little barbaric, a little worn and used and bracingly clean and attractive.'

With the Chieftains riding high, Island Records re-released the group's first four albums in February to coincide with a major BBC television documentary profiling them for the arts programme *Omnibus*. Even the communist English newspaper *Morning Star* managed to get into the act and find socialist merit in The Chieftains 'What is striking about The Chieftains is that they are beginning to achieve in the capitalist West, a status for instrumental folk music usually only accorded to groups in the Socialist community.'

After having to cut short the previous winter's world tour because of exhaustion, The Chieftains set up some travelling ground rules to ensure it would never happen again. From now on they agreed to pace themselves so they were never away from home for more than three weeks at a time. But with scores of offers flooding in every week, the efficient Jo Lustig loathed to turn down work, leading to bitter arguments. Ultimately, band members always had the upper hand over their frustrated manager as their contract gave them final say for bookings.

When Lustig started planning an ambitious six-week tour of the States that April they balked, refusing point blank to do more than three. It was left up to Chieftain leader and spokesman, Paddy Moloney to liaise between both sides and as a self-confessed workaholic he found himself in a dilemma.

'There were two sides of me pulling against each other,' explained Moloney. 'One was trying to persuade the band to do it and the other was thinking the same as they were. Do I lose out on the management side or do I lose out on the popularity side?

'You see, I understood where Jo was coming from but he couldn't understand where the band was at. I had to tread a very awkward line because I was thinking of the music and what I wanted to hear. I wasn't going to get swallowed up into something they didn't want to do and risk losing the band. At that time there were festivals and things being sacrificed that were brilliant, because they came at the wrong time. Jo could never understand members of the band from a family point of view and I wasn't going to neglect them because we were a democracy.'

Moloney refused to give in to Lustig's continual shouting and screaming down the phone, which led to little Aedín Moloney nicknaming him Jaws. Eventually the manager was forced to back down and the tour was scaled down to three weeks.

Just before leaving for America in April, The Chieftains played a sell-out concert at the Royal Festival Hall on the River Thames and proved that they hadn't lost their traditional edge.

'The music of old Ireland worked its magic once more and sent young fans skipping down the aisles and onto the stage for a good natured jig around the musicians,' wrote *Melody Maker*'s Chris Welch.

While noting that The Chieftains' American success had given them improved stage presence and confidence, he chided Seán Potts for constantly interrupting Moloney's 'amusing if rambling announcements'.

Crossing the Atlantic for their second major North American tour in six months, The Chieftains now found themselves a major draw everywhere they went. Even though there was very little alcohol consumed before a show, their concert riders now insisted on promoters providing a case of Guinness and Harp lager in their dressing rooms for hospitality after the shows.

The tour began with a sell-out show at Avery Fisher Hall, before moving on to the Symphony Hall in Boston and concerts in Buffalo, Pittsburgh, Cleveland, Baltimore, Chicago and Washington. It was then back to New York where they sold out Carnegie Hall on April 22 in a show described as 'vibrant' by *Variety*. Travelling by bus, the early tours were taken at a far more leisurely pace than the later ones would be.

'There was always great fun,' remembers Seán Potts, who hated flying. 'I used to love the bus travel if we were doing the east coast from Boston down to Washington. We used to stop off for the odd jar but nowadays it's fly, fly, fly.'

Heading west, The Chieftains finished up the tour with two standing room only shows for San Francisco promoter Bill Graham in Winterland. The climax of the tour was Los Angeles where they found themselves fêted by Hollywood in the wake of the success of *Barry Lyndon*. Composer Leonard Rosenman, who shared composing honours with Moloney for the Stanley Kubrick film, threw a party in their honour with guests like Larry Hagman, Tatum O'Neal and veteran actor Burgess Meredith.

'We were all mad about their music,' says Meredith. 'Paddy's a most joyful man and we became good friends and he would always come and stay with me when he was in Hollywood. I've spent some of my best moments with Paddy. I think he's wonderfully creative and a fine artist.'

At The Chieftains concert in Santa Monica the California governor of the time, Jerry Brown, turned up with his then girlfriend singer Linda Ronstadt (now singing with The Chieftains and Los Lobos on their 1996 Galician album *Santiago*) and went backstage to be photographed with the group. Also backstage was Robbie Robertson and Garth Hudson of The Band who had come to check out traditional Irish music.

'Garth asked us to a party after the show,' remembers Moloney. 'He drove us all to his studio in an old Mercedes where we had champagne. They played us their new album and it was great music. Terrific. I think they wanted us to record some tracks and it was an awful pity that we didn't have any time to do it. That would have been historic.'

During that tour, The Chieftains' inexhaustible publicist Charles Comer set up a total of 89 interviews for Paddy Moloney, who showed a natural flair for publicity and the art of the soundbite. It was during these early American tours that Moloney and Comer came up with a highly effective publicity formula to ensure sell-out shows.

'Paddy and Charlie made a great combination,' says Shanachie Records' boss Dan Collins. 'Paddy would start doing pre-interviews, four or five days in each city, before the gig. This would get newspaper articles appearing and the seats started selling. They worked very hard on this. When Charlie's finishing up a tour his voice will be hoarse and almost gone. At his level he's the best at what he does.'

Back in Ireland The Chieftains' incredible rise to international stardom had not gone unnoticed with many people assuming that they must be making big money. Asked by *The Irish Times* if he was now in the sur-tax class Moloney laughed, saying, 'Not at all. With seven members, after all, the money has to go a long way. We've all gone full-time these past few years and everyone manages all right. But nobody's making a fortune.'

Moloney claimed that the group's expenses alone for the recent American tour came to more than $60,000.

'I couldn't believe it,' he said. 'But we got it all on paper properly accounted for.'

It was during this brief time off in Dublin that The Chieftains collaborated with Art Garfunkel on his third solo album, *Watermark*. The former partner of Paul Simon, who had now embarked on a solo career, had first heard Chieftains' music when he went to see *Barry Lyndon*. A few months later he went to their Buffalo show and immediately knew he had to have The Chieftains' sound on his new record.

'I heard the edge of Paddy's uilleann pipes and it went straight to my emotional centre,' remembers Garfunkel. 'I felt it's a great colour that's never used in the rock 'n' roll palette and I felt I had to use it.'

The superstar singer came backstage after the show to introduce himself to the band and offered to fly them all out to the famous

Muscle Shoals Studios at the end of their tour to record backing tracks for his version of *She Moved Through the Fair*. Although Moloney could see the importance of a superstar collaboration with Art Garfunkel, he realized it contravened their new three-week touring rule.

'I thought, "Here we go again. Another big opportunity missed," ' says Moloney. 'I said, "Oh God, Art, the band won't do that. The only way it's going to happen is if you come to Ireland." '

To Moloney's surprise Garfunkel instantly agreed and within a few weeks he was in Dublin with his girlfriend staying in a huge suite at The Shelbourne thanks to special arrangements made by Paddy and the hotel's management. Although Garfunkel's original plan was to stay for two days and do an evening recording session at the Lombard Studios, he stayed ten. Today Garfunkel is a little vague about that first trip to Dublin, but his tour guide Paddy Moloney remembers it well.

'Art had a ball,' says Moloney. 'He thought Dublin was the greatest with all the bars and the restaurants. We had one really memorable dinner at King Sitric, the famous restaurant in Howth. From then on he was always sneaking into Ireland for his little visits.'

During his trip Garfunkel recorded three Chieftain backing tracks for *Watermark*, including a version of *She Moved Through the Fair*, which Sinéad O'Connor would later sing on *The Long Black Veil*. On his return to Hollywood to mix the album at the Cherokee Studios, Garfunkel was thrilled with the results.

'You move to the ends of the world to make sure your record really happens,' explained Garfunkel. 'When I was back in the studio hearing Paddy's pipes I was just full of joy. My ears told me that it was one of the greatest sounds that I had ever heard. There was so much heart in it. They are the Irish soul.'

After their breather in Dublin, The Chieftains flew out to Australia to fulfil the dates they had missed the year before. All The Chieftains were very excited about going halfway around the world to Australia and New Zealand for the first time.

'I couldn't believe it when I heard we were going to Australia for two weeks,' remembers Seán Keane. 'I said "Are you serious? We're going to Australia?" '

'We used to work twice as hard as we do now,' explained Moloney. 'But we had to because there wasn't that much money coming out of the records in those days. Lustig came in strong. He wanted his 25 per cent which was a huge amount to take off the top before the band saw anything. And then we had to pay our own expenses. I used to go in and argue with him and say, "I'm not doing it unless you get the hotels thrown in." There were terrible arguments. We always went for expenses and sound to be provided. You see it wouldn't make any difference to him but it made a lot of difference to us.'

There were growing disputes between Moloney and Lustig during the Australian tour and at one point a concerned Derek Bell had a serious talk with the prickly manager about his future.

Bell: 'Lustig said he was leaving us and I said, "Well, what will happen to The Chieftains without you?" And he said to me, "As long as Paddy bloody well wants there to be Chieftains, there will be Chieftains. When he wants it no more you're gone." And I think that's a bit of truth.'

During the turbulent tour there were calmer seas when The Chieftains went sightseeing on their days off Melbourne, Sydney and Perth and Michael Tubridy even managed to trace some long-lost relatives. At the end of the tour Moloney had a day off in Perth and decided to go shopping for presents. While he was in a department store he mysteriously felt an overwhelming compulsion to buy baby clothes.

'I thought, "What the hell am I doing this for, as there was no reason for me to be looking for baby clothes," ' said Moloney. 'That night I called Rita to tell her I'd be home the following day when she suddenly said, "I might have some news for you when you get back." '

Amazingly, Moloney arrived home to discover that Rita's news was that she was pregnant with their third child.

* * *

With future tours already lined up for Europe, Australia and New Zealand, The Chieftains were committed to spending six months or more on the road every year for the foreseeable future. Bodhrán player Peader Mercier was now in his 60s with ten children and was feeling the pressure. On their return from Australia, Moloney and Mercier discussed his early retirement and the elderly bodhrán player was more than happy to agree.

Now Moloney had the problem of finding a replacement for Mercier with just weeks before he was due to go into a London studio to record his most ambitious album to date, *Bonaparte's Retreat*. With time running out Moloney remembered a young bodhrán player called Kevin Conneff whom he had met a few years earlier. Tracking down Conneff to the Instamatic Printing Company in Dublin where he now worked, Moloney telephoned, inviting him to come to London the following week and play on a couple of Chieftains' tracks for the new album.

'I was working in the darkroom when I got the call from Paddy,' remembers Kevin. 'I said I would have to square it with my boss first. When I asked him for a week's holiday he told me it was okay as long as I had all my work cleared up and there was nothing in my in-tray. It meant working overtime to clear my work but I did it.'

* * *

Kevin Conneff was born on January 8th, 1945. He was raised in the Liberties, right in the heart of Dublin. When he was just ten days old Kevin had a delicate operation for a cleft lip. Although Kevin was later to develop a normal boy's interest in boxing, his mother was advised by the family doctor that her son should never be a boxer.

His father Thomas Patrick Conneff was a picture frame maker and gold leaf artist who found it a constant struggle to support his wife Margaret and their six children, of which Kevin was the youngest. When Kevin was two, his brother Tony died of meningitis and his earliest memories are of being taken to see his sick brother on his death bed.

There was always music coming from the gramophone and wireless when young Kevin was growing up. His father loved the legendary Irish tenor John McCormack, who brought *Mother Machree* and *When Irish Eyes are Smiling* to America in the 1920s – half a century before The Chieftains arrived with the real thing. When McCormack or Caruso came on the wireless everything had to stop in the Conneff household so the singer could be given due reverence. And at weekends Kevin joined the family around the old wireless to listen to popular Irish music programmes like *Take the Floor* and *Ceili House* and his sister Áine would step dance to the traditional music.

'There was a great love of music in general,' says Kevin. 'But unlike other members of the Chieftains I didn't hear traditional music from the womb.'

Indeed, when he was growing up in the 1950s Kevin preferred listening to the pop stars of the day like Johnny Ray and Eddie Fisher. Right across the road from the Conneff's house on Hamilton Street lived Breandán Breathnach, a renowned traditional music collector who wrote the landmark work, *Folk Music and Dances of Ireland*, as well as starting na Píobairí Uilleann (Uilleann Piper's Association) of which Paddy Moloney was also a founder-member. Kevin remembers thinking that the traditional music which he heard when passing their house was 'corny and weird'.

Kevin was sent to the Weaver Square School where he was taught by nuns before he was old enough to go to the Christian Brothers' St Theresa's Primary School a stone's throw away from his home. An average student, Kevin enjoyed playing Gaelic Football and won the interschool singing competition with a stirring version of the song *Bells Across the Meadow.*

At the age of 12 he went to the St James' Street Secondary School, next door to the Guinness brewery. Showing little academic interest, Kevin disappointed his parents by refusing to take his qualifying examinations and left school at 15 to make his way in the world.

'A lot of my pals had left school and had money in their pockets,' he explained. 'They were able to go places and I didn't want to be left out.'

Spotting a newspaper advertisement for a photographic assistant based with the Irish agents of a printing machine company located in Cleveland, Ohio, Kevin applied and got the job. It paid just 30 shillings per week, out of which he gave his parents 20 shillings for his keep. At the beginning there was little photography involved and Kevin's duties included sweeping the floor, laying down rat poison and running errands. But Kevin was keen to learn the trade and within a couple of years he had risen to be a qualified lithographic plate maker and printing lay out artist.

The job also gave Conneff his first introduction to traditional music at the age of 18, through his work mates. Every week a group would club together to hire a car to drive to one of the many fleadhanna cheoil (music festivals) around Ireland. When he was invited to accompany them to the 1964 All-Ireland fleadh ceoil in Mullingar he readily accepted.

Remembers Conneff: 'I simply went along for a great time and to have a drink for the first time in my life. And girls would have been looming large at that stage too, but not close enough unfortunately. So this seemed to be a place where perhaps one might meet girls.'

During the weekend Conneff and his friends were sitting on a rail in the square in Mullingar when a group of traditional musicians came over and started playing. 'I was totally bowled over when I first came close to traditional music,' remembers Conneff. 'There were these old guys wearing Sunday suits about ten years out of fashion, caps and the wrong coloured shoes. Before I would have described them uncharitably as a bunch of culchies. But they were playing such incredible music. I was just staring at their fingers on the fiddles and the flutes and I just realized that they were very very talented, and they probably didn't know it. They were just enjoying themselves.

'And I've never forgotten that image of traditional music and the sheer joy and respect that I had in a matter of moments as I looked at those men playing. I was hooked.'

From then on Conneff started going to fleadhanna cheoil every weekend and picking up songs which he started performing in the traditional Seán Nós style or a cappella. He also bought his first bodhrán for £3 at a fleadh ceoil in Newscastle West, Limerick, so he could accompany two friends who played whistle and accordion. A few years earlier, Conneff had first heard the bodhrán accompanying a singer doing a song on the radio from the John B. Keane play *Sive* and had heard Seán Ó Riada play it with Ceoltóirí Cualann. He was amazed at the power and range of the simple goat skin drum.

'It had as much rock 'n' roll balls in it as Little Richard in top gear,' says Conneff. 'And it was a much simpler thing. It just absolutely floored me.'

Conneff soon mastered the bodhrán and began playing it with his friends at fleadhanna cheoil around Ireland. After one informal session during the Oireachtas competition at the RDS in Dublin, Kevin met Paddy Moloney for the first time when the famous piper came over, patted him on the back and said, 'I'll be talking to you sometime.'

At this point music started taking over Conneff's life as he became a regular on the Dublin traditional music circuit, visiting O'Donoghue's Pub and the Church Street and Thomas Street Pipers' Clubs.

'The clubs were dry,' explained Kevin. 'So what we did was, if we spaced out our money well enough through the week, we might have enough for a couple of pints in O'Donoghue's and then make our way to Church Street or wherever.

"O'Donoghue's was a traditional music mecca in those days. I could just go in after work and hear the greats of traditional music. I was lucky enough to see the piper Séamus Ennis and wonderful singers like Joe Heaney or Caitlín Maude just playing for the hell of it. In the jazz world they would be the equivalent of Charlie Parker. It was a great era. You'd have a pint and suddenly you'd find yourself in a singing session with these legends.'

For summer holidays, Conneff and six or seven of his friends would hire a car and tour traditional musical areas like Kerry or Clare, camping or sleeping rough in hay barns and generally roughing it. They would also head off west to Roscommon or Sligo on St Stephen's Day, the day after Christmas, to hunt the wren. The Wren Hunt is an ancient Celtic tradition where the men and boys of the parish dress up in ragged costumes and blacken their faces. They then go around houses and pubs singing, dancing and playing instruments to get money for food and drink on the pretext of waking and burying of a wren, the smallest bird known in Celtic folklore.

'It was a wonderful time,' says Conneff, who would sing the traditional *Wren in the Furze* to such great effect on The Chieftains' *Bells of Dublin* album many years later. 'We wouldn't dress up but we'd go around the pubs and get involved with those musicians that did and join in their sessions.

'Even though it was the middle of winter we'd sleep in the hay barns and snuggle down in the hay. When we woke up in the morning there would be literally frost on the hay but it wouldn't have bothered us because, being exhausted and with the help of alcohol, we would have slept very soundly.'

When the folk revival of the mid-1960s swept through Dublin, Kevin Conneff and a group of like-minded friends of his decided to start their own club devoted to traditional singing. They found a pub called Slattery's on Capel Street and negotiated to have the basement bar for their Listener's Club every Wednesday night. Admission was free and Conneff even printed up membership cards at work to add some class. The Listener's Club soon became so popular it outgrew the tiny basement and they had to move upstairs to a larger bar. The new bar was a more ambitious affair with a small admission so Conneff could book out of town traditional musicians to perform.

After a row over the way it was managed Conneff finally quit the Listener's Club and stepped back a bit from the traditional scene. For a year he put traditional music on hold and began listening to jazz and classical music and going out more to films and plays. But his interest was rekindled when a friend took him to a new folk club called The 95 Club on Hardcourt Street off St Stephen's Green.

'I realized how much I had missed traditional music and became involved in the scene again,' he explained. 'I started singing again and got spots in the different folk clubs around Dublin.'

After losing its premises The 95 Club briefly reopened in a basement in Parnell Square before moving to the original Listener's Club site at Slattery's Pub, where it was renamed the Tradition Club. For the next few years Conneff and a couple of friends ran what was probably the longest-running and most respected traditional music club in Dublin, booking a wealth of traditional musicians including Kevin's future colleagues, Paddy Moloney, Seán Keane and Michael Tubridy.

'The whole thing was run very idealistically,' says Conneff. 'On a bad night we would have to dip into our own pockets to try and make the musicians' fee a little bit more respectable than the takings would allow.'

Using material from his printing job, Conneff designed and printed by hand the Tradition Club posters himself with the motto 'Ceol agus Amhránaíocht ar an Seán-nós' which means 'Music and Song in the Traditional Style'.

'I also needed to add in large red print "Only Listeners Welcome" because we were determined the musicians and singers would be shown the respect they deserved and not to be merely background music.' In the Tradition Club music took first place and the audience were expected to be quiet in the bar during performances.

'It can be very irritating if you have a solo piper or a fiddler playing,' he said. 'You will always have a certain buzz of conversation and of course people ordering drinks but we'd try to keep it down.'

Sometimes that meant bribing a rowdy party with a round of drinks to leave and many a barman would resent being asked to be quieter and revolt by noisily banging down glasses.

Paddy Moloney's life-changing call to come to London and play the bodhrán on a couple of tracks of *Bonaparte's Retreat*, came in the middle of the record-breaking summer heat wave of 1976. When he arrived in London, temperatures were in the nineties and there was no air conditioning at the Island Studios. The Chieftains were recording in the adjoining studio to the Jamaican hand Burning Spear and the sounds of reggae would often drift through the walls. A couple of days into the recording Moloney asked Kevin out for a drink at a pub in the nearby Portobello Road.

Remembers Conneff: 'We were having a glass of Guinness when I discovered that instead of just the couple of tracks Paddy had asked me to do in Dublin, he now wanted me to stay for a whole week and play on all of them.

'Well, you could have knocked me off the barstool with a feather when Paddy said, "I'd like you to make it permanent. Would you consider it?" I felt absolutely flattered and complimented because I'd just been playing the bodhrán as I always did and I didn't think I was doing anything special. But Paddy obviously liked what I did. In fact at the time I never even realized Peadar Mercier was leaving.'

Conneff said he'd need time to think about the personal implications of being a Chieftain and spending six months or more on the road every year. At that time he was 31 years old, had a good job and felt responsible for looking after his elderly mother who he was living with at the time. He also felt a moral dilemma in joining a commercial group after devoting so many years to playing and promoting Irish music in its purist form without being paid.

'There was a certain reluctance to go from an idealistic situation regarding traditional music to beating the bodhrán on the stage for a living,' explains Conneff. 'I wasn't to be singing with The Chieftains at that stage.'

Conneff admits to having been 'an inverted musical snob' some years earlier who considered The Chieftains a sell out.

'It was fashionable to knock The Chieftains,' says Conneff. 'The very fact that they had come up with a different sound and were making records meant that they'd gone commercial.'

Conneff got his come-uppance at a party given by an artist friend of his called Brian Bourke at his house in Mount Merrion.

'There was a great, exciting bunch of people at the party,' says Kevin. 'Artists, poets and a great collection of people. Suddenly somebody said, "Put on a Chieftains' album." And I said, "The Chieftains? Have you nothing else?"

'And Brian Bourke came over to me and said quietly, "I bet you have never actually *listened* to The Chieftains." And he was right. I'm sure I blushed because he hit the nail on the head. And as a result of this very stern rebuke I did and realized that The Chieftains were an absolutely fantastic group. I saw that they were musical geniuses in their own right and for me to have any kind of haughty opinion was absolutely ridiculous.

'In fact this hostile attitude to The Chieftains is still very prevalent in Ireland. I've had many Irish people coming up to me after a concert in America to say how much they loved us, but they never would have gone to see The Chieftains play in Ireland.'

After discussing Paddy Moloney's offer with his mother, friends and work mates, Kevin agreed to throw in his lot with The Chieftains. As the newest member of the band Kevin Conneff would bring a modern new sensibility to the group. Ironically, his first appearance on stage with them at the Crystal Palace Festival supporting Eric Clapton, was a clear signpost to The Chieftains' new direction.

13

Round the House and Mind the Dresser

Aedín Moloney remembers the day when, as a nine-year-old, she was in her biology class studying tadpoles when her mother burst into the classroom to announce that her daughter had to leave immediately for London. Before her teacher Miss Dunhill could say a word, Rita in her customary long hippie dress, grabbed Aedín and bundled her into a waiting taxi. On the way to the airport Rita explained that they were off to see her father play the Crystal Palace Festival with superstar Eric Clapton.

'That afternoon I was sitting at the lake at Crystal Palace with my feet in the water, one of 20,000 people watching my father on stage,' remembers Aedín. 'Later I saw Eric Clapton play and I vividly remember his long hair and beard. I thought it was wonderful that my daddy was on the same bill as Eric Clapton.'

The star-studded Crystal Palace Festival was Kevin Conneff's first gig with The Chieftains and the first time he had ever played outside the small folk clubs of Dublin.

'I got the thrill of an audience,' he said. 'Having them go wild for you was something I'd never experienced and it was great to be playing with the cream of musicians.'

Later backstage, Jo Lustig took Conneff to one side for a chat. The experienced manager told Conneff that committing himself to The Chieftains would mean hard work and lots of travel but added that he would probably make a good living.

* * *

Bonaparte's Retreat was released to ecstatic reviews in October. Critics applauded The Chieftains for keeping the traditional faith and not letting their new-found success compromise the music. A quantum leap forward for The Chieftains, *Bonaparte's Retreat* was a concept album themed around Ireland's little known role in supporting Napoleon against the English.

'It's my tone poem which was inspired by reading the history books and seeing the Irish connection with the French,' explains Moloney. 'It's about how the Irish asked for Napoleon's help and then how they went over to help him out with our common problems with the neighbours.'

Moloney's musical collage begins with a lament for the flight of a group of Irish chieftains called The Wild Geese who were forced into exile in the 17th century, and whose descendants later offered their services to Napoleon in his battles with England. The intensely emotional piece vividly details Napoleon's rise and fall through the eyes of Ireland. It evokes the repeated requests for French assistance to help Ireland and finishes with Napoleon's exile to the island of Elba and the end of Ireland's dream of freedom as the Bourbon monarchy is restored.

Bonaparte's Retreat was the first Chieftains record to include the human voice and featured Dolores Keane singing three haunting narrative verses a cappella, adding a new depth to the music.

'Dolores was a sweet beautiful 17-year-old girl from Galway with the most melodious voice,' says Moloney. 'Of all the great lady singers I think Dolores is still the best.'

Dolores was living in London when she was invited to appear on *Bonaparte's Retreat*.

'I was The Chieftains' first singer,' quips Dolores. 'I thought it was a great honour when Paddy asked me to be a part of this major work.'

On the last track Paddy successfully managed to incorporate step dancing on a rousing series of Kerry slides called *Around the House and Mind the Dresser*; the traditional warning to dancers not to crash into the furniture. Eight dancers were invited to the studio to perform but thirty turned up.

'Although there was only room for ten on the floor these whacked into their job with a heavy vengeance,' wrote Garech Browne on the album's sleeve notes which he co-wrote with Ireland's ambassador to Spain, Richard Ryan, who is also an accomplished poet.

In *Around the House and Mind the Dresser* Moloney leads The Chieftains in the stirring chorus: 'If I had a wife, the plague of me life I'll tell you what I would do, I'd buy her a boat and put her afloat and paddle me own canoe.' Paddy got the words for this from Irish Shanachie and storyteller Eamonn Kelly.

Jokes Moloney: 'That's what I sing for Rita when she gets on my nerves or when things go wrong. She has some songs about me but we won't repeat them.'

* * *

Bonaparte's Retreat was released in October to coincide with a major UK tour where they played top flight venues in Manchester, London, Birmingham, Newcastle, Leeds, Edinburgh, Aberdeen and Glasgow. Ironically, the week before the tour started The Chieftains played a school gymnasium in Downpatrick, Co. Down, with a basketball net hanging over their heads.

Quipped Derek Bell at the time, 'It's a bit different from the Royal Albert Hall – but maybe the acoustics will be even better.'

In December The Chieftains returned to America for the third time that year and the constant climatic changes were taking their toll on Paddy Moloney's frail uilleann pipes. In Ontario the reeds of Moloney's pipes cracked as he carried them from his hotel's central heating into the freezing conditions outside. Moloney was devastated. The reed had been made by his teacher Leo Rowsome and he'd been using it for more than 17 years without a problem. As Rowsome had died in 1970 he knew it would be very difficult to get another set of reeds that tuned to his satisfaction.

'Reeds are my curse,' says Moloney. 'If they go wrong you are in terrible trouble. It's brutal. You're supposed to make your own reeds, but I never managed to master the art, and frankly never had the time.'

To make thing even worse, the concerts at the Symphony Hall in Boston and at the Massey Hall in Toronto were to be recorded for a live album. Moloney, who was very unhappy about his reeds, says he never felt at ease for the shows.

In Boston Island Records' Chris Blackwell turned up and to Moloney's embarrassment witnessed a full-scale panic when Seán Potts' tin whistle disappeared minutes before they were due to perform.

'There was a terrible uproar,' remembers Moloney. 'Seán said he'd left his whistle on the grand piano and he thought somebody had stolen it. In the end he had to play another whistle and he wasn't happy at all.'

The whistle was eventually found lodged deep inside the piano during the interval and Potts merrily piped through the second half of the show. But in the end only one track from the Symphony Hall show was usable as the mobile recording equipment had somehow picked up radio signals from a nearby hospital. The balance of the album came from the Toronto concert.

Chieftains Live was released the following year and gave record buyers an infectious taste of the group's stage show for the first time. Complete with Paddy Moloney's jovial banter and humorous remarks between tunes, the album managed to capture The Chieftains in full musical flight.

'Good evening Ladies and Gentlemen you're all very welcome to our concert of traditional Irish music,' says Moloney introducing *George Brabazon*, the first of the album's three Carolan pieces. Other tracks include Martin Fay and Derek Bell's moving duet on *Carrickfergus*, *The Foxhunt*, *O' Neill's March* and *Ríl Mhor*.

The album gives a taste of Moloney's self-effacing introductions like this build-up for *Kerry Slides*.

'Now we're all in great spirits here tonight so we decided that we'd like to go down to Kerry. And down in Kerry incidentally they have all the great music. They have all the hornpipes, jigs, reels, hop jigs, slip jigs and all them things, polkas. And they also got slides. And we'd like you to enter into the gas or a bit of a hooley that we're having on stage here, I hope. And away we go now with three or four fast moving Kerry slides.'

When the album was released the following year Moloney was unhappy with it.

'It's a good album but it could have been a great one,' said Moloney with his perfectionist's ear. 'I don't know what they did to it technically but I know it plays too fast.'

*　*　*

Jo Lustig had now been managing The Chieftains for almost two years and his relationship with the band had badly deteriorated. Always hands on, Paddy Moloney liked to 'manage the managers' and this led to constant heated arguments over the phone. There was also increased tension within The Chieftains as Seán Potts clashed with Moloney, accusing him of being selfish managerially and not giving the other members of the band due recognition.

'Paddy and I were very close but we argued terribly,' remembers Potts. 'I was the eldest in the band so I'd call him out and challenge him. I was always the one that had to tell him to step down or whatever because none of the others would do it.'

Paddy Moloney says that The Chieftains' chemistry at that time was intense with so many diverse characters.

'Seán Potts had a very strong personality and Keane tagged along with him,' remembers Moloney. 'Martin was always Martin. Martin was always close to me and backed me all the way. Mick Tubridy was very close and Derek's my best friend in the band.'

Stepping into a long established band, new boy Kevin Conneff was also having a difficult time adapting to his new life. The Chieftains maintained a strict travelling routine where they always sat apart on planes and each stayed on different hotel floors. There was little socializing on the road between members of the band. After concerts Moloney and Derek Bell might go out for a Japanese or Thai meal or a couple of the others might meet for a drink but otherwise the only time they all met up on the road was at sound checks and performances.

'I nearly went crazy,' remembers Conneff. 'I'm a fairly gregarious person but I found that I wasn't getting close to anybody in the band and I didn't want to because my close friends were in Dublin.'

During his first few years with The Chieftains Conneff socialized with the road crew, often finding himself in an uncomfortable position if something went wrong with the equipment. For more than a year he was miserable and seriously considered returning to his printing job.

In March 1977 Rita Moloney gave birth to an 8 lb baby boy who was named Pádraig and the news came that Seán Keane's wife Marie was also pregnant. It was hard for The Chieftains' wives to run the household and bring up their children while their husbands were off on the road for more than half the year. In the early years The Chieftains' wives occasionally joined them on the road but this practice was discontinued after a show in Donnegal.

'It didn't quite work out,' says Moloney, refusing to elaborate. 'We just decided that it wasn't a good idea to bring wives or families on tour.'

But Rita Moloney, Marie Keane and Bernie Potts became close

friends as they had a lot in common with young children and supported each other while their husbands were away.

'Marie and I would often meet up with the kids and go out together,' says Rita. 'She used to phone me up to see how I was getting on while Paddy was away which I really appreciated.'

That spring The Chieftains were enjoying a relatively quiet spell with occasional showcase concerts like performing on the Olivier Stage at the National Theatre in London. But behind the scenes Jo Lustig was hard at work arranging a British summer tour followed by the biggest American tour of their careers.

'It was going to be amazing,' said Lustig. 'After going through a lot of personal problems with Paddy and the band, with all the arguing and people threatening to leave, I set up this wonderful summer tour of America. I had booked them for the Carnegie Hall again, the Universal Amphitheater as well as all those wonderful summer theaters where they have those Sunday celebrity concerts.'

A few weeks before they were due to leave for America Moloney telephoned Lustig to announce The Chieftains would not be doing the tour as Séan Keane didn't want to be away from home for the birth of his new baby.

Remembers Lustig: 'I said, "Paddy, he's had children before. If necessary we'll get a nurse."

'So I said to Paddy, "These people have booked you because of my reputation not yours. If I cancel this tour I resign. I can't take it anymore. It's not worth it." They wouldn't back down so I resigned. I didn't want to but I cancelled out.'

Paddy Moloney says cancelling the tour was the only way to keep The Chieftains together and the end certainly justified the means even if it meant losing a manager and being dropped by Island Records. Paddy made his decision at a concert in Ennis, Co. Clare, at the Old Ground Hotel. He has never forgotten it and never regretted it.

'Jo nearly cried,' remembers Moloney. 'The Greek Theater would have been the biggest thing we had ever played at. After that the record company felt that was it. They couldn't understand the attitude.'

It didn't take long for Moloney to get a new contract with CBS Records and staunchly defends his decision to put family before business.

'So we could have made more money and we could have been

more popular. Perhaps we'd all have been retired long before now if we had done it that way. But we didn't. We stuck to what we wanted to do.'

Even today the group all acknowledge a debt of gratitude to Lustig for launching their professional career.

'We were happy enough plodding along and playing concerts here and there,' says Keane. 'Lustig turned the whole thing around and made us realize what we had. He got the best out of us. He put us up there and then we took it from there.'

From that point on The Chieftains would go through a revolving door of managers as Paddy Moloney could never allow himself to relax the reins of control. From its very beginnings he had doggedly led the group and would never take a back seat to any manager.

'Paddy doesn't seem to be able to delegate anything,' says Derek Bell, who is the closest band member to Moloney. 'We all say he's a workaholic and he has to oversee everything himself. He's on the telephone all day and then his whole bloody time's gone. You only have to spend a morning in his house and hear how often the phone rings. It's just as well he doesn't have to practise 12 hours a day like a concert pianist.'

Lustig, who has now left music management to become a successful film producer, says he found Moloney impossible to manage.

'He was most difficult,' states Lustig. 'Musically wonderful but otherwise forget it. I mean I'm quite fond of Paddy but he's impossible. That's why I do films today. A film doesn't give me trouble.'

* * *

Outwardly, Lustig's departure did little to change The Chieftains as they attempted to carry on as usual, but there were cracks now starting to appear in the band. Lustig agreed to stay on through July to help The Chieftains complete a British tour he had set up for July to tie in with the release of *Chieftains Live*. The group's first live album received great reviews despite Moloney's reservations about its quality. *Melody Maker* highly recommended it for 'those who like their Chieftains having a knees up,' although it deplored the cover photograph which made band members look like cardboard figures.

In September, after the birth of Keane's son Darach, The Chieftains did tour North America, and continued to have amazing success. But inwardly at least, there were signs of tensions.

When the English magazine *Folk News* carried a gossip item in its Deep Throat column saying that two members of The Chieftains were expected to leave within a year due to 'friction', Moloney immediately had Claddagh's press officer Pat Pretty call a press conference to deny it.

'I was worried about the band and people thinking we were breaking up,' remembers Moloney. 'There was a rumour that Seán Keane was about to quit so I promptly called a press conference. Luckily I was able to push the whole thing underneath the carpet and within 24 hours it had blown over.'

Moloney's damage control had been so successful that the following week the Dublin magazine *Hot Press* reported that there was no substance to the rumours, adding that it believed the initial source to be Irish. In a story headlined, 'Chieftains Deny Rumour of Split,' *Hot Press* carried a detailed report of the press conference. 'The Chieftains are presently touring Canada, but Pat Pretty said that in response to the report, Paddy Moloney had asked each member of the group about their future plans. All had denied to him any intention to leave. Nor has any resignation been tendered.'

It was at this point that The Chieftains began to face a backlash of resentment from purists and music historians which has continued to this day. Dublin's *Hot Press* actually put The Chieftains on trial in a two-page spread in September entitled, 'Whither have you come o Chieftain men & what have you done.'

Since turning professional The Chieftains had easily become the most successful Irish musical group in history. They had paved the way for other Irish groups like The Bothy Band and Planxty as well as personally conquering thirteen countries on three continents and selling more than 250,000 records. Now Moloney found himself pilloried and being forced to defend his place in traditional music.

Speaking to *Hot Press*, Moloney explained: 'Once you build up to a certain popularity, there's nothing else to do at that point but to start knocking and they're going to town on us lately.'

Moloney pledged The Chieftains would carry on playing their music and fired a clear warning shot across his critic's bow threatening never to play in Ireland again.

'We're going to take our international policy a little more

seriously now,' he said. 'If people don't accept what we're doing there's no point in being here.'

U2's manager Paul McGuinness found himself in a similar position in Ireland a decade later when his band achieved global success.

'I think it comes with the territory,' said McGuinness. 'The Irish word for it is begrudgery and everyone knows what it means here. When anyone achieves success the people with whom they used to be compared with suddenly turn on them and try and bring them down to size.

'Paddy has an amazing energy and professionalism and, quite frankly, the musical environment from which he sprang was full of a lot of lazy people who would rather have a quiet life and spend as much time as they could in pubs. And he's the opposite.'

Rita Moloney says that the petty jealousy and feelings of resentment against her husband are still there and it is something they have both learned to live with.

'We're a nation of knockers,' she says. 'I think there are certainly people who don't like Paddy's success, whether it be the fact that he's written about all the time, or the fact that they think we've made a lot of money, which we haven't. In other words he's not a great musician because he's not struggling. But they seem to forget all the years he did struggle.'

In October Paddy Moloney could no longer contain The Chieftains' internal problems after Seán Keane publicly announced he was leaving for 'personal and family' reasons. In a story carrying the banner headline 'Keane Quits The Chieftains', *Melody Maker* seriously questioned the band's future.

'Keane would appear to be another casualty in the pressure this unprecedented popularity has caused them,' wrote *Melody Maker*. 'The news comes as a further complication in what has become a difficult time for the band after their dramatic rise to international acclaim and stardom in the last couple of years following 14 years of gradual and low-key development.'

Keane promised to stay with The Chieftains and help them fulfil engagements until a replacement could be found. But things got even worse for Moloney when Seán Potts, Michael Tubridy and Kevin Conneff all announced just before Christmas they were planning to leave too.

Remembers Moloney: 'Martin Fay's the joker of the group and

he sent me a Christmas card with three people standing under a lamppost and he'd written "The New Chieftains." '

Hitting rock bottom Moloney turned to his family for solace and to provide him with the strength to carry on.

'I had so many bloody Christmases where I should have been miserable but thank God I have my wife and family so I can switch off like that and just go into my own world. In those days I could just do it and those were crucial times. I always said to myself, "Look, I can play my old tin whistle, I can play my pipes. I can put another band together in the morning if I have to. Thank God it never came to that." '

14

The Ace and Deuce of Pipering

The New Year saw a recharged Paddy Moloney come out fighting. The persuasive piper managed to calm the troubled waters, and agreed to give his troops more musical credit than they had ever received before and their new 1977 album, *Chieftains 7*, reflected this.

Their first CBS album went back to basics, delivering a set of effectively simple no-nonsense traditional tunes and for the first time since *Chieftains 1*, the group recorded at home at the new Dublin Sound Studios, which had full Dolby capabilities.

'I felt the time was right for each member of the band to contribute their own musical ideas,' explained Moloney. 'It wasn't that I was drying up or there was any shortage of ideas. I just felt that we had all come a long way and were experienced enough to each do something.'

Chieftains 7 is the group's personal musical scrap book. Paddy Moloney leads off with a rousing selection of reels and a hornpipe he calls *Away We Go Again*. Martin Fay's contribution *Hedigan's Fancy*, is a slip jig named after his favourite pub in his hometown of Cabra. Seán Potts' air and two reels comprise a set named *No. 6 The Coombe*, which was the home of his grandfather John Potts, and is dedicated to his uncle Tommy Potts.

Seán Keane arranged three of his favourite tunes for *Friel's Kitchen*, named after the Milltown Mowbay pub which was the scene of many a 'mystical' experience between the fiddler and legendary piper Willie Clancy. Michael Tubridy immortalizes his late aunt Mrs Crotty of Kilrush on *Oh! The Breeches Full Of Stitches*, on which he plays her concertina. And the flautist also introduces The Chieftains' first recorded version of *O'Sullivan's March*, which he used to play with the FCA Pipe Band as a boy in Kilrush. Moloney would later re-record *O'Sullivan's March* as the theme music for the 1995 film *Rob Roy* starring Liam Neeson. Moloney had Derek Bell arrange a piece called *The Fairies' Lamentation and Dance*, a tone poem spotlighting each of the Chieftains' musical personalities.

Reviewing *Chieftains 7*, when it was released in April, *Melody Maker's* Colin Irwin saw it as 'a deliberate move towards recapturing the atmosphere of the group before they became superstars.

'No longer with a big British label and no longer with high-powered management they've reverted to the old style of cover and of identifying by numbers. And almost in defiance of the stories about disenchantment in the band due to Paddy Moloney's domination, Seán Potts, Martin Fay, Seán Keane, Michael Tubridy and Derek Bell have all been credited with individual arrangements of certain tracks; in fact never can Moloney have remained so much in the background on a Chieftain record,' wrote Irwin.

Even though the other members of the band had contributed musical ideas to the album, Moloney was still musical director and producer and was certainly in command in every other area; managing the group, booking gigs and dealing with the new record company Columbia.

'The change in record companies naturally caused a bit of unrest,' admits Moloney. 'But the only real difficult part was all the rumours that were going around. Even in England where the rumours started we were having great gigs. We may have been facing major problems but they were internal ones and the band was still going up and up.'

On March 15th, The Chieftains played the first of what would become their traditional St Patrick's Day concerts in New York. Although the show was two days prior to St Patrick's Day, they sold out every one of the Avery Fisher Hall's 2,742 seats. The highlight of the set, that lasted two and half hours, was the finale, *Drowsy Maggie*, when each Chieftain took the spotlight for a solo.

'They had the crowd dancing in the aisles,' wrote *Billboard*. 'Something that doesn't ordinarily happen in staid Avery Fisher hall.'

On his return to Ireland Moloney was commissioned by the director of the Irish National Ballet Company, Joan Denise Moriaty, to supply the music for a ballet version of *The Playboy of the Western World*. As part of the long-term project The Chieftains agreed to perform the score live for a major international tour of the ballet the following year.

'It was a massive undertaking,' says Moloney. 'I had to find out about ballet in order to prepare for it.'

For the early rehearsals the dancers were choreographed from a two-and-a-quarter-hour tape culled from Chieftain records. But in three full dress rehearsals The Chieftains performed live with the ballet dancers to synchronize the timing which proved difficult.

The Playboy of the Western World was premiered at the Dublin Theatre Festival in the autumn for a week-long sold-out run and recorded for future broadcast by RTE. Two years later The Chieftains and the National Ballet Company would tour *Playboy* in Belfast, London and France, culminating in a two-week run off-Broadway in New York.

In the summer of 1978 Paddy Moloney achieved his long held dream to move out of Dublin, buying a house and land in the tiny village of Annamoe, tucked away in the breathtakingly scenic Wicklow Mountains. Moloney bought the house from an Irish-American couple called Jack and Peg Davitt, whom he had met two years earlier at a party in Washington. Davitt had mentioned that he had a cottage in Annamoe and invited Moloney to look it over. The minute he saw the three-bedroom house he fell in love with it.

Although they retained the Milltown home as a Dublin base, Paddy and Rita and their three children now planned to spend most of their time in Annamoe.

Lying off the main road, the house was just ten years old and set in its own grounds adjoining a property owned by the English film director John Boorman, who was delighted with his new neighbour.

'I knew Paddy for years through Garech,' says Boorman. 'When we became neighbours we started seeing quite a lot of each other. He's come to my house and he'd always have his whistle in his pocket and play something after dinner.'

A do-it-yourself fanatic, Moloney tried to create a more homely aged look for his modern home by putting in wooden beams and rough plastering the walls and installing panels of the local Douglas fir timber as flooring throughout the house.

'This is literally the house that Jack built,' he boasts. 'I added the music room myself and put down the foundations.'

The music room is Moloney's favourite where he composes and has his grand piano facing an enormous picture window.

'You can see seven mountain ranges from here and the view

changes colour every day,' he says. 'In many ways it's a ridiculous place to put a house, but it's beautiful. We got snowed in one Christmas and it was the best time of my life.'

The whole house is furnished in old pine and one of Moloney's favourite pieces is an 18th century settle bed where he keeps his extensive, and treasured, collection of musical instruments including his old ukulele, his concertinas, a mandolin and a Chinese yangching.

In the same way that he visualizes music Moloney saw exactly how he wanted the ambiance of his new house right down to the last detail. One of his pet projects was to create an art gallery on a drop level on the ground floor which would be centred around a tall stone from a nearby quarry.

'I just thought it would be great to have a large stone piece in the middle of the whole place to give a feeling of earthly power,' explained Moloney. 'One night I dreamed of the particular stone I wanted and when I woke up I drew it out on a piece of paper.'

The following day Moloney went to see his father-in-law, Faley O'Reilly, the last of the quarry men who had already cut the stone to build an identical fireplace to the one he remembered as a boy in his grandmother's house. Moloney then gave him the drawing of what he would later call 'my phallic symbol'.

'We were walking through the quarry and he said, "Jesus Christ, Moloney, what are you up to now?" ' remembers Paddy. 'Suddenly I saw this thing and I couldn't believe it. It was almost covered over with grass but I knew immediately it was my stone. It must have been intended as a gatepost at some time or other. That was another one of the premonitions and dreams that I have continually.'

Moloney arranged to have the huge granite stone hauled back to his house and sunk five foot into the foundations, where it now rises a full twelve foot by the wine cellar.

The peace and tranquillity of Annamoe stand in stark contrast to the frenetic jet setting pace he faces from morning to night when he's out on the road.

His work schedule was crippling during the months he schemed and battled to keep The Chieftains on course. The piper spent much of his time in London meeting music executives and making new contacts to further the group's career.

Explaining his business philosophy to *The Irish Times*, Moloney said: 'The music business is a machine that has to be used properly if you want to survive.'

During one of these trips he was introduced to a young Englishman called Pete Smith, who was co-managing the folk rock star Al Stewart who had a huge hit in America with *Year of the Cat*. Duly impressed by Smith, Moloney asked him to take over The Chieftains' English management.

'I had a short period of time managing The Chieftains while they were at CBS Records,' says Smith. 'But in the end Paddy just wanted to have one management focus and having one person in America and another in the UK didn't suit him so we parted company albeit very amicably.'

On the San Francisco leg of The Chieftains' 1978 tour two 17-year-old female Chieftains fans started chatting to the ever flirty Derek Bell at a Harp convention party after the show. The following night the girls, one of them named Steffie, returned and sought out the band again during the interval. Steffie, who was a harpist, immediately hit it off with Derek as they discussed the instrument.

'Paddy and I chatted to them and we gave them free tickets for another show at the Great American Music Hall,' remembers Derek. 'They were quite charming.'

A few months later, when he was next in San Francisco, Derek was asked to give a lecture to the American Harp Society. Arriving at the venue he was met by Steffie, who happened to be working as a volunteer for the society.

'And by some accident of fate she was the one appointed to look after me,' explained Derek. 'Steffie had to make sure I didn't get lost in the grounds and fail to turn up for the crucial lecture. From then on we were inseparable.'

By the end of his stay Derek had fallen head over heels in love with Steffie and went to meet her mother to show his intentions were honourable. When Derek flew back to Ireland Steffie promised to join him in Dublin later in the year to see if she could live in the city.

That autumn The Chieftains went into Olympic Studios in Barnes, outside London, to record their new studio album. Eric Clapton happened to be recording there too and he and Moloney renewed their friendship.

The cover of *Chieftains 8* is a striking photograph of the Giant's Causeway, one of the seven wonders of the world. Inside The

Chieftains were in fine form although this would be the swan song for both Seán Potts and Michael Tubridy.

The new record demonstrated that however much pressure Moloney might be under he always retained his keen sense of humour. For example he dedicated the song *If I had Maggie in the Wood* to Princess Margaret in an early morning live radio interview, when he was asked for his comments about Princess Margaret allegedly calling the Irish 'pigs'. Carefully reserving his judgment, Moloney told the reporter that he would make his own musical statement at the next concert. 'After all,' he thought at the time, 'Maggie likes a drop like the rest of us.'

A few days later Moloney unveiled his reply to the English princess in an almost rock 'n' roll song sung by Kevin Conneff. The piper's cheeky lyrics, to what would become a Chieftain show stopper, were:

> 'If I had Maggie in the wood
> I'd do her all the good I could
> If I had Maggie in the wood
> I'd keep her there till morning.'

By *Chieftains 8* the group was developing a set recording routine. They would usually go into the studio in the autumn between tours with new material, which would have been previously selected and arranged by Moloney. Once in the studio the tracks were recorded with the minimum of rehearsal to retain a fresh and spontaneous feeling.

'There was no fiddling around with trying things out or whatever,' explains Kevin Conneff. 'We try to keep it that way because I think it shows in the recordings afterwards that it's not rehearsed to death, which it can be. You can spend two weeks rehearsing three tunes or whatever and go in and play them and they sound worn out.'

It is very rare for The Chieftains to do more than three takes on any track and no album has ever taken longer than a week to record.

'You have to take the warts as well,' says Seán Keane. 'Because if there's a fault by someone on one part of the track and then something good on another, if you play it again someone else will probably do something wrong. So If you don't get it down the first three takes, it's going to get worse or totally staid.'

Producer Paddy Moloney was now highly proficient at studio mixing, which was done by hand in those days before computers became an essential part of studio equipment.

'You might have ten fingers moving at the same time,' explained Moloney. 'You had to drive the machines and I had to push things up if I wanted more of one instrument or pull things down if I wanted less. You had to do everything yourself.'

Moloney's set piece for *Chieftains 8* is a breathtakingly beautiful tone poem in homage to the stirring power of the sea. *Sea Images* is an epic piece and closer to classical music than traditional. In his six-minute composition Moloney's uilleann pipes swirl up into waves of sound and seem to crash down on the surf of Conneff's bodhrán.

Explained Moloney: 'I was trying to paint a picture of the sea and about how friendly and cruel it can be. And in the middle of it I've got a disaster. I have all these disturbing sounds which are all done with Chieftain instruments.'

In an excellent review of *Chieftains 8*, *Melody Maker* complimented the group for not resting on their laurels and continuing to experiment and expand.

'It's a recurring problem for someone with instrumental virtuosity in a specialized style to maintain the freshness, and therefore audience interest, particularly when they've been going as long as The Chieftains,' said the review.

Melody Maker applauded The Chieftains for stealthily keeping to the traditional course and not being tempted to resort to 'gimmickry' and 'desperate experimentation' to appeal to fans. The reviewer concluded that Moloney was painstakingly treading a balance between 'academic fulfilment and enterprise'.

At the beginning of December as The Chieftains toured the UK to promote *Chieftains 8*, Paddy Moloney told journalists that the new CBS contract has given the band 'a new zeal', Moloney told journalist Colin Irwin that the group had never been stronger.

Wrote Irwin: 'Moloney himself is sometime so ebullient it's sometimes difficult to tell the natural from the professional.'

Chronicling The Chieftains' recent 'traumatic times' Irwin noted that even their once unquestioned position as Ireland's premier folk band was now being 'severely challenged' by up-and-coming outfits like The Bothy Band, Clannad and DeDanaan, which featured Dolores Keane.

Noted Irwin: 'But Paddy Moloney, a man of staggering resourcefulness who could surely do treble somersaults on a high wire whilst playing *Flight of the Bumblebee* on the uilleann pipes and sell tickets on the door, has rallied his troops.

'It's become fashionable to knock The Chieftains; indeed it's the inevitable reward of anybody who breaks through from a specialist audience to grand-scale acceptance. Where recently they've looked to be playing from memory, at the Albert Hall last Thursday they showed the passion and relish for the music that's so crucial to the strength of Irish music, but is so difficult to maintain if you're constantly playing in formal fashion on world tours.'

* * *

1979 was a watershed year for The Chieftains which finally set in place the personnel that would bring a lasting stability to the band. Kevin Conneff had changed his mind about leaving and was back as a full member of the band, but Michael Tubridy announced he was leaving to go back to his job. The quiet flute player had started suffering from stage fright and longed to return to his old life.

'I'm sure it's worse now than it was then,' says Tubridy. 'But even in those days it was pressure all the time. When you spend so little time playing music it's very important that you do it well on the stage. For me there was so much build up to performing that I began to get worried and concerned about going out and performing. From my point of view that was the biggest pressure.'

Tubridy also hated all the travelling and living out of suitcases that being a Chieftain demanded.

'Sometimes you'd hardly have time to open your suitcase on a lot of these journey,' he explained. 'It's inevitable if people want to see you play but it's just a totally different way of life.'

With an impending major North American tour in March, followed by a two-week run of *Playboy of the Western World* with the Irish Ballet Company, Moloney persuaded Tubridy to fly to New York just for the ballet.

'I agreed because whereas they could get somebody to fit into the group for concerts it would have been very awkward to do this with the ballet,' he said.

Tubridy appeared with The Chieftains when they toured the ballet for critically-acclaimed week-long runs in Dublin, Belfast, Sadler's Wells in London and Paris. He then returned to his engineering job in Dublin while the rest of the band flew over the Atlantic for the tour which would wind up in New York with *Playboy.*

This North American tour would prove to be a nightmare of uncertainty for Moloney, who was now wearing the hats of leader, manager, tour promoter and agent. As if he didn't face enough problems already, some of the worst storms on record threatened the Canadian leg of the tour. On a flight to St Johns, The Chieftains' jet was forced down in Nova Scotia by 110-mph gale force winds and Seán Potts, who hated flying at the best of times, panicked.

'I thought we were gone,' says Potts. 'The plane was turning upside down and I was saying my prayers.'

The pilot managed to make an emergency landing at the airfield in the small town of Mungton and the shaken passengers were told to remain in the plane until the storm had subsided and they could take off again.

'We were told there was no way we could get off this flight,' says Martin Fay. 'Seán says, "watch me." And he got up and left us in the plane.'

Potts somehow managed to find a taxi to take him the 80 miles to Halifax, where he could reunite with the band, and settled down happily in the back seat with a book and fell asleep. Suddenly he was awoken as the taxi started lurching across the road.

'The winds were so bad that the cab was blowing from one side of the road to the other,' says Potts. 'I thought, "Now I'll be killed on the ground." '

When the storm died down the taxi driver drove a still shaken Potts to the nearest airport where he summoned up the courage to catch the next flight and meet up with the rest of the group in St Johns.

'I missed the sound check but I did the gig,' said Potts. 'That frightened the life out of me and was when I really decided to leave The Chieftains.'

Reunited with Tubridy in New York, The Chieftains found themselves the toast of the town. Taking some time off to relax and sightsee, Moloney was joined by Rita, his son Aonghus and daughter Aedín on their first trip to New York.

On their return to Dublin, Seán Potts told Moloney he was finally quitting The Chieftains and this time he was adamant.

'It was a hard decision,' says Potts today. 'After three years I was beginning to get mentally tired of the travel. I'd only be back a week or so and I'd be off again packing my bags. That did not suit me at all.'

Potts, who was still on a leave of absence from the post office, had the luxury of knowing he could return to his old job without losing any seniority or his pension.

'I think it would have been a horse of a different colour if I'd had no job to come back to,' explained Potts, who would retire from the post office six years later to devote his life to traditional music.

Moloney was sympathetic to his old friend's decision and there was no animosity between the two musicians who would still visit each other's houses to play sessions and spend New Year's Eve together with their families.

'I knew Seán hated the travelling and that it wasn't agreeing with him because he was so nervous,' says Moloney. 'There were occasions when I said to myself, "My God, Seán shouldn't be travelling." '

The departures of Chieftain 'stalwarts' Tubridy and Potts were announced publicly in *Melody Maker* in May. According to the music paper Potts was to be replaced by tin whistle player Michael O'Halún, for the group's upcoming British tour, and Irishman Maurice Cassidy was named as the group's new manager.

'There have been various rumours of unsettlement within the ranks,' wrote Colin Irwin. 'But the group has withstood the turbulence and survived relatively unscathed until now.'

Appointing Cassidy, who would later help to produce the enormously successful *Riverdance*, took a huge burden off Moloney's shoulders.

'It was hell when I was managing the group,' admitted Moloney at the time. 'There was a tremendous strain in the first six months of 1979 with the touring and looking for new members – they don't grow on trees.'

Maurice Cassidy says he joined The Chieftains during a particularly turbulent time in the group's history.

'I think at that time Paddy wondered whether the band would survive,' says Cassidy. 'Paddy really has been the cornerstone in keeping the band together over the years and supplying creative management.'

Cassidy set about restarting The Chieftains in America and introduced them to the Columbia Artists' booking agency who would handle US tour for the next few years.

That summer Moloney was looking long and hard for a flute player to replace Michael Tubridy when he remembered his old musical partner Matt Molloy, who he had duetted with at the Old Sheiling so many years before. As a former member of The Bothy Band and Planxty, Moloney was well aware that Molloy's reputation as an unparalleled traditional flutist would enhance the band's credibility. The shrewd piper was looking to build a Chieftains mark II to take the band forward into the next century.

'Of course I miss Mick, and of course I miss Seán,' Moloney told an English journalist at the time. 'But I think a change can be very healthy, and we were lucky to get Matt who has shaped us differently.

'Yet I don't think we've really changed our policy or our attitude since we started. We're never going to be millionaires and we still have a priority of music first and earning a living out of it second.'

15

Boil The Breakfast Early

Matt Molloy was born on January 12th in the year of the Big Snow of 1947 – in Ballaghaderreen, Co. Roscommon, deep in the rugged countryside of the west of Ireland. The Molloy family had produced gifted traditional players for generations and Matt's grandfather John Molloy, father Jim Molloy and Uncle Matt, whom he was named after, were all flute players.

Jim Molloy was brought up on a small farm outside Ballymote, Co. Sligo, before moving to America to seek employment in the late 1920s. In Pittsburgh, Jim met and married Kathleen Cahill from Shraigh, Co. Mayo but in the mid-1930s the couple returned to Ireland and settled down near Ballaghaderreen, Co. Roscommon.

The youngest of three boys, Matt got his first taste of the distinctive regional style of traditional music from his father. The area was renowned for its fiddle players like Michael Coleman, James Morrison and Paddy Killoran who had all gone to America at the turn of the century. These musicians recorded traditional music on the newly invented 78's in the 1920s which found its way back to their home town and was an influence on Matt, and other musicians of his age group.

'They have their own particular style of playing here,' explained Matt. 'To put it simply, the music has its own accent.'

Matt attended the local Christian Brothers' School in Ballaghaderreen where he joined the marching band. When he was 12 his father began giving him flute lessons.

'My father saw me struggling and took pity on me,' remembers Matt. 'He started to teach me polkas and simple jigs and reels and let me play his flute which he had brought back from the States many years before.'

When he started showing promise on the flute, Jim Molloy and his neighbour Peadar Nooné, who was a fine fiddle player who loved the Irish language, would take Matt and his friends to the newly established fleadhanna cheoil, then springing up all over Ireland. It was at these music festivals that Matt started meeting other young musicians and listening to different musical styles.

'I lived in an isolated pocket of traditional music,' explains Matt. 'It was just a few families that played the music and knew one another but we never saw the big picture.'

Going to the festivals with his father in the early 1960s, Matt gained confidence musically and began entering and winning competition after competition. Matt finally retired unbeaten after winning Irish music's two biggest competitions in the same year; the Senior All Ireland Fleadh Ceoil and An Oireachtas.

In 1964 at the age of 17 Matt moved to Dublin to live with his elder brother Johnny, who was working for Aer Lingus. Matt had successfully applied for a coveted place on the airline's new training scheme for aircraft mechanics and technicians. And he was sent to Dublin's Bolton Street School of Technology to begin a four-year full-time course in aeronautical engineering.

Among the musicians Molloy played with in those days was Paddy Moloney, who was already actively involved in The Chieftains, the fiddler Tommy Peoples and the young piper Liam Flynn from Kill, Co. Kildare, who had also been taught by Leo Rowsome. The four of them were regulars at the Old Sheiling in Raheny, which was owned by Irish millionaire Bill Fuller and featured ballad sessions organized by singer Dolly MacMahon who also acted as master of ceremonies. Both Fuller and MacMahon were lovers of traditional music and tried to feature it as much as possible.

'The audiences were just beginning to educate themselves in traditional music,' says Dolly. 'Although Matt and Liam Flynn were excellent musicians they had not been fully discovered. So when I was at the Old Sheiling I invited them to play one or two nights a week and they were extremely popular. Suddenly people who hadn't been aware of traditional music realized that there was something marvellous happening.'

It was at the Old Sheiling that Molloy struck up a friendship with Paddy Moloney during the long periods of inactivity between their ten minute traditional spots.

'We used to have a couple of pints and share a few tunes,' says Molloy. 'Because, let's face it, we played for 20 minutes out of the full night and you could do that in your sleep. And neither did you really have to be sober to do it.'

In those days Matt Molloy was a real fashion plate and a favourite with the ladies.

'Matt was very different in those days,' says Dolly MacMahon. 'He was always immaculately dressed in a suit, white shirt and a fancy tie and he had jet black hair. He was terribly handsome but he was also very shy. A lot of women were mad about him.'

Dolly, who is married to Radio Éireann's Ciarán Mac Mathúna, had her own weekly traditional radio show and often played Matt Molloy's music. 'I loved his music and I used to play it so often that I'd get calls asking if Matt Molloy was the only flute player in Ireland. I would say, "Yes, there are others, but Matt's the best." '

One day Molloy received a call from the leader of the Siamsa Ceili Band John Joe Gardiner who came from Sligo and had played with Matt's grandfather, father and uncle. Gardiner, now an old man, had heard about the flute player's growing reputation and was determined to get a third generation of the Molloy family into his Dundalk-based band.

'We used to call him The Boss,' remembers Molloy. 'He was a big burly man and he had a great presence about him. He smoked a pipe and he was a real character. I had great fun with that band and we played all over the country.'

By the beginning of the 1970s Matt Molloy had passed his aeronautical exams and was working full-time for Aer Lingus as part of a crack team overhauling 747 jet engines. Music was still a sideline to him and he never even considered turning professional as he felt there was no money to be made as a traditional musician. It was while working for Aer Lingus that Matt met his future wife Geraldine at a company dance.

'We'd been eyeing each other up and then we finally met at a dance,' remembers Geraldine. 'We knew through mutual friends that we'd both be there and then we started courting.'

As traditional music took off in the early 1970s, Molloy began playing at the newly established folk clubs like Kevin Conneff's Tradition Club. Matt was at the centre of Dublin's now vibrant music scene and in 1973 he, along with fellow musicians Tommy Peoples, Donal Lunny, Paddy Keenan, Tony MacMahon and Tríona Ní Dhomhnaill, decided to go out and perform their own shows.

'We got this brain wave,' explained Matt. 'At this stage we were all fairly well known in the traditional music scene so we decided to go to different parts of the country and organize a concert on an occasional Friday night.'

Recruiting local traditional music enthusiasts, who would rent the hall and run the concerts, Molloy and his friends began staging shows the length and breadth of Ireland.

'They put our names up and we'd draw the crowds,' says Molloy. 'And we'd get our cut from the proceeds and drink that over the weekend. So basically it was just a wild weekend and you weren't coming home stony broke. So it was a nice handy little idea and we all had a good time doing it.'

In the beginning the Friday night shows just featured the musicians playing solo spots but soon they started refining their presentation by bringing everyone out to play together in a rousing finale. This proved so popular with audiences that Matt and the other musicians decided to form themselves into a group they called The Bothy Band and go professional.

Now that Matt Molloy and Geraldine were married, with a year-old son Peter, it was a difficult decision for him to lay his career on the line for the uncertainties of playing traditional music for a living.

'A job with Aer Lingus was regarded as a secure pensionable job and one to mind,' says Molloy. 'You would not become a millionaire but you were nicely secure. But I just felt there was more that I could do and I wanted to give it a shot.'

Aer Lingus granted Matt a six months' leave of absence in 1974 so he could get his feet wet and see if he could make living out of music. The Bothy Band was formed in 1975 featuring Matt Molloy on flute, Paddy Keenan on uilleann pipes, Donal Lunny on vocals, bouzouki and guitar, Tríona Ní Dhomhnaill on vocals, clarinet, harmonium and bodhrán and Micheál Ó Dhomhnaill on vocal, guitar, organ and harmonium.

Over the next four and a half years The Bothy Band established themselves as one of the most exciting traditional groups on the scene. They made four successful albums and were regulars on the European club and festival circuit and had one successful American tour. Their fast-paced music was powered by Donal Lunny's hard-driving bouzouki and guitar rhythms. It was with The Bothy Band that Molloy firmly established himself as Ireland's most exciting young flute player as he took his instrument soaring to new heights, and in 1976 he recorded his first solo album called *Matt Molloy*.

In the late 1970s Molloy and the rest of The Bothy Band found themselves thrown far deeper into the excesses of the rock 'n' roll lifestyle than The Chieftains ever were.

'It was wild times,' says Molloy. 'For the first few years it was all new and exciting fun being with a band on the road. When you're fairly young you're fit and well able to take on the rigours of staying up all night, travelling all day and then playing the next night and staying up all night again.'

The Bothy Band spent weeks on the road touring Britain and Europe in a beat-up old Commer van and for a while it was like one big party.

'We'd be the first into the bar after a show and the last out of it,' says Matt. 'We'd be playing sessions all the time. And you can do that for quite a long time and not worry too much about when you eat or sleep.'

In mid-1977 the excesses of the road caught up with Molloy when he was diagnosed with tuberculosis and was forced to rethink his life. Seriously ill without any health insurance he felt irresponsible, feeling that he had let his family down.

'I was coming in off the fast lane and found myself in a TB ward,' remembers Molloy. 'I suppose a lot of contracting TB came through being run down by the drinking and late nights.'

Fortunately, Molloy's highly sensitive flute playing technique had given him an early warning that there was something wrong after he detected problems with his breathing and his phrasing. When he visited a doctor he was accused of being a hypochondriac but he insisted there was something wrong with his lungs and eventually the TB showed up on an X-ray.

It took two years for Molloy to make a complete recovery and get off medication and he was bedridden in the TB sanitorium for two months.

'I had lots of time to think,' he remembers. 'I just decided things would have to change one way or the other and something had to be done.'

On his release from hospital Molloy got back on track with The Bothy Band and held a series of meetings to decide the future policy of the band. They decided to continue on a more organized business footing but the improvements in the band were short-lived.

'We were so untogether,' admits Molloy. 'There was a joke among our friends that every concert would be our last. It was very explosive but it did tend to put an edge on the music. 'We'd make decisions and then the thing would fall apart on us. We decided it was time to take a break.'

In the summer of 1978 The Bothy Band decided to take six months to rethink its future but reunited early the following year to tour England and Ireland. After a highly successful tour, musically and financially, the band finally broke up and Molloy went back to playing solo around the clubs.

'We disproved everybody and we did stay together for four and a half years which was far longer than anyone had anticipated.'

In April 1979 Donal Lunny invited Molloy to join the second incarnation of the traditional band Planxty to record an album called *After the Break* followed by a tour. Molloy agreed but after completing the tour he went back to his solo career.

Then out of the blue Paddy Moloney called Molloy to invite him to guest on the upcoming Chieftains tour of Ireland in August.

'Nobody had to twist my arm to play with those people,' jokes Molloy. 'I'd played with Paddy for years and I also knew Seán Keane quite well and I had a great respect for their music. They're just top traditional players and there it is.'

* * *

Matt Molloy's first appearance with The Chieftains was at an open air concert at the 1979 Edinburgh Festival when they opened for music legend Van Morrison. The band then went on to complete an 11-date Irish tour. When the tour finished, Matt Molloy went into Dublin's Windmill Lane Studios to sit in on the sessions for *Boil The Breakfast Early* or *Chieftains 9*. Molloy still only considered his stint with the band temporary and had arranged a 20-date English club tour with piper friend Liam Flynn in October.

'And then I got this word that The Chieftains were going to the States and I was part of it,' remembers Molloy. 'And I remember ringing up Paddy and saying, "What is this? I didn't know I was part of it."

'Paddy said, "Didn't I tell you about joining the band?"

'I said, "No, Paddy, I think I'd remember something like that." '
And so Liam graciously agreed to find another musician for his
tour, and Matt became a fully-fledged Chieftain.

16

By Papal Request

On the morning of Saturday September 29th, 1979 Derek Bell woke up a bundle of nerves. Not only would he be making history by playing for Pope John Paul II, on his first official visit to Ireland, he also had to meet his girlfriend Steffie, who was due to arrive that morning from San Francisco. The lovestruck harpist had already warned Steffie, whom he calls 'The Snow Leopard', that they would have to dash straight to Phoenix Park from Dublin Airport in order to make the performance.

'When she came out of customs she was in a bad state,' remembers Bell. 'Steffie had had a terrible row with the immigration man trying to get in. She's half-American and half-German so I don't know if that rattled the immigration man but he was extremely rude to her. If she hadn't been able to pull out a wallet full of money to show she could support herself she never would have got in and I would have been left there waiting.'

Leaving the airport, Derek and Steffie headed straight out to Phoenix Park to join the rest of The Chieftains and their families. Although it was still early the roads were already paralyzed with traffic as the whole of Dublin converged on the 15 acres to witness history being made with the first reigning Pope ever to set foot on Irish soil.

As performers The Chieftains parked their cars close to the stage, displaying their special stickers. Everyone had brought a picnic lunch as once in Phoenix Park there would be no way to leave until after the Mass.

'I couldn't believe all those people,' remembers Seán Keane. 'It was a very emotional occasion.'

As Paddy Moloney led The Chieftains past the colourful assembly of bishops and cardinals to the stage he looked out over an estimated 1.3 million people, the largest audience in history. To add to the excitement The Chieftains knew they would be seen by an additional tens of millions of television viewers all over the world.

'It was like having a sea of people in front of you,' remembers Moloney.

At first Moloney was concerned about whether their public address system could cope and the audience could even hear them, as there was a disturbing delay between the end of each number and the ensuing applause.

'They heard every note,' says Moloney. 'It was a very moving to play to such a huge audience. We played a 20-minute set and then the Pope's helicopter came flying in low and there were roars from the crowd. As he landed and came out of the helicopter we played *Carolan's Welcome* from *Chieftains 9, Boil the Breakfast Early* as his greeting.'

During the Papal Mass The Chieftains were sitting right beside the altar ready to play their part in the Offertory. Kevin Conneff struck up his bodhrán followed by Moloney's pipes and the other instruments as the ceremonial gifts were brought up to the Pope on the altar.

'I had a feeling of great happiness,' sighs Moloney as he relives the scene. 'During the mass we played for ten minutes and they reckon a thousand million people saw it all over the planet. It was a beautiful day and we were really privileged. There was excitement. No fuss. Just happiness.'

With his strict Catholic upbringing, Moloney felt the deep spiritual significance of playing in front of God's representative on earth.

'It reminded me of the parable of the loaves and fishes,' he explains. 'You know there was great feeling in Phoenix Park that day. It was a magic feeling, a happy feeling. The album of the mass that was released afterwards sold platinum in Ireland.'

Making one of his first appearances with The Chieftains, Matt Molloy remembers the Pope's visit as a landmark in the group's career.

'A million and a quarter people or whatever,' sighs Molloy. 'Just sitting up there and there are people as far as the eye can see. And then when they started singing. I mean the hairs just literally stood up on the back of your neck. It was a thrilling moment. A very emotional thing. And as cynical as one might be, and I can be, you were in awe of the occasion.'

The Chieftain who remained unmoved by playing in front of the Pope was Martin Fay who kept his customary cool. 'To me it was another show and we weren't going to let ourselves down.'

But ironically when The Chieftains actually met the Pope face to face in the Vatican six months later, Martin Fay was paralyzed with nerves. The private audience with the Pope came about when The Chieftains were in Turin and they were invited to play for him. It was in the middle of winter and as Italy was snowbound all flights had been suspended so The Chieftains were forced to take the night sleeper train from Turin to Rome. When they arrived at the Vatican The Chieftains were escorted into a large auditorium full of people and were asked to play before the Pope's arrival.

Then the Pope came into the hall and there was complete silence as he took his seat just a few feet away from The Chieftains on stage. They struck up their instruments once more and launched into a memorable set of traditional music. They played again several times during the audience. Afterwards, Pope John Paul II personally greeted and posed for photographs with each member of the band and said he loved their performance.

'I could feel this incredible charisma coming from this man,' remembers Moloney. 'He spoke to us all individually and held onto my hand all the time he was with us. He told me, "Ah, The Chieftains. I have all your albums and I love your music from Ireland."'

The pontiff told Derek Bell that he was certain that St Patrick had come to Ireland to work as a missionary because he loved the country's music.

'I told him he was doing a great job,' jokes Bell. 'He came up and shook hands with each of us and we kissed the ring and he went onto the next fellow. It wasn't just kiss the leader and bugger off as sometimes happened. He actually came around to each person. That I did like.'

However, when the Pope greeted Martin Fay, the wise-cracking fiddler found himself totally lost for words.

'I was probably the only one in the group who was absolutely tongue-tied when the pontiff approached me,' admits Martin. 'I just didn't know what to say. It's this charisma thing again. Like if I met Prince Charles tomorrow I'd say, "Hello, Prince Charles will you have a pint?" I wouldn't be shaking or anything like that. But when I met the Pope I was.'

*   *   *

At the end of October The Chieftains set off on a seven-week tour of America, ushering in the beginning of a new era for the group. Finally there was complete harmony in the band as newcomer Matt Molloy found his feet with The Chieftains.

'The first thing I discovered was that the band was pretty well organized thanks to Paddy,' remembers Molloy. 'But it was easy and very nice because Paddy did all the work. He did the worrying and we did the playing.'

Martin Fay says that the rest of the band are quite happy to sit back and let Moloney guide their career.

'Well Paddy formed the group so you'd have to say he was steering things,' explains Fay. 'At the beginning it was very demo-cratic kind of thing but now Paddy is the figurehead or spokesman. And he's welcome to it. It's not particularly that he's the only one capable of leading us, it's just that nobody else wants to do it. And Paddy's doing a great job. I'd never take that away from him.'

Arriving in New York they had two days off before the opening show at Carnegie Hall and for the first time Molloy realized just how aloof and private his new colleagues were.

'We were in a sweet old-fashioned hotel,' remembers Molloy. 'It had been a few years since I had been in New York and I had forgotten about the hustle and bustle that is Manhattan. During the two free days nobody rang me up to see whether I was alive or dead. I thought I'm going to have to figure this out.'

For two long days Molloy stayed in his hotel room alone reading newspapers, playing music and going out to a local diner for meals.

'I didn't drink or anything,' he says. 'I just played a few tunes and locked the door when it suited me. I was just curious to see which way this ball is bouncing.'

Molloy soon realized how the band's deliberate aloofness from each other on the road was one of their biggest strengths and the glue that has kept them together for so long. Seeing the warmth and humour of a Chieftains' show might give the false impression that the band members regularly socialize with each other but that isn't the way they do things.

'The golden rule is that we keep our own different spaces,' says Seán Keane. 'Give the other man his space. Invariably before a concert we end up in each other's dressing rooms. Maybe we won't see each other before going on stage. But if we do get together it would have been a *craic*. And that's it. If you consciously work on that, you don't even think about it any more. We go our own way.'

Keane says that any six people spending as much time on the road as The Chieftains are bound to get on each other's nerves and points out that there are few bands that have stayed together as long.

'We tend to measure ourselves with the Stones as far as longevity is concerned,' he explains. 'The life and music are totally different of course. Different worlds altogether. But I suppose we're unique as far as Irish bands go.'

Derek Bell says that the idea of the band staying apart from each other on different hotel floors dates back to the early days when life on the road was wilder for The Chieftains.

'People used to come home at four in the morning from this or that club,' says Derek. 'I didn't want the fellow next door banging his door and waking me up. It also makes for a certain amount of quietness if half of us go to sleep and the rest go out on the town and you get all those doors banging when they come back. So it's a very sensible decision and suits everyone.'

Even at meals The Chieftains mostly sit apart from each other in a hotel dining room.

'Coming down for breakfast in the morning, I wouldn't dream of sitting with one of the other guys,' admits Keane. 'Just pick your own table and that's it. Great.'

Kevin Conneff says that although he greatly respects all his band mates he probably wouldn't be close friends with any of them if he wasn't a Chieftain.

'Over the years I've obviously established a relationship with the other members of the band,' he says. 'But I could safely say that if I wanted to hitchhike around the world I wouldn't choose any of them as a companion.'

As The Chieftains' popularity increased, their touring schedule became more and more hectic with less time off between concerts.

'Tours are no longer sane,' says Derek Bell. 'Once you used to do a concert and there was a couple of days off before the next one. It was very easy going. Now you're shipped off every night in a plane like a herd of cattle. It's a different town every night. After three weeks of that you're fit for the nuthouse.'

The happiest Chieftain on the road is Martin Fay who unlike some of his band mates others never complains about the travelling.

'Fortunately I like travelling,' he says between puffs of a cigarette. 'If you didn't, this job wouldn't last a month. I don't like being away from home anymore than the other guys but a job's a job. I look on it that if I was a tradesman I'd be away for about two weeks from the boss.'

* * *

When *Boil The Breakfast Early* was released at the beginning of 1980 critics hailed it as a fresh departure for the group with Kevin Conneff and Matt Molloy being heavily featured. Moloney had reinvented the band, without compromising the music in any way, and the new record introduced his new streamlined musical vehicle ready for the 1980s.

The new Chieftains' record also introduced Windmill Lane Studio sound engineer Brian Masterson, who from now on would play a major part in all subsequent Chieftains' albums. Tall, genial and curly-haired, Masterson had first seen the Chieftains five years earlier playing on the same bill as the heavy metal Dublin rock band, Skid Row.

'I have to be honest and say that I went to see Skid Row,' admits Masterson in his office at Windmill Lane. 'And then these guys came on, they sort of sat around in a circle and I was absolutely entranced by their music.'

When the young recording engineer was initially asked to work on *Boil The Breakfast Early* he was filled with trepidation.

'I'd heard all these terrible stories about Paddy and how particular he was,' said Masterson. 'If he had a sound in his head, God help me if I wasn't able to translate it in the studio. But it went really well and we've had a great working relationship ever since.'

Masterson says that one of the biggest problems in recording The Chieftains is capturing the uilleann pipes as they can suddenly jump a note, or even an octave, without any warning. 'The pipes are just the most contrary instrument. Paddy and I have evolved a technique over the years where we pre-record drones as we're striving to get as close to perfection as we can.'

Among the many highlights of the album was *Carolan's Welcome* which Moloney had arranged especially for the Pope's visit to Phoenix Park.

'I'm not so sure that it was Carolan but it was the one I picked up in a book,' quipped the piper.

Boil The Breakfast Early came from an old tune that Moloney used to play with Leo Rowsome. The ninth Chieftains' album is also memorable for introducing Kevin Conneff's bell-clear tenor in a moving version of *When a Man's in Love*. Kevin's beautiful singing style would play an increasingly important part in the group. And there was even a guest appearance from Seán Keane's local Rathcoole Pipe Band Drum Corps

'The rejuvenation of The Chieftains has been an education to behold,' wrote *Melody Maker*'s Colin Irwin after a triumphant Chieftains' concert at the Albert Hall in February. 'Just a year ago they looked a skeleton of the band they used to be. And now they've come up with their freshest album for years.'

Clearly on a roll, Moloney retreated to his new home in the Wicklow Mountains in the early spring to write his first ever complete film score for *Tristan and Isolde*, based on a ninth-century Irish legend, filmed in Ireland and starring Richard Burton and Kate Mulgrew. Moloney composed 75 minutes of music for the film. 'Just walking around my garden gave me a great feel for the whole story. You let your imagination run wild and you get into a great mood to come up with music.

'You must remember I've hoarded so much music in my head during my life. The only way I can explain it is that it's like a deep well with a stone over the top, containing all the music that's been with me for years. I've got that music in me. I don't know where it comes from but it's there. When I get inspiration that stone's pulled away to release the music trapped inside.'

A world away from the solitude of the heather-strewn Wicklow Mountains, Moloney found himself in New York for the Chieftains' annual St Patrick's Day Concert and their first ever appearance on the top-rated ABC network *Good Morning America* show, seen by millions coast to coast. In his first national television interview Moloney introduced the band and then played some of the new record.

That night Marianne Faithfull, who had just released her comeback album *Broken English*, went to see The Chieftains with her guitarist and songwriting partner Barry Reynolds.

'It was a wonderful sort of magic,' remembers Marianne. 'We'd been on our own rock 'n' roll tour which was quite hard and I'll never forget going to see The Chieftains and being transported into another place far, far away from *Why D'You Do It*.'

The hectic North American tour saw The Chieftains playing in 15 cities in just 17 days with the final show at The Bottom Line described as 'breathtaking' by *Rolling Stone*.

In June 1980 *Rolling Stone* magazine profiled The Chieftains telling its young readership that 'in importance and fame The Chieftains are the Rolling Stones of their field'.

Moloney, now 42, was in fine form for the *Rolling Stone* interview jesting about opening for the Pope, saying, 'we didn't get a fair crack; it was his gig.' He also reiterated his dream of using Chieftain music to help demolish ethnic stereotypes in America.

Said the piper: 'One thing we're all very particular about is getting away from this false impression of what Ireland's all about. That's some of the passions that I set out on 20 years ago: to get away from shamrocks and heather and Mother Machree and all that sort of . . . shit.'

Appealing to the young American music fans, Moloney explained how The Chieftains had brought traditional music into modern times without compromising it.

'I think it's important that you play today's way today,' he explained. 'What we're doing doesn't interfere with the authentic way of playing music or what it's about; it's bringing it forward even more. It's been sort of lying flat and just carried on over the last hundred years. What we're doing along with other great performers and groups, is bringing it out and keeping it alive. It's living now.'

* * *

On the evening of July 22nd, 1980 Paddy Moloney and Rita were asleep in their bedroom in Annamoe when the piper had a terrible nightmare and woke up at one in the morning in a cold sweat.

'I had an awful dream,' remembers Moloney. 'Peter Sellers was standing at the end of my bed with a glass in his hand smiling. He looked just as he had done the first time I had met him. I woke up

Rita and said I was having this terrible dream about Peter and I didn't know why.'

Rita calmed Paddy down and made him a cup of tea and then they both went back to sleep. But the next morning when Moloney turned on the radio he was startled to hear on the eight o'clock news that Peter Sellers had suffered a massive heart attack and died.

'He died at 1:00 a.m. which is exactly the time I saw him in my dream,' says Moloney. 'It was rather weird and chilling.'

17

Cotton-Eyed Joe

In December 1980 Paul McCartney telephoned Paddy Moloney to ask him to lay down a track of uilleann pipes for a new song called *Rainclouds*, which would form the B side of his *Ebony and Ivory* collaboration with Stevie Wonder. Moloney found himself in a quandary as he and Rita were due to fly out to Bombay for the wedding of his old friend Garech Browne at the same time as the session. The romantic Guinness heir had fallen in love with a beautiful Indian princess called Purna Hashad Devi Jadeja of the State of Morvi and was planning an exotic, no-expense spared Hindu wedding. To celebrate, Moloney had composed a special tune on his tin whistle which he planned to play at the ceremony as a wedding present. Although he was loath to let Garech down, Moloney also realized the vital long-term career benefits of a second collaboration with McCartney.

'Rita and I both wanted to go to Garech's wedding, which I understand was incredible,' says Moloney. 'But at that stage of my career I thought that doing another track with McCartney would be very important.'

Early in the morning on December 8th as Moloney was leaving to catch the first plane to London he heard the tragic news that John Lennon had been gunned down by Mark Chapman outside the Dakota Building by New York's Central Park.

'As soon as I heard John Lennon had been shot I rang up the studio,' remembers Moloney. 'They said everything's on course so you might as well come over.'

When the piper arrived at Air Studios off Oxford Circus where in 1973 they had recorded *Chieftains No. 3* he found the Beatles' long-time friend and producer George Martin already there.

'We just sat around and talked about how sad and terrible John's death was, and then put down the 16 bars required for the middle of the song, with George in control,' said Moloney. 'Then Paul came in and he was in an awful state. He said that the press had been outside his house since 5:00 a.m. and that he'd been pestered so much at home that he just had to get away. He managed to lose the reporters and sneaked into the studios up the back stairs.

'We just sat around talking about John. I remember Linda came in at one point and she had been crying. It was very very emotional. By this time a lot of musicians and friends of Paul had arrived in the studio. Finally about two o'clock in the afternoon Paul said, "Look, Paddy, do you want to come out to the house and stay?" But I said, "No, I'll leave you to it." I knew he was very upset. Afterwards a lot of people said they thought it was unusual that Paul had gone into the studio after John's death. But I thought, "What else would he do?" '

Ultimately, Garech's fairy tale wedding was postponed until early the following year when Moloney's piece, aptly called *Garech's Wedding*, was played on tape. It also was included as a track on the next Chieftains' album *Chieftains 10*.

Casting out his musical net even further into the Celtic world, Moloney asked Derek Bell to research Manx harp music for the album. The brilliant harper came back with a wonderful medley that is one of the highlights of the album.

Moving even further afield, *Cotton-Eyed Joe* saw The Chieftains making their very first foray into American country music. Although The Chieftains had made numerous visits to America since turning professional, they had somehow never played Texas. But in February 1981 Chessley Millikan lined up six concerts in ten days all over the Lone Star State culminating in a show at Willie Nelson's Grand Oprey House in Austin.

'We had the most brilliant time of our lives,' laughs Moloney, who along with the rest of The Chieftains was named an honorary citizen of the city. 'It seemed like a different country and not like America at all.'

It was Chessley Millikin who first introduced The Chieftains to *Cotton-Eyed Joe*, the wild show-stopping stomper that the traditional group would make their very own.

'I played it for Paddy on a jukebox,' remembers Millikin, who later guided legendary Texas guitarist Stevie Ray Vaughan to stardom. 'I thought it would be a good tune for them.'

Moloney couldn't believe his ears when he first heard *Cotton-*

Eyed Joe as he instantly recognized the similarity to a traditional old Irish reel *The Mountain Top*, as well as to *Did You Wash Your Father's Shirt*, a little ditty that his grandmother used to sing when he was a child. 'It was the same tune and it was one that obviously went across from Ireland. After hearing it I put together a quick arrangement and got Derek on the piano. We played it at that very night's concert.'

The Austin crowd loved The Chieftains doing a hoe-down and from then on Texas became a staple part of their American touring route.

'The Chieftains are princes of Texas,' declares country singing star Nanci Griffith, who would later collaborate with the group. 'They're well loved here and my mother is a huge fan who has all their records.'

A week after returning from America The Chieftains went straight into Windmill Lane studios to record *Cotton-Eyed Joe* as the title track of the new record. On it Seán Keane's barn-stompin' fiddle seems to go into overdrive and the piece ends with Paddy Moloney's laughing into fade out.

By the early 1980s Moloney was more relaxed with The Chieftains than he'd been in a long time, and although tours were still hectic the musicians were having more fun on the road. After one memorable concert at the Olympia in Paris, Moloney and Fay went out on the town with *Irish Times* writer Joe Breen.

'Unfortunately for the band's elder statesmen everywhere they tried was shut,' remembered Breen. 'In desperation they decided to try a rather stylish-looking premises. Inside was an old woman with vacant eyes at a cash register, an Incredible Hulk look-alike covered in a raincoat and five beautiful women. Around the bar were imitation Greek sculpture while in the corner was an ornamental staircase that led to the second floor. Without saying a word the Irishmen knew where they were.

'After an expensive round of drinks they were sure of it and when the blonde barmaid lifted her skirt to reveal her thighs as casually as if she were brushing back her hair the Irishmen took a deep swallow, turned wide-eyed to each other and began talking in Irish.

'Three rounds later the novelty of being in a brothel was becoming a nightmare and the Irishmen walked out onto the wet Paris night before the sales pressure became too severe.'

Ironically, just a few months later in London, Paddy Moloney accidentally found himself mixed up with the legendary Happy Hooker, Xaviera Hollander. The piper was having lunch at the legendary Soho bar El Vino's with Garech Browne and Gloria Mac-Gowran, the wife of the late Irish actor Jack MacGowran. Over lunch they were joined by Garech's friend, the late *Evening Standard* columnist Stan Gebler-Davis, who was doing an interview with Xaviera Hollander to publicize her infamous autobiography, *The Happy Hooker*. Garech began chatting to fellow Irish aristocrat Lord Carbery who was on the next table, and who had just been made Chief Knight of the Knights of Saint Patrick. 'So Paddy proceeded to play him a jig called *The Knights of Saint Patrick* on the tin whistle which he happened to have with him at the time,' recalled Gebler-Davis a few years later in his *Evening Standard* column. 'The management absolutely declined permission for this recital. Miss Hollander – who it transpired was a frequent patron of the New York Metropolitan Opera when she was running a whorehouse in that city – asked for another tune, but was refused permission. No music in El Vino.'

The journal immediately penned an angry column giving a blow-by-blow account of the luncheon. As a result, the next day one Irish paper printed a huge photograph of Moloney alongside the banner headline 'Chieftain Thrown Out of El Vino's with The Happy Hooker.'

'Somebody rang me up at one in the morning on Holy Thursday saying, "Paddy, have you seen the front page?," ' he remembers. 'It was dreadful.'

Moloney explained to Rita how the story had been distorted and he was thinking of suing but his main concern was for his mother whom he knew regularly read the paper. 'It was funny later but I was furious at the time.'

The following day was Good Friday and Moloney could feel the snickers from on-lookers as he made his way to the Pro-Cathedral to play at a special mass with Seán Potts.

Said Moloney: 'The bishop, who was quite amused by the whole affair, was there and said, "Don't be minding what they say. I know all about *The Happy Hooker*." '

He was further vindicated when he was stopped after the service by a newspaper man who said encouragingly, 'Paddy, you were quite bloody right. They had no bloody business to chuck you out for playing an auld song.'

The chief of the Chieftains' good name was fully restored when Saturday's *Irish Independent* pictured him playing at the mass with Seán Potts.

That summer the Moloney family attended a rock festival organized by their close friends Desmond and Mariga Guinness in the palatial grounds of their Leixlip Castle. Playing on the bill were English rock groups Squeeze, UB40, The Police and a young unknown Dublin band called U2.

'We used to spend a lot of time hanging out with the Guinness's,' says Aedín Moloney, then just 13. 'We were invited to stay for the weekend and there was going to be a big party at the castle after the music finished. On the way back to the party I said to my dad, "I'm going to introduce you to Sting." And that was the first time they met.'

After dinner at the castle Paddy Moloney took out his tin whistle to start a session and was soon joined by Sting and his fellow Police members Stewart Copeland and Andy Summers.

'I remember we found an old harpsichord and Sting started playing Bach and Mozart and I joined in on the tin whistle.'

The Police were having such a good time that they decided to stay the night, totally forgetting about catching the red eye airplane to Holland they were booked on for a concert the following day. They were short of a room for Sting to sleep, so Aedín volunteered to give up her four-poster bed and move in with her parents.

'It was all very innocent,' she remembers. 'But a year or two later I wrote an article in a newspaper about it and they used the headline 'Sting Slept in my Bed.' It was a gas. I was kicked out of my bedroom so he could sleep there.'

* * *

That autumn Paddy Moloney was commissioned to write a joint score for The Chieftains and the RTE Symphony Orchestra for an Irish television mini-series called *The Year of the French*. Based on the novel by Thomas Flanagan, the story follows a wandering poet called Owen McCarthy on his travels through Ireland at a time in history when the French had volunteered some military assistance against 'our neighbours who had taken up residency in our country' as Paddy puts it. Composing for a full symphony orchestra was a 'terrifying' challenge for Moloney at the time.

'It had taken me a few years to build up the courage to write an orchestral work,' he explains. 'But I love a challenge.'

During one rehearsal one of the violinists took out her knitting in the middle of the performance after finishing her piece. 'This disheartened me,' Moloney recalls, 'but it made me even more determined to achieve a better performance.'

By the time he went into RTE's own studio to record the score, Moloney was far from happy. As producer, he had warned the television executives that a fully-equipped professional studio was required but his suggestion was vetoed as too expensive.

After the sessions, which a furious Moloney felt had not gone at all well, he met with the RTE executives and refused to release it as an album, demanding that it be re-recorded under the careful eye of Brian Masterson at Windmill Studios. RTE grudgingly gave in to Moloney's demands but he was not out of the woods yet.

The session to re-record *The Year of the French* was booked at Windmill Studios a few mornings later. Engineer Masterson had carefully miked up the Symphony Orchestra and The Chieftains for sound and was about to call the first take when a representative from the musicians' union burst into the studio. He took Moloney to one side and said that his members wouldn't play unless they were paid extra money.

'I couldn't believe what I was hearing,' said Moloney. 'I said, "Look, let me put it this way. You are costing me an extra two weeks out of my life that I can't afford. I don't get any extra money for this, why should you?" '

Moloney then threatened to call off the recording there and then but finally an agreement was reached and the recording went ahead with the RTE Symphony Orchestra giving an excellent performance which was later acclaimed by the critics when the album was released. *The Year of the French* also saw The Chieftains make their acting debut by playing cameo roles as 18th century musicians.

That same year, Derek Bell took centre stage with the release of his infamous solo album, *Derek Bell Plays With Himself*. The multi-instrumentalist, who has an eye for the ladies, says when the record company – or Garech, to be exact – first suggested the title, he thought it was a joke.

'And they took my laughter for consent,' Bell told *Hot Press* writer

Liam Fay many years later. 'None of the nuns would buy it, you know. My music had always been popular with nuns, but not that album. But, as I always say, they couldn't be very good nuns if they saw the joke in the title.'

Derek Bell Plays With Himself was even featured on BBC TV's *That's Life* as a comic misprint by presenter Esther Rantzen and the harpist says he has even been stopped by over-zealous customs officers who think the cover picture of Derek posing next to various types of phallic-looking oboes is pornography.

Says Bell: 'There was talk of re-titling it to *Derek Bell Plays Eight Instruments with Himself* but I never really liked that. The other has a better ring.'

* * *

In late 1981 The Chieftains boarded an Aer Lingus jet from New York to Dublin and found themselves travelling with the world-famous classical flautist James Galway. The burly Belfast musician had been an early fan of The Chieftains and of Moloney's whistle playing as reported by the *Irish Times* diarist Quidnunc, and he already knew Matt Molloy, but it was his first meeting with the rest of the band.

'It was a real head-on collision,' laughs Galway. 'By the time we got to Dublin we'd planned ten records and drank the bar entirely dry. It was murder. That's the only way you could describe it.

'I told Paddy, "Listen, you've got to stop making all these Chieftains 10, 11, 12, 13, 14 and 15, or else you're going to be cataloguing that book 1001 Irish melodies on disk. I said it's time to do something different." '

Galway, famed for his golden flute, credits Chieftains' music for helping him through a period of homesickness when he moved to Germany to play with the Berlin Philharmonic in the mid-1970s.

'It was like having a little bit of Ireland with me in Berlin when I wasn't feeling particularly German,' remembers Galway. 'They were like secret cult and I used to listen to a lot of their music over there.'

That Christmas James Galway accidentally found himself The Chieftains' special guest at their very first *A Traditional Irish Christmas Concert* at New York's Lincoln Center.

'We came over and did our Christmas show in the States with

the Wren Boys,' explains Moloney. 'I wanted to bring the old traditions of an Irish Christmas to New York with set dancing and
dressing up in straw costume as is the custom on St Stephen's Day.
It's all in the video of our *Bells of Dublin* Christmas album. And
this was a full 15 years before *Riverdance.*'

Moloney recruited some Co. Clare-style set dancers from Hartford, Connecticut, and arranged for them to come to New York to
perform with The Chieftains.

The Christmas concert started with a tape of the pealing bells of
Christchurch Cathedral welcoming The Chieftains onto the stage
which was covered in Christmas wreaths and holly.

'Everybody goes mad when they hear those bells ringing,' says
Moloney. 'You couldn't have a better welcome.'

The Christmas concert featured transplanted Irish actor Milo
O'Shea re-enacting a slapstick version of David vs. Goliath against a
background of Chieftains' music and a moving recital of Christmas
poetry by actress Geraldine Fitzgerald. Half an hour before the
curtain was due to go up for the sold-out show, Moloney got a call
from a frantic James Galway who was in New York and wanted
tickets.

'I said, "No problem. Why don't you bring the flute?",' recalls
Moloney. 'At the end of the first half I called him up on stage and
he joined in with us for a real jam.'

This unscheduled appearance would be Galway's very first in an
ongoing musical collaboration with The Chieftains and the musical
chemistry between them was spellbinding.

'People know that I'm not a traditional player,' explains Galway.
'But I can fit into that group. We give each other something and
we always have a great time on stage.'

The show climaxed in a grand finale with all the Hartford dancers
donning traditional strawboys and girls uniforms to join The Chieftains on stage for a medley of Christmas carols.

New York Post music critic Ed Naha was ecstatic about the show.

'If there's a more joyous sound on all the earth than the music
of The Chieftains, I'm not aware of it,' he wrote. 'Armed with tin
whistles, pipes, harps, drums, fiddles, flutes and goodwill, The
Chieftains pull melodic gems out of the treasure chest of traditional
Irish music with astonishing grace and ease.'

* * *

That Christmas was the first in many years where Paddy Moloney could relax and savour his tremendous accomplishments over the past two decades. With the gelling of the band's new line-up, Moloney considered that the Chieftains were playing tighter than ever. Now returning home from an exhausting winter tour of America and Europe, Moloney looked forward to a quiet Christmas spent with his family in Annamoe.

His son Pádraig was now five and Moloney had bought the little boy a piano as a Christmas present and arranged for lessons.

'I was the same age myself when I got my first tin whistle,' said the proud father. 'The little one is taking lessons.'

Christmas in the Moloney household is a special time and although Paddy admits to being a workaholic for the rest of the year, Rita forbids him to do any work over the festive period.

Explains Rita: 'After Paddy left Claddagh I said: "That's it. No more work over the two weeks of Christmas. He starts drifting back in after the New Year but it's about the only time that we have Paddy entirely to ourselves." '

As The Chieftains' fame and success increased, Paddy and Rita Moloney prided themselves on maintaining their working-class roots and staying down to earth. Although he freely rubs shoulders with presidents, rock stars and film actors, Paddy is happiest at home out of the spotlight doing odd jobs around the house. His daughter Aedín is convinced that their pet tabby cat Carmen and dog Bizet have somehow managed to exert their influence on Chieftains' music.

'It's all part of Paddy's homelife and who he is and where he comes from,' says Aedín. 'He's at his happiest when he's at home and working on his music. Christmas Day is about the only day that he actually doesn't do any work, but even then I wonder if he's thinking about what he has to do.'

Every Christmas Eve the Moloney family goes to Midnight Mass at the Old Church in Milltown where Paddy plays for the congregation on his pipes and tin whistle, joining in with the choir and organ.

After the service the family drives the 26 miles back to Annamoe where tradition dictates that before retiring to bed they leave biscuits, and a bottle of stout as gifts for Santa Claus, or 'Santy', as he is referred to in the Moloney household. And if anyone dare question the existence of Santa Claus Paddy will get very upset.

Next morning the Moloney family get up and go downstairs to gather around the brightly lit Christmas tree to discover what gifts 'Santy' has brought them. And without fail each year Paddy receives a specially gift-wrapped present from the midlands of Co. Laois where his grandmother came from.

'It's marked "Holy Water",' laughs Moloney. 'And it's the absolute Rolls Royce of poteen or moonshine as they call it in the States. It's a great drink. They've legalized a version of it that you can buy but it's not the real thing. The real poteen is untouchable. Magic.'

After present opening Paddy, Aedín, Aonghus and Pádraig drive into Dublin to visit relatives and exchange more gifts and by the time they return to Annamoe, Rita has Christmas dinner on the table ready to serve.

'From then on it's eat, sleep and be merry,' says Aedín. 'Ignore the saints and stretch out.'

On St Stephen's Day the whole Moloney family go for a long walk in the Wicklow Mountains where they talk over old times and plan for the future.

'It's the only time we're all together without anybody else,' says Aedín. 'It's wonderful and every year it's exactly the same and we are all together.'

Up to a couple of years ago Paddy and Rita Moloney hosted an annual New Year's party, which over the years grew into an institution. In the old days during the Christmas period the ever social Moloney issued impromptu invitations leading to hordes of strangers arriving at the party.

Tradition dictated that Seán Potts and his wife Bernie would arrive with a group of traditional musicians to entertain. Other regulars include Seán Keane and his wife Marie, Johnny Morris and Thelma Mansfield, and their neighbours John Boorman and family.

'We always used to go over and spend a few hours at Paddy's house on New Year's Eve,' says Boorman. 'All sorts of people turned up there and the music just went on continuously with musicians moving in and out. At a certain point it becomes transcendent, just extraordinary.'

At one memorable Moloney New Year's party Rita had stayed in the kitchen drinking tea with a couple of chauffeurs who had brought a couple of famous guests, as she was furious with Paddy for inviting so many people without telling her. When it came time to ring in the new year Moloney got out his accordion and shepherded everyone outside to the field at the back of the house so he could play the traditional Auld Lang Syne.

'We had a ball,' says Moloney. 'It was all dancing and jumping around after the 12 o'clock bells had gone.'

Back in the kitchen Rita was making small talk with the chauffeurs and opening bottles of champagne for the guests outside.

'Just before midnight this man suddenly arrived at the front door,' says Rita. 'I thought he was another chauffeur because he had a cap on and dark glasses. He came into the kitchen and I gave him a stool to sit on. I introduced myself and he said his name was Jack. I wished him a happy new year and poured him a cup of tea.'

As the strains of Paddy's Auld Lang Syne filtered into the kitchen Rita offered the chauffeurs a glass of champagne. Two of them politely declined but Jack said he would love one.

'I said, "Well, I'm going to have one too because I need one after this husband of mine invited all these people without asking me." '

It was an unusually warm night outside and the party was jumping as Paddy and the traditional musicians entertained the guests who by now were dancing on the patio.

'We were having a good old time,' remembers Anjelica Huston. 'Everyone was in a great mood and we were doing the traditional thing of dancing out of the front door and in the back door.'

A conga line led by Paddy Moloney swept into the kitchen where Rita was sitting, now drinking champagne, with the chauffeurs.

Rita: 'They all came in and someone said, "Oh Jack. You've decided to come in." I thought to myself, "Oh, the chauffeur's in a bad humour." And with that somebody told me that I had Jack Nicholson in my kitchen and all that time I thought he was a chauffeur.'

After being discovered Nicholson came and joined the party.

'We were having a wild time,' says Anjelica. 'Everybody was singing and kids were sleeping under the tables. Then we all did a party piece where everybody does a bit and I was called on to sing. So I sang this old Irish ballad called Mrs McGrath and that was really fun.'

But when it was Jack Nicholson's turn for his party piece he just sat there.

John Boorman did a rendition of a verse called *There was an Old*

Farmer. 'Everybody has to do something. A thing. Anything. And Anjelica, well she knows a lot of Irish songs of course, but Jack sat firmly behind his sunglasses.'

* * *

Ironically it was the little Wicklow village of Annamoe that would provide the catalyst for The Chieftains to make valuable contacts in Washington D.C. Every summer the Moloneys' long-time friends Jack and Peg Davitt, who had sold them the house in Annamoe, invited the family to stay at their Cape Cod home. Jack Davitt, who had been Head of the Justice Department under the John F. Kennedy administration was very well connected in political circles.

'We first met Senator Kennedy at Hack's Bar with the Davitts,' remembers Rita Moloney. 'We all got on very well. Hack's an incredible man. He's American, has no teeth and usually speaks with an East Coast American accent. But when he speaks Irish, his voice is pure Connemara. It's a great bar he runs, but when he's had enough of mixing drinks for his customers, he closes the bar and sends everyone home.'

One night Paddy and Rita Moloney were in Hack's Bar with Seán Keane and his wife Marie when the Senator came in and joined them. Soon other friends and family came in, and an impromptu session of songs and music started up. The Senator then invited everybody to visit the Kennedy's Hyannisport compound the following day to meet his mother Rose.

'That was an extraordinary experience altogether,' remembers Keane. 'Ted was there and it was a real family occasion.'

'Rose was outside on the verandah and Ted invited me out to meet her,' Moloney adds. 'We spoke about pipes, and she asked if mine were the Irish elbow-blown type. Her husband Joe had brought out a piper from Ireland in the 1940s. When I told her they were elbow pipes, she decided to come in and join the party, and she instructed Ted to make sure we had enough to drink. The children danced and we had a rare old party, and almost stayed for dinner.'

'Paddy and The Chieftains came over to sing a few Irish songs,' Sen. Kennedy told the author. 'My mother loved to have family and friends join around the piano and sing along, and having The Chieftains there was a special treat.

'At one point, my mother began playing *Sweet Adeline* on the piano. Of course, that was my Grandfather Honey Fitz's theme song while he was Mayor of Boston. Grampa must have sung it a thousand times. Paddy joined in on his whistle, and it was one of the best versions of *Sweet Adeline* I have ever heard. Paddy even persuaded my mother to try her hand at the penny whistle, much to everyone's delight.'

* * *

In the summer of 1983 Mick Jagger requested that The Chieftains open for the Rolling Stones when they played an open-air concert in front of an audience of 83,000 at Slane Castle outside Dublin. On all the other legs of their record-breaking European tour the hard-rocking J. Geils Band preceded the Stones to the stage, but Jagger insisted that The Chieftains open the concert with their traditional music.

The Chieftains were delighted to be playing with 'The Greatest Rock 'n' Roll Band in the World,' especially Seán Keane, who'd recently become a Stones fan after hearing the Stones blasting away on the juke box in a smoky Montparnasse basement bar after a concert in Paris.

'Obviously I'd heard the Stones as a kid in 1963 but I'd never paid much attention to them as folk music was my prime concern,' remembers Keane. 'That night in this club I just suddenly stopped and I was listening to this great *Jumpin' Jack Flash* and *Honky Tonk Woman*. I said to myself, "Jeez, there's something in that." '

As if in a trance Keane then pulled out his fiddle and bow in the bar and started playing along to *Tumblin' Dice* as the rest of The Chieftains' entourage cheered him on.

Reported *Irish Times* journalist Joe Breen, who was an eye witness: 'Their eyes, wearied by a lack of sleep and a surfeit of drink, suddenly sparkled with a satisfaction that said loudly, "That's our boy." '

The night before the July 24th Slane Castle concert Mick Jagger and Jerry Hall were guests of Garech Browne at Luggala. Although it was the middle of the summer there was a log fire blazing in the front room as the assembled guests reminisced about Garech's parties in the old days. Far quieter than his hell-raising image might suggest, Jagger was the first guest to retire to his favourite passage bedroom where there was a big log fire burning.

When Paddy Moloney arrived at Slane Castle he drove up the hill past the thousands of fans who had camped over night for the huge open air concert. There was already that expectant air of excitement that accompanies every Rolling Stones Show and he headed straight to the lavish backstage area which promoter Bill Graham had organized.

Before the show Paddy Moloney, his daughter Aedín and Garech Browne chatted backstage to Mick Jagger, already dressed up in his colourful costume. Kevin Conneff, himself a big Stones fan, had brought a bodhrán especially to present to Charlie Watts, whom he knew through Chessley Milikin.

'Charlie was very taken by the sound of the bodhrán and how it was played,' says Conneff. 'So I presented him with one at Slane Castle.'

A few years later the Stones' drummer showed his gratitude by giving Kevin two early 19th century hand-illustrated books on bird watching, a hobby that both percussionists were passionate about.

'Charlie's a thorough gentleman,' says Conneff. 'But he admits to this day that's he still trying to get the hang of the bodhrán.'

Slane Castle was the first time that Matt Molloy had met his one-time heroes the Rolling Stones in person and he was very impressed.

'It was incredible,' says Molloy. 'Because I was a Stones' fan when they started off. I was into blues singers but when it came to rock 'n' roll it was the Rolling Stones. Other than that it was traditional music.'

When The Chieftains took the stage at Slane Castle the young audience gave its local heroes a roaring welcome as Moloney led the band to a memorable performance. The sun was shining as The Chieftains' delighted the rock 'n' roll audience with a breathtaking display of jigs, reels and hornpipes. And when they closed the show with a dazzling display of traditional pyrotechnics on *Cotton-Eyed Joe* the dancing fans were screaming for more.

When the Stones mounted the stage to play their set Paddy Moloney was out on the side of the stage listening intently. During the Stones' performance he was joined by his old friend Phil Lynott of the Dublin band Thin Lizzy, who would soon tragically die of a drug overdose.

'I watched the show from side-stage, and was joined there by Phil, and both of us shared the glass of whiskey I brought on during the performance. That's the last time I saw Phil.'

* * *

A few weeks later American rocker Jackson Browne finally crossed paths with The Chieftains when they found themselves together on the same bill at the Lisdoonvarna Festival. The serious quietly spoken singer-songwriter, who was currently riding high in the chart with *Runnin' on Empty* had hired a 707 jumbo jet to fly him and his huge entourage to the west of Ireland for the festival.

'Paddy and I finally hooked up at the Lisdoonvarna Festival,' remembers Browne. 'We worked out a version of *The Crow and the Cradle*, which I guess is an old Irish ballad, and the audience loved it.'

Browne was so delighted to finally be playing with Moloney that he invited him to come and play with him on his two upcoming shows at London's Hammersmith Odeon.

'He's a brilliant soloist,' says Browne, who still has the tapes from those performances. 'You know it's funny because you don't have Paddy sitting-in the sense that many musicians sit-in. Paddy has a vast repertoire of traditional melodies and I don't think it's really like jamming around. He's able to fit any number of traditional melodies to contemporary music. To contemporary songs. I mean he works that way.'

Browne became close friends with the traditional piper in London, forging a lasting personal and musical relationship. While they were in London Moloney showed him his favourite haunts and talked traditional music with the American rock star.

'We got on very well,' says Browne. 'Paddy's a very funny guy. He's got a tremendous amount of energy, a great sense of humour. Tremendous drive. He works real hard and I enjoyed his company very much.'

Apart from his music Paddy Moloney now started branching out into the business world to negotiate a corporate sponsorship with Guinness. In one of the first sponsorship deals of its kind The Chieftains signed a lucrative deal to endorse Guinness, often affectionately known as 'The National Product,' in return for underwriting some of the costs for the spring tour of America in 1983.

As part of deal The Chieftains became the centrepiece of a big-budget Irish television advertising campaign.

'Paddy was a tough negotiator,' remembers Trevor Jacobs, the Guinness account director for Dublin-based Arks Advertising who masterminded the campaign. 'He knew his business. Unlike other artists I've worked with, Paddy was always very clear about his career and where he was going for the next couple of years. This was useful and allowed us to build a campaign around The Chieftains incorporating those elements of uniqueness and pre-eminence we were looking for.'

Moloney wrote special Chieftains' music for the commercial, which was filmed at Slane Castle and during selected performances on their American tour that summer by the late Irish film director Tiernan McBride using Brian Masterson for sound. In the television ads each of The Chieftains, with the exception of Derek Bell who didn't drink Guinness, were seen sipping a creamy pint and giving a testimonial.

The commercial starts with Chieftain's theme music as the group prepare to go on stage to play. A dramatic voice-over builds up the atmosphere saying:

> 'The beat of the bodhrán
> The cream of the head
> The unmistakable taste
> The unmistakable song
> The Chieftains.'

Other ads in the series, which had carried the slogan 'The Chieftains' Greatest Hit,' rhapsodized about 'The sound of the harp' and 'The dance of the fiddle' declaring that, like The Chieftains, Guinness has a style and taste of its own.

In Washington D.C. the Guinness sponsorship led to The Chieftains entering the hallowed world of international politics by becoming the first group to play a concert in the Capitol Building. The historic concert launched the late House Speaker Thomas 'Tip' O'Neill's sponsorship fund to further the study of international relations, underwritten by the Guinness-Harp Corp.

After the black tie concert Tip O'Neill slapped a smiling Paddy Moloney on the back as his old friend Senator Ted Kennedy reminisced about old times.

'The last time I saw you guys was at my mother Rose's house,' the Senator told Paddy. 'Isn't it nice to be in the Speaker's house this time?'

The Guinness campaign was a tremendous success, running for three years in the Republic of Ireland. It was even immortalized by the group's friend Christy Moore who lampooned the ads with the infectious hit song *Lisdoonvarna*, which carried the lyrics, 'Six creamy pints came up on a tray before The Chieftains would play.'

18

The Chieftains in China

To celebrate The Chieftains' third decade in 1983, Paddy Moloney hatched an ambitious plan to go to China and become the first ever Western group to play on the Great Wall. For years The Chieftains had been billed as Ireland's Musical Ambassadors, but Moloney was now determined to do something unique to write The Chieftains into musical history and take them to new heights of international recognition.

Three years earlier the Chinese Embassy in London had taken a box at the Royal Albert Hall for *The Sense of Ireland Festival.* The Chinese diplomats had enjoyed The Chieftains' performance so much that they invited Paddy Moloney to visit China. As the Chinese did not have an embassy in Dublin the logistics of such a trip seemed impossible. But when full diplomatic relations between the two countries were restored in 1981 and an embassy was opened, Moloney decided to pursue the offer.

'They weren't quite sure what to make of me,' remembers the piper, who felt he wasn't being taken seriously by the diplomats. 'I think they thought I was a happy-go-lucky sort of character as I was so joyful when I met them. I don't think they thought I was serious.'

In 1982 Moloney stepped up his campaign to go to China after playing with the Tianjin Ensemble of Chinese musicians and dancers at the new National Concert Hall in Dublin. Paddy had not only organised their trip to Ireland, and the concert, but also found them accommodation they were thrilled with, and he and Rita entertained them at home. To his delight Moloney discovered before the show that the Chinese musicians used the same tonic solfa notation that he employed. He then realized how easy it would be to communicate musically with the Chinese as he taught them the old Irish tune *An Gaoth Aneas*, which both sets of musicians performed together later that night to a standing ovation.

'One of my greatest ambitions had always been to try and visit China,' states Moloney. 'I've always been fascinated by Chinese music since I first heard it as a child. I often wondered if reincarnation might have something to do with it.'

When Moloney first suggested The Chieftains tour China he met resistance from the other group members who didn't share his vision as there would be no concert fees.

'They all said, "Well, I don't see anything coming out of China," ' remembers Moloney. 'It certainly wasn't the money as it ended up costing us. But then think about it. First band in the West ever to go. Big government thing. Make an album. Big spin-offs. Make a video that's been shown twice a year on the BBC ever since. Something to talk about in the newspapers. It's the biggest publicity campaign that you can ever do. I mean you'd pay thousands for it.'

Eventually Moloney's sheer determination and persistence paid off and the Chinese agreed to cover their expenses.

Matt Molloy maintains that once Moloney gets an idea in his head he will doggedly pursue it to the ends of the earth.

'A lot of musicians blow hot and blow cold,' says the flautist. 'What seems like a great idea tonight might have gone to hell in the morning. But if Paddy chats up an idea and gets it into his head, he runs with it. He's very motivated and sometimes too much so. But there you go.'

Before setting off for China, Moloney requested that The Chieftains perform with local orchestras during the three-week trip. He then sent each orchestra the music of *Planxty Irwin* and *An Gaoth Aneas (The Wind from the South)* to learn and in turn received some music from China called *Full of Joy.*

'The fellow in Beijing that concocted that piece had been inspired by a recent decree that said all Chinese must be happy in their work,' explained Derek Bell. 'They didn't want their western brothers to see them miserable so they sent us over *Full of Joy*. It became our signature tune in China.'

The organization required for the trip was immense. Accompanying The Chieftains to China were wives Rita, Marie, Geraldine and Steffie, and an eight-man film crew headed by director Alan Wright, who had just finished making the film *Wagner*, starring Richard Burton, and Windmill Lane Studio's Brian Masterson was there for sound as some of their performances were to be recorded for an album. Garech Browne gladly accepted an invitation to join the trip with Princess Purna and Chieftain tour manager Mick O'Gorman and publicity man Charles Comer made up the party.

From the moment The Chieftains' Swissair DC10 landed in Beijing on April 23rd they faced the formality and stiffness of Chinese protocol, which at times could be overbearing. At the airport they were greeted by two interpreters who had been assigned to them throughout the tour.

'We couldn't even pronounce their names,' laughs Rita Moloney. 'We called the little one Shirley Temple because she was a bubbly girl and the tall one Doris Karloff as she was always grumpy. She used to drive us mad as she was so bossy. But later, when she got to know us, she became very friendly and even cried when we left.'

On the first night of the trip The Chieftains were guests of honour at an official banquet at the Peace Gate Restaurant with the Irish Ambassador John Campbell. During the banquet an official proclamation from the China Performing Arts Society welcoming The Chieftains was read out by its manager Hou Dian.

'Friends and comrades,' began Dian speaking through an interpreter. 'The month of April in our capital city Beijing is a season full of warmth and blooming flowers of Spring. And we are very glad that in such a splendid season we are greeting the Irish artists of The Chieftains who have come to give performances in China. Please allow me to extend a warm welcome to all the Irish distinguished guests.'

When The Chieftains were finally relaxing towards the end of the dinner, the Chinese contingent suddenly stood up and started to leave.

'We thought we had done something wrong as it was only 9:00 p.m.,' says Rita. 'The ambassador later explained the Chinese were so formal that when the Minister of Culture, who was sitting with us, decided to leave, everybody else did too.'

There was an official government banquet every night of the trip during which Paddy Moloney would be expected to give a speech.

'They would be very controlled and formal,' says Moloney. 'But towards the end of the trip we had gotten the word around that we're not formal and we like to have fun and sing.'

On the second day of the trip two buses collected The Chieftains to drive them the 50 miles through the mountains to the town of Badaling where they were to perform on the Great Wall. The party had been awoken at seven in the morning to get an early start and Garech Browne and Princess Purna were less than happy.

'Poor Garech and Purna didn't know where the hell they were,' jokes Seán Keane. 'Getting up that early in the morning was real shock therapy because they are not used to it.'

Brian Masterson, who was officially with the film crew, decided to reassign himself to the musicians' party as he could see they were getting preferential treatment.

'I quickly jumped camp in China to join The Chieftains' bus,' he explained. 'As they were guests of honour everything was great for them and they went to all the nice places. The poor old film crew were really just tolerated by the Chinese and obstacles were put in their way. After a couple of days I saw what was happening and said, "Can I go in your bus?" We had great times after that.'

When they arrived at the Great Wall it was a scorching hot day and also a holiday so it was packed with sightseers. Derek Bell, who was carrying his harp, was very worried that it would be damaged by the crowds as they made their way up the narrow steps to one of the castle-like blockhouses dotted along the wall.

'We nearly caused a riot,' laughs Moloney. 'All the people were trying to get up the stairway to one of the turrets to see what was happening and there was a dreadful crush.'

Once they got to the top of the wall The Chieftains brought out their instruments and started to play an old Irish tune as the curious Chinese onlookers watched in amazement.

'I don't know the name of the piece we played,' admits Moloney. 'But I thought it would be a nice appropriate piece as it had a swinging lilt to it. For the gas we called it *Off the Great Wall*.'

After only ten minutes The Chieftains had to call a halt to the music as more and more people started climbing up the wall to see what was going on. But they did manage to record and film their performance of the piece.

The strict government itinerary called for them to spend four days at each of the three cities selected for the tour. At each concert they would perform a number of songs with the local orchestra as a finale. Arrangements had been made for rehearsals prior to each show in the local conservatory of music.

'They don't understand a word of English and we don't speak a word of Chinese,' says Moloney. 'Yet there was no language barrier. It was just music. Some of their instruments I've never even seen before. But using the tonic solfa was a great help, and I also discovered their other system of musical notation which uses numbers. I had worked out the arrangements for both groups in advance, so once we all got going it was just like a little hooley in the West of Ireland.'

At each show an interpreter faithfully translated Paddy Moloney's introductions to the audience and then struggled gallantly to pronounce The Chieftain's names in Chinese. As part of his programme of music, Moloney decided to deliver a mixed bag of Chieftains' music.

'We gave them some Carolan and little solo pieces from each member of the band,' said Moloney.

At first The Chieftains had no way of knowing if the Chinese liked their music as they were not demonstrative and there was little applause if any.

When Bell decided to personally investigate whether the Chinese liked Chieftains' music he was told that during a recent London Symphony Orchestra visit most of the audience had walked out in the middle of the second half.

'When we played nobody left so that's how we knew they had liked us,' says Bell. Paddy adds, 'At the end of each concert we got a standing ovation. That's usually quite a good hint.'

From Beijing the Chieftains travelled to Suzhow where they became the first group since the revolution to be allowed to play in the city's historic gardens, which were especially opened for their performance.

'It was a beautiful place,' says Moloney. 'Poets used to come there and read their poetry and musicians used to play but they have been closed up since 1949. It was a great honour that they agreed to open it for us.'

During their stay The Chieftains were accompanied by the assistant director of the Chinese Performing Arts Society who started singing Moloney some traditional Chinese tunes.

'Once he sang me a beautiful love song,' remembers Paddy. 'You'd swear you were listening to a song from the West of Ireland. I could directly relate it to the traditional sean-nós singing. If I'd had more time I would have recorded it. Maybe some day I'll get around to it when The Chieftains are less busy.'

The video crew were on hand to film the whole trip but on several key occasions the cameras ran out of film and missed some of the high points. Unfortunately this happened on the day The Chieftains went to the Yangtse River and started an impromptu session on the boat.

'We started playing and Rita and Marie Keane grabbed hold of the Chinese guides and got them dancing to the old set dance *The Walls of Limerick*,' chuckles Moloney. 'Unfortunately the film crew ran out of film. It was priceless to see the representative of the minister of culture doing his Irish steps.'

On another occasion Paddy asked their guides to take them to see local musicians and were taken to a peasant farm house where an old farmer lived with his two sons, their wives, grandparents and children.

'Some musicians came by and they started to play for us,' remembers Moloney. 'At first they tried some very fancy opera stuff but then they broke down and did their own music. I played the whistle and it was great fun.'

Each part of The Chieftains' day was planned down to the very last minute by the Chinese authorities but invariably someone in the party would be late and throw off the itinerary.

'It would drive them around the bend,' laughs Moloney. 'Someone was always 15 or 20 minutes late and this would upset their itinerary as the traffic – mostly bikes – had to be reckoned with.'

By the end of the three weeks Moloney noticed that all the times on the official schedule had been quietly moved half-an-hour forwards to compensate. Matt Molloy says that although he had a wonderful time he was also exhausted by the time The Chieftains' train arrived in Shanghai for the final concert.

'We had to rehearse and play with a different orchestra in each city,' explains the flautist. 'It was very difficult as there were interpreters who weren't versed in music trying to transfer our ideas to the Chinese and vice versa. It could be a bit exasperating at times. But it was all worth it for the last 20 minutes of our show when we had the Chinese orchestra up on stage with us playing the Irish pieces. It brought the house down. The communication was there.'

The final concert in Shanghai was filmed by Chinese television and later shown to an estimated viewing audience of 700 million. The Chieftains' visit was big news in the Chinese Republic with newspapers reporting on the Irish visitors daily. Leading politicians and diplomats attended the concerts and the tour helped cement future relations between Ireland and China.

The vice chairman of the Musician's Association of China, Sun Sheng, said he had been deeply affected by The Chieftains' visit.

'I think through The Chieftains' music I have seen the images of the Irish people,' he declared. 'Music knows no boundaries for it is a unique and comprehensible language.'

On the final day of their stay the Mayor of Shanghai gave The Chieftains a lavish 15-course farewell lunch including pheasant and Peking Duck. The Irish musicians were placed at the top table with the mayor and other guests of honour. All through the meal the small glasses of the delicious Chinese spirit Maotai were quickly refilled after the traditional Chinese toast, 'Gambei' – 'Bottoms up!'

Remembers Matt Molloy: 'Early on in the game we realized that to get another shot you had to propose a toast because then they'd come out and refill everyone's glass for the next toast. So Gambei was the thing.'

As the meal progressed The Chieftains party started playing a game of inventing various Gambei's so their glasses would be refilled. They began toasting the flute players in China, the cultural exchange bureau and any other Chinese organization that came to mind.

'We started running out of ideas,' says Molloy. 'Finally Seán Keane stood up and announced he wanted to toast the person who invented the Gambei.'

For the first time since their arrival their Chinese hosts loosened up and even joined The Chieftains and their wives in an Irish step dance. Rita partnered the elderly mayor of Shanghai and six-foot-six-inch Seán Keane towered a full two feet over Shirley Temple, the group's interpreter.

The luncheon then became an international drinking match between the Irish and the Chinese as diplomatic relations between the two countries reached new levels of cordiality.

'The funny part was that we were able to drink them under the table,' boasted Derek Bell. 'At the end the bloody government officials were getting shaky and tipsy and were trying talk to us although they didn't know a word of English. It was getting to be really comical but it goes to show that for drinking there's no one to beat the Irish.'

But the Chinese were not quite sure what to make of publicity man Charlie Comer when he began leading the Irish contingent in a rousing medley of old bawdy English vaudeville songs.

'Charlie was definitely a talking point for the Chinese,' says Molloy. 'He was wearing a Rolling Stones' leather touring jacket with that logo of Mick Jagger's lips and the poor Chinese had never seen anything like it.'

After the banquet, as The Chieftains were back in the hotel preparing for the evening flight to Hong Kong, Moloney was visibly moved when he triumphantly declared to his fellow Chieftains, 'We did it, lads. We did it.'

* * *

Hong Kong was a great week for all The Chieftains, their wives and families and friends, and holds many happy memories for them. One in particular was when they were driving from the airport, and Garech's bag fell out of the boot of the car, and his boots could be seen hopping off the road through the busy tunnel. 'Dear Jesus,' said the promoter, 'please tell me this is not happening.'

After two shows in Hong Kong The Chieftains flew on to Australia where they went straight onto the stage at the new Melbourne Concert Hall without any sleep. While in Australia they introduced their new Chinese tune *Full of Joy* to the audiences who loved it and from then on it would become a staple part of The Chieftain repertoire.

The seemingly indefatigable Chieftains played 10 concerts in 14 days in Australia before returning to Ireland with a large assortment of Chinese instruments they planned to learn and incorporate into new material. On his return Paddy Moloney told RTE Radio that China had had a huge influence on The Chieftains.

'I'm thinking of the possibility of using some of the Chinese instruments and possibly some of the music in some film scores that I have coming up,' he explained. 'It's great music. I mean it's all there. It's beautiful.'

A year earlier Paddy Moloney had been commissioned to

compose the score for the Canadian film *The Grey Fox* by Philip Borsos. Starring Richard Farnsworth, the film was the true story of Bill Miner who spent 33 years in San Quentin for robbing a stage coach at the end of the last century. On his release he goes to the newly invented cinema to see *The Great Train Robbery* and gets the idea of robbing a train. For the moving cinema scene, which is the climax of the film, Moloney adapted his composition *Sea Image*.

'It needed a lot of expansion,' explained Moloney, who won a Canadian 'Genie' for the score and was nominated for a Grammy. 'The disturbing sounds of the rolling waves suited what Philip Borsos wanted to do for the train sequence.'

The Grey Fox was the first film score that Brian Masterson worked on with Paddy Moloney at Windmill Studios. The sound engineer says that traditional music is perfectly suited to film as it is so highly evocative.

'To be terribly simplistic, there are two sides to Irish music,' explains Masterson. 'There are the slow airs which are very filmic and paint pictures and the reels, jigs and hornpipes that are terribly energetic.'

Masterson says these two elements are the foundations of Moloney's film music but adds how technically difficult it is to write music to fit the action in a film.

'In *The Grey Fox* it is just amazing when you see these great shots of these old trains coming along through the mountains in Canada and you hear Paddy's fantastic dance rhythms which just mesh and work brilliantly.'

19

The Ballad of the Irish Horse

On February 13th, 1984, The Chieftains celebrated their 21st birthday with a special champagne concert at Dublin's National Concert Hall. Ex-Chieftains Michael Tubridy and Seán Potts were reunited with their old band mates for the sold-out concert which was also a fund-raiser to send an Irish team to the Blind Chess Olympics in New Jersey.

There was also a tinge of sadness as The Chieftains played *The March of the King of Laois* in memory of their old friend Luke Kelly of The Dubliners, who had recently died. The grand finale of the evening saw a rousing medley of jigs and reels where The Chieftains were joined on stage by set dancers and drummers and pipers from the Rathcoole Pipe Band.

From the stage the victorious Chieftains toasted the audience with champagne as a huge birthday cake bearing the words, 'Congratulations Chieftains: 21 years in Show Business' was carried onto the stage.

As Paddy Moloney blew out the candles with the bellows from his uilleann pipes, he seemed to have achieved his life-long dream of helping to preserve traditional music for future generations to come.

At 47, Moloney had taken traditional music to almost every corner of the globe and turned The Chieftains into an Irish institution. They constantly filled the top concert halls of the world with record sales in the millions. And although they rubbed shoulders with world leaders, film stars and rock 'n' rollers they all managed to remain relatively unchanged by success, keeping their working-class roots and traditions.

Yet for Paddy Moloney fame could be a difficult burden to bear at times. Since the formation of The Chieftains, Moloney had become a legend to many and the living embodiment of traditional music.

But ironically it was his very success as a champion of traditional music that had driven a barrier between the piper and some other traditional players. For Moloney now found, to his deep regret, that he could no longer go into a session unnoticed to play with the musicians he had cut his musical teeth with.

'I used to go around the country and play,' says Moloney. 'Go into sessions and sit in with this one and that one. Great tunes there. Then all of a sudden I noticed that the more popular I became, the whole attitude of the other players I used to sit down and play with changed.

'It's nothing malicious. It's just all of a sudden they see you up there playing on the big stages and on television making money and this, that and the other. Therefore when you sit in amongst musicians they become uneasy in front of you. Don't ask me why. Or else they're being over-nice. People that I've known for 20 or 30 years. Sometimes when I walk into a room I get the feeling that there's a little bit of resentment.

'So as great a success as one might have with The Chieftains, you have to suffer other things. Losses, like a more friendly attitude with fellow musicians you used to play with on a non-commercial basis. I miss it terribly. It's dreadful. And you also find that those things cannot be planned. You can't buy them. Spontaneous sessions. I'd love to seek out these people and go back in like the good old times and have a few tunes but it doesn't work that way anymore.'

Being an instantly recognizable celebrity in Dublin can also create problems for Moloney when he goes out to dinner with his family, and autograph hunters descend on their table. Even so, the piper makes it a point to be friendly and find a kindly word for everyone.

'In Dublin you have to watch where you go,' he explains. 'Especially from the family point of view.'

Moloney's daughter Aedín, now an accomplished actress, loved the attention when she was growing up, but her two brothers hated it. The eldest, Aonghus, never spoke about who his father was to anyone when he was at college and as a child Pádraig had wanted to shoot pestering fans if they tried to accost his father.

'I remember once going in Bewleys Coffee House in Dundrum for a coffee while Rita was doing her shopping,' says Moloney. 'And everyone in the place was grand except one guy. The minute I sat down he came over. "How are you?" And then his greasy hand – he'd been eating chips – was on my shoulder. There was a smell. That was it and then he went away and I thought, "Thank God."

'Two minutes later he was back. "Do you know so and so?" He was a musician from somewhere. I had two mouthfuls and left. That was the end of my coffee.

'I don't get annoyed over those things any more. I just think they're funny and you have to put up with that kind of thing. And you get worried when it stops because that means you're out of business.'

The Chieftains have always prided themselves as being a band of the people and over the years they have carefully developed an open door policy where any fan can come and meet the group personally after the show. This has helped cement the intense loyalty of Chieftain fans, especially in America, who come and see the band year after year.

Larry Kirwan, lead singer of the New York-based Irish rock band Black 47, has been a lifelong fan of The Chieftains and cites them as a big influence.

'To me they are the Grateful Dead of traditional music,' says Kirwan. 'They've been there, they're out there and they're very accessible because they're always around. I've always thought of them in that sense and that's a compliment.'

Celebrities were also going out of their way to court Paddy Moloney and The Chieftains. That February Moloney had met the film director Ron Howard backstage after a concert in Pasadena. Howard, who starred in the 1970s' television hit *Happy Days*, had invited Moloney to compose the score for his upcoming film *The Rainbow Warrior*. Although that movie about Spanish whaling ships was never made, Howard found inspiration for his later film *Far and Away* from a Chieftains' song he heard that night. Ten years later he would invite the group to record for the movie soundtrack.

Moloney also recently discovered that another actor in *Happy Days*, Henry Winkler (who plays The Fonz), had been a fan of The Chieftains for years. He and Moloney were eventually to meet at Carol Bayer-Segar's house in 1996.

During their stay in Hollywood Moloney cannily negotiated a barter deal with Arnold Askenazy, the owner of the prestigious L'Ermitage Hotel. The arrangement was for The Chieftains to play as part of the hotel's 'Salon Series' for 30 specially invited guests in exchange for free accommodation for each member of the group. Stefan Grapelli and James Galway also do this series.

'He is giving each of us a $400-a-night suite for the six days we will be in Los Angeles,' Moloney told *The Irish Independent*. 'We just have to play a one-hour performance.'

During his time in Los Angeles Moloney became good friends with film stars Burgess Meredith and Larry Hagman, who lived next to each other in Malibu, and Moloney often went to their homes.

'We are always delighted when Paddy drops round,' Burgess Meredith told the author. 'Larry and I were mad about his music and completely engaged by him as a musician and a person. His group were wondrous and not like any other musicians I'd ever seen. They were all laid back and free and easy and played this beautiful music.'

While they were at L'Ermitage The Chieftains viewed four hours of rushes from an upcoming National Geographic special on Irish horses for which Moloney had been commissioned to write the score. The sheer grace, speed and elegance of the thoroughbreds naturally fitted in to Chieftains' music.

For the rest of the US tour Moloney jotted down his inspiration for *The Ballad of the Irish Horse* for Chieftains and symphony orchestra on anything that came to hand wherever inspiration hit him. It would take almost a year for Moloney to compose the 52 music sequences needed.

'When you get the tunes you have to write them down,' he explains. 'Wherever. I often use the sick bags in airplanes if I'm on a long flight. I have many a score on sick bags.'

'Derek's a genius,' says Moloney. 'Very quick. After I've finished my composing and arranging, Derek comes down for a day or two and scores it out for me. I do the arrangements, which are very important, and select the instrumentation and colour I require. Then Derek writes it all out for me.

'For *The Ballad of the Irish Horse* I came up with 16 bars of a melody,' he explains. 'I'm very much into melody and I don't like music that can't be remembered afterwards. I took that 16 bars and expanded it into all sorts of counter melodies and different rhythms.

'It was amazing because Derek told me that I had written 16th century Irish harmony without knowing anything about it. I didn't know what I was doing and I have no idea where it came from. It just popped out. Derek was fascinated.'

The main theme of *The Ballad of the Irish Horse* was given its premiere during The Chieftains' first live performance with a full symphony orchestra in Milwaukee. It was a major breakthrough for The Chieftains to play with a full orchestra and they performed selections from *The Year of the French* and *Tristan and Isolde*. From then on The Chieftains would regularly perform with orchestras all over the world as Moloney more and more incorporated his traditional ideas into serious classical music for films.

'The sound is mighty with a full orchestra,' said Moloney. 'My film score music with The Chieftains and orchestra has grown immensely over the years. But I've condensed it and broken it down into an hour and 15 minutes. That's enough time to inflict that music on an audience. Then the rest of the concert is The Chieftains.'

Ironically, Moloney would give his first public performance of the theme of *The Ballad of the Irish Horse* to a small gathering of traditional music lovers in Dublin. The famed piper was the special guest at a traditional session which included ex-Chieftain Seán Potts, his son Seán Og and piper Ronan Brown.

'The Chieftains' chief began with a couple of good piping jigs,' wrote Mick Slevin in the traditional piping journal *An Píobaire*. 'The playing was careful without being slow. Paddy's playing did full justice to the tunes, gradually warming up to lovely flowing piping. The Donnycarney boy then played a theme piece composed by himself for a new film on Irish horses. It was comprised of an air, hornpipe and jig. This was pleasant but what really made the ears rise to attention was a stunning, beautifully phased Caisleán Uí Néill. A tea break followed giving the punters a chance to chat.

'The night ended at 11:00 p.m. and we departed reluctantly but full to the gills with a feast of "craic" and music. Paddy Moloney – come again soon.'

Moloney was also trying to recreate the warmth and excitement of a traditional session in The Chieftains' show and he began regularly featuring Michael Flatley, the American-born seven-time world championship step dancer. With his dazzling displays of intricate high steps, Flatley, then 25, added new excitement to The Chieftains' stage shows. This went on for several years with Michael touring the world with the band. In fact, it was during a concert in London that Michael met his wife Beata. Jean Butler followed Michael as the band's solo dancer making her debut with them at Carnegie Hall. This was still a full decade before they would capture the world's attention with the hit show *Riverdance*.

'The idea of putting show dancing on a stage definitely came from The Chieftains,' says Jean Butler's sister Cara, who now regularly dances with the group. 'I think the beginnings of the whole *Riverdance* concept were started by Paddy at his traditional Christmas shows when he had the wren boys and girls dancing.'

* * *

During The Chieftains' frequent trips to London it became a custom for them to meet friends at The Bar at the Ritz Hotel. Once frequented by Winston Churchill, who conducted World War II strategy meetings at his special table across from the bar, it had over the years became a favoured drinking spot for the likes of Charlie Chaplin, Graham Greene and Ian Fleming. In the mid-1980s the Louis XIV style bar was still a favourite haunt of writers, film stars, politicians and the occasional traditional musician.

'We used to go there at about 5 o'clock in the evening and hold court,' remembers Moloney. 'There were lords and ladies and all sorts of funny people there, and people from the recording industry would join us. They were flabbergasted by this carry on.'

On one memorable occasion Moloney and Garech Browne were in the middle of a pheasant lunch when Marianne Faithfull came breezing into the Ritz.

'She took one look at me and said, "Ahhhh Paddy Moloney. I don't believe it." '

Marianne joined her friends and started drinking the bar specialty Vodka Riccis and as things got livelier she asked Paddy if he would play her favourite song, *Love is Teasin'*.

'But The Bar at the Ritz,' Marianne says, 'is just about the one place I can think of where you couldn't just take out a whistle and blow.'

So Paddy and Marianne went off behind the bar to try and find somewhere to play, eventually winding up in a tiny broom cupboard.

'There were pails and brooms and dusters and mops,' laughs

Marianne. 'And we went in and locked the door. I sat on a bucket and Paddy leaned against a broom. We just had a session.'

Moloney remembers playing the old song *Love is Teasin'*, which Marianne had asked for, and which she would record for *The Long Black Veil* almost a decade later.

'I was going to play for the whole bar but they wouldn't let me,' says Moloney. 'After I played her the tune we went back to lunch.'

On another occasion Paddy was with Rita and Derek Bell having lunch at Rugantino's with Garech Browne and Lord Gormanston. During lunch they began chatting to a man on the next table who had introduced himself as Laurence. When, at 3:00 p.m. closing time, the party decided to move on to a Soho after hours drinking club, Laurence tagged along.

Over drinks, Laurence Daly explained that he was General Secretary of the National Mine Workers Union, which was then involved in a bitter fight to bring down Margaret Thatcher's government with a wave of crippling strikes. Daly confided that he was in hiding at present so he would not have to negotiate with the government. But his main concern was finding himself drinking with ruling class aristocrats like Lord Gormanston.

'He decided that the only way to overcome this problem was to officially swear in Nicholas Gormanston as a member of the Ukraine Worker's Union,' recalls Rita. 'Which he did and gave us all communist badges with all the other paraphernalia.'

As the afternoon heated up the owner was having so much fun that she decided to close down and make it a private party. Later on, passing Buckingham Palace, Derek and Paddy decided to play a tune for the Queen. 'We got out of our taxi, and played our own version of *Rule Britannia*, much to the amusement of all concerned.'

* * *

By 1986 Paddy Moloney was still manager of The Chieftains and things had settled down to a profitable routine. Now carefully billed by Charles Comer as 'An Irish Institution,' the group played 120 concerts a year and changed at least half their material every year. They did a US tour every March and then ventured out to various parts of Europe before returning to America in the summer. In the winter they headed off to the warmer climes of Australia, Japan and the Far East.

Moloney steered the Chieftains' ship on a straight course and, although there was the odd 'little tiff' among group members, morale had never been better. Tradition dictated that all concert proceeds were split equally among the six Chieftains.

'Matt Molloy calls me "the mammy",' says Moloney proudly. 'I keep the whole thing ticking on. You have managers and agents coming and going and my job has always been to keep it all together.'

Moloney is driven, working tirelessly to further The Chieftains with always at least half a dozen projects for the group on the boil.

One of the things audiences most love about The Chieftains is their on stage humour, much of which is self-depreciating. Moloney and 'Ding Dong' Bell are constantly cracking jokes at each other's expense and both men's natural flair for comedy helps keep Chieftains' performances fresh and unpredictable.

'There's a lot of fun on stage,' says Seán Keane. 'And the audience senses that we're out to have a good time. Sometimes I'll play a bum note just to gain somebody's attention or to annoy someone or whatever. It keeps a great atmosphere going on stage.'

One of the high points of The Chieftains' act is Derek Bell's medley of piano rags for which Moloney feigns an Oliver Hardy-like irritation to the audience.

Explained Derek: 'That all started as a joke on Paddy at a party we had to go to in Denver once after a concert. As there was no harp available Paddy said I should play my particular solo on the piano. So as a joke I played some old rag or something and Paddy loved it so much that he introduced it into the concert. Now the joke is to find one that will fox him on stage and give him a few surprises.'

Another long-running gag off-stage between the two on tours involves the saga of Micky the Muck. The character of Micky the Muck, which is Gaelic for Micky the pig, originated as a story Moloney used to tell his children when they were growing up.

'At first I used to tell Derek, "Some day Micky the Muck is going to come and destroy you," ' says Moloney. "Don't look under your bed or he'll get you." '

Stepping up his campaign, Moloney started leaving little stickers around for Bell to find, saying, 'Micky was Here', 'You're for the Chop' and 'Pig Power Rules.'

'Paddy's got it into his head that his pig's got miraculous powers,' says Bell shrugging his shoulders. 'Well I say Micky is only fit to be used as bacon to eat in the morning or to make the bags for bagpipes out of. Pigskin. Then I started the Big Cat's Club to keep the pigs in order by eating them where necessary. It has leopards, tigers and pumas then I went one better by starting a Big Bear's Club with grizzlies, brown bears and pandas. And they're eating all his blinking pigs for all he's worth. And so it goes on.'

Kevin Conneff pretends to see nothing funny in two grown men talking about pigs and pandas and constantly chastises them for being silly. But to keep things going Matt Molloy deliberately tries to annoy the percussionist by making a point of always asking how Micky is doing, which prompts the reply from Derek that Micky is fine and 'about to finish Paddy's pipes off'.

'You see Kevin's the schoolmaster,' quips Bell. 'He makes sure the ties are straight and I haven't spilled the soup down my front.'

This good-natured ribbing is an integral part of The Chieftains interaction on the road and helps them get on with each other during the long gruelling months they spend tramping around the world.

'I think it's a lot more like family than just about anything else,' explains Derek Bell. 'Well, it has to be but having said that it has to be qualified. Part of the secret is never getting too close to be in the way and not being too remote to be uncommunicative. It's as simple as that.'

After so many years on the road The Chieftains have evolved a code of survival on their lengthy tours which is frequently misunderstood by outsiders as stand-offishness.

'I well understand how people feel on a tour,' says Moloney. 'You don't know what's going through a fellow's head, and if it's something irritating him or something wrong at home, if he's on a tour it's difficult to deal with it. It's like being in prison.'

On the road with The Chieftains during their 1989 European tour. (Courtesy of Marian van de veen-van rijk)

The young Paddy Moloney all dressed up for his confirmation. (Courtesy of Paddy Moloney)

Paddy Moloney's first-ever public performance. Paddy (pictured second from left) appeared with Leo Rowsome's school of young pipers in a 1947 concert at Dublin's Phoenix Park. (Courtesy of Paddy Moloney)

Paddy Moloney's wedding to Rita O'Reilly on September 14, 1963, almost didn't take place after the young bride refused to ride in the big American car sent to collect her. Pictured behind the bride and groom (left to right) are Sean Potts, Martin Fay, Sean Ó Riada, unknown, Michael Tubridy, Sean O Se, and Ronnie McShane. (Courtesy of Paddy Moloney)

Sean Ó Riada leads Ceoltóiri Cualann in a live radio broadcast on RTE in the mid-1960s. (Courtesy of Paddy Moloney)

Actor and friend Richard Harris made a special appearance with The Chieftains at their 1989 St. Patrick's Day concert at New York's Carnegie Hall. (Courtesy of Chuck Pulin/Star File)

The Chieftains travel hundreds of thousands of miles each year to bring their unique brand of Irish music to every corner of the globe. (Courtesy of Marian van de veen-van rijk)

Paddy Moloney and the Chieftains hang tough for the cover of their crossover album *Another Country* in 1992. (Courtesy of Caroline Greyshock)

The Chieftains make a St. Patrick's Day appearance on NBC's "Today" show in 1986 with presenter John Palmer. (Courtesy of Chuck Pulin/Star File)

Matt Molloy can often be seen play-
ing a rousing session at his popular
Matt Molloy's Bar in Westport,
Ireland. (Courtesy of John Glatt)

Martin Fay keeps dry during a shower before playing in a live telecast of
the National Independence Day concert on the White House West Lawn
in 1995. (Courtesy of John Glatt)

Kevin Conneff and his daughter Peggy go for a walk near their home deep in
the scenic Wicklow Mountains. (Courtesy of John Glatt)

Sean Keane relaxes outside his local thatched bar in Rathcoole with his friend Brian McEvoy. (Courtesy of John Glatt)

Derek Bell didn't let a rain shower spoil his mood before the 1995 Independence Day concert on the White House Lawn. (Courtesy of John Glatt)

The Chieftains became highly successful international spokesmen for Guinness Stout in the eighties. (Courtesy of John Glatt)

The Chieftains officially launch Matt Molloy's Bar with an impromptu free concert on the bar roof. (Courtesy of Liam Lyons)

Paddy Moloney shares a joke with Senator Edward Kennedy after the
Chieftains became the first musical group ever to play the Capitol Building in
Washington, D.C., in 1983. (Courtesy of Chuck Pulin/Star File)

The Chieftains pictured with former Speaker of the House Thomas "Tip"
O'Neill at the Capitol Building in 1983. (Courtesy of Chuck Pulin/Star File)

Longtime friend Marianne Faithfull made a guest appearance with The Chieftains during their St. Patrick's Day show at New York's Avery Fisher Hall in 1995. (Courtesy of Chuck Pulin/Star File)

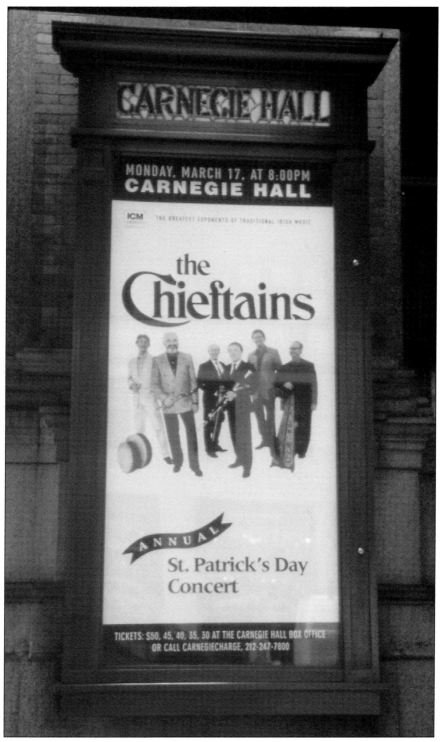

St. Patrick's Day with The Chieftains has become a New York institution.
(Courtesy of Chuck Pulin/Star File)

The Chieftains proudly hold their gold records for their best-selling Christmas album *The Bells of Dublin.* (Courtesy of Chuck Pulin/Star File)

Paddy Moloney receives his fifth Grammy for *Santiago* in 1997. (Courtesy of Chuck Pulin/Star File)

The Chieftains are firm favorites whenever they appear on The Nashville Network's "American Music Shop." Here Paddy Moloney poses with country legends Don Williams and Ricky Skaggs. (Courtesy of TNN)

Rock star Sting made a guest appearance on the Grammy-winning *The Long Black Veil*, singing "Mo Ghile Mear"/"Our Hero" in Gaelic. (Courtesy of Claire Carnegie)

Paddy Moloney and Canadian singer-songwriter Sarah McLachlan pose backstage during their 1995 United States summer tour. (Courtesy of John Glatt)

Country star Ricky Skaggs and The Chieftains playing "Cotton Eye Joe" during the 1995 Independence Day concert on the White House Lawn. (Courtesy of John Glatt)

The Chieftains appeared live on a "House of Blues" telecast in June 1995 to promote *The Long Black Veil.* (Courtesy of John Glatt)

Paddy Moloney and Matt Molloy share a joke with Mel Gibson during the Hollywood premiere of *Braveheart* in June 1995. (Courtesy of John Glatt)

The Chieftains during a guest appearance with the cast of ABC-TV's "One Life to Live" in 1996. From left to right: Laura Koffman, Susan Bedsow Horgan, Gina Tognoni, Sandra Grant, Crystal Chappell, and Susan Haskell. (Courtesy of Steve Fenn/ ABC)

The Chieftains—the world's greatest exponents of traditional Irish music. (Courtesy of Caroline Greyshock)

20

Broadening Horizons

In January 1985 *The Chieftains in China* album and video were released to critical acclaim almost two years after the trip. At a champagne press reception at the Chester Beatty Library in Dublin, the Chinese ambassador to Ireland Xing Zhongxiu, cheerfully posed for pictures with Paddy Moloney. Later The Chieftains played *Full of Joy* for the press and Garech Browne gave a speech which was praised for its brevity.

At the reception Moloney told Dublin's *Hot Press* magazine that The Chieftains could no longer survive by just playing in Ireland. Explaining himself he asked why a BBC-made six-part tribute to celebrate the group's 21st anniversary had not been screened by RTE.

'We would prefer to stay here,' he told *Hot Press*. 'But there just isn't a living to be made in Ireland at the moment. In fact, the band must spend more than half of the year outside of Ireland in order to make it pay.'

Although Moloney had been ruled exempt from income tax on his composing royalties, he, along with the other members of the group, seriously considered moving to Boston and becoming tax exiles in 1985 as they were being so heavily taxed.

'We were looking at our whole financial situation,' explained Moloney. 'One doesn't mind having to pay taxes but there's something wrong when 90 per cent of your income is coming from abroad and then Irish tax man takes more than half.'

There was a group meeting to discuss leaving Ireland permanently and become US residents but when it came to a vote two members were against the plan and the idea was abandoned.

'I personally would have gone,' admits Matt Molloy. 'But we are a partnership and it was either six for it or nothing. That was the only fair way.'

The flute player still feels strongly that The Chieftains are inadequately compensated for the goodwill they create for Ireland as unofficial ambassadors.

'One of my pet grievances is that there's no sympathy for us getting off our collective arses to scour the highways and byways of the world to create a market for our music,' says Molloy. 'And we've had little thanks from the government. You get a token acknowledgment. A nod of the head, "You've all done great, lads." The fact remains that we do a lot for Irish tourism and a lot of people in government know it. But they don't show it in a concrete way.'

Ten years on Paddy Moloney says he's glad The Chieftains never emigrated to America.

'When I say on stage that Dublin is the best city in the world I really mean it,' says the piper. 'I just love floating around in Wicklow and recharging my batteries. After a long hard tour abroad you just find yourself settling back into your own self again. You get thoughts about music that you had years ago and tunes come into your mind. So when you are approached by a film company to compose a score you can go back out there with a fresh mind.'

* * *

Another welcome escape from the pressures of the music business for Paddy Moloney were his regular visits to Brittany, where he stayed with his old friend Polig Monjarret. During their 25 year friendship the two men had developed close bonds through a common love of Celtic culture.

'I call Polig the godfather of Brittany,' declares Moloney. 'He's done so much to revive the music and the language.'

In the mid-1980s Monjarret suggested that his friend buy a place in Brittany, as he was going there so often, and found him a small maisonette in the village of Bubry.

'He got me a little converted shebeen in the middle of the country,' says Moloney. 'We have the bare necessities. A kitchen, two bedrooms and a loft. And a nice garden which Rita loves. However, I wouldn't give it to my worst enemy, but we're happy.'

In an attempt to retain his anonymity Moloney told Monjarret to keep his new home secret, but word soon leaked out in the village.

'The mayor heard that I was coming and said, "Paddy, we want to see you in the town hall on Wednesday." I asked him why and he replied that he wanted to officially welcome me to Bubry and make me an honorary citizen.'

Protocol dictated that Paddy's mother Catherine, who was now in her 80s, be present at the ceremony so she caught the next ferry over with her grandson Pádraig. And she was all smiles as her famous son was welcomed by the leading citizens of Bubry and presented with bouquets. For his thank you speech Moloney whipped out his tin whistle and played a rousing jig for the assembled guests.

'Later we had to join in the Breton dancing whether we knew how to do it or not,' laughs Moloney. 'It was a wonderful day.'

Now every summer Paddy and Rita spend a couple of weeks relaxing in their Bubry home, which at Rita's insistence does not have a telephone.

'We're away from everything,' says Moloney. 'There's nobody pestering me on the telephone and once I get there my mind switches off.'

One night that summer Moloney was at a small dinner party at Polig Monjarret's house celebrating the publication of his collection of more than 3,000 Celtic tunes. In a labour of love Montjarret had devoted 12 years of his life to collecting the tunes, for his *Traditional Tunes From Lower Brittany*, plus an additional 7 years to transcribe them.

During the evening Monjarret joked that after *The Chieftains In China*, Moloney might consider a follow-up called *The Chieftains in Brittany*. Then looking over to his friend Christian Michielini, the managing director of Brittany Ferries, Monjarret added, 'And, of course, Brittany Ferries will sponsor it.' When Michielini agreed, the seeds for *Celtic Wedding* were planted although they would take another full year to flower.

Once The Chieftains committed to the album, Monjarret visited Ireland several times to help select tunes from his book. It took hours of pouring through different tunes before they finally came up with the right ones to fit Moloney's concept for the record. For he had decided to musically recreate the ritual of a 14th century Breton wedding ceremony.

'Polig gave me all the stories and the background behind all the tunes,' explains Moloney. 'There was so much material in his book it was a difficult to narrow it down. I had my own visions on how

I wanted to present *Celtic Wedding*. There was one long 20 minute piece which was a tone poem. Polig told me the whole story of what used to happen in a Breton wedding from the 14th century onwards. How the piper would come in when the couple were courting, and what he'd play all through the ceremony right up to the Roast Tune, which the piper plays during the wedding meal. And I put the whole thing together.'

To Moloney, *Celtic Wedding* marked a spiritual rebirth of The Chieftains as it was the first of his on-going musical voyages of discovery to trace the influences of Celtic music around the world. In future years he would explore the traditional music of Galicia, and its connections with other parts of Spain, Cuba and Mexico as part of a larger body of Chieftains' work.

'*Celtic Wedding* reminded me of the very first Chieftains' record,' explains Moloney. 'We recorded it in the tiny Landsdowne Studio in Dublin and we had to stop recording every now and again because someone would be demonstrating electric guitars downstairs. It was difficult. Whenever a motorbike or a lorry went by the wall would start to shake. It was really incredible that we got the whole album recorded in a week, but with expert Brian Masterson we got through it.'

Polig Monjarret attended the recording sessions and taught Kevin Conneff the song *Ev Chistr 'ta, Laou!* and his daughter Nolwyenn can be heard singing the hauntingly beautiful *A Breton Carol*, which she would later perform live on The Chieftains' Christmas album *The Bells of Dublin*.

To add to the authenticity of the record Moloney invited Breton dancers and musicians to come to Kerry and recreate a wild Breton party in a local ballroom. The result was the highly infectious *Dans Bro-Leon*, which features the memorable chorus, 'And it is not nice Jack, to stuff yourself so much (with food and drink).'

Moloney, who at the time was shopping around for a new record deal for The Chieftains, says that *Celtic Wedding* was the album that persuaded the German multi-national record company BMG to sign the group to a world deal on its prestigious RCA Victor Red Seal label (whose US president was Michael Emerson the ex-manager of James Galway).

'It was that album that sold us to BMG,' says Moloney. 'They loved it and they decided they were going to sign the band.'

To celebrate the release of *Celtic Wedding*, The Chieftains went on a two-week tour of Brittany with a hundred Breton musicians, dancers and singers. Driving around in a large bus, the tour, sponsored by Brittany Ferries became more of a travelling musical party.

'I kept asking my dear friend Polig for an itinerary,' explains Moloney, 'as we always like to leave information with our families. Eventually he sent me this so-called itinerary which had no hotel information. All it said was: '11:00 a.m. leave hotel; 12:00 p.m. restaurant; 3:00 p.m. finish lunch; 5:00 p.m. champagne reception; 6:00 p.m. sound check; Dinner 7:00 p.m. to 9:00 p.m.; concert 9:30 p.m.'

'It was like a menu and it never said where we were going to be. All it mentioned was the great times we were going to have. In the end I just said one meal a day is enough, Polig.'

Sound engineer Brian Masterson remembers one particular concert on Mid-Summer's Day in a small village in the heart of the champagne region.

'The Chieftains were playing on the steps of this huge crumbling 14th century chateau,' says Masterson.

'It was an amazing concert and they were playing brilliantly. They played one encore and the crowd were going mad for another. They were really tired and they'd given a great concert so they weren't going back again.

'Then word came down to The Chieftains that these old French aristocrats who owned the chateau would throw us a champagne reception in the chateau if we did another encore. So wham, The Chieftains are back on stage.'

After the show The Chieftains climbed up the ancient stone steps to the chateau to find a glorious banquet laid out for them on long trestled tables.

'That night was just amazing,' recalls Masterson. 'There was all this lovely food and champagnes and wines like we'd never tasted. And then of course out came the instruments again. These guy just never stop. I don't know how they do it but they do.'

* * *

That Christmas Burgess Meredith was the special guest at The Chieftains' *Traditional Irish Christmas Show* at the Brooklyn Center for the Performing Arts.

'It's going to be a real cracker,' Moloney told *The New York Daily*

News in a media blitz organized by Charlie Comer which helped sell out the tour.

The veteran film star was delighted to be joining The Chieftains on stage for the first time and decided to recite a verse called *The Elegant Wino* against a backdrop of Chieftains' music.

'When Paddy told me about this I agreed to do it,' said Meredith. 'The main thing was to have a good time.'

In addition to the actor, Moloney had arranged for world champion step dancer Michael Flatley to lead a locally based dancing troupe dressed up as straw boys and girls and a choir of carol singers from Queens.

'A Chieftains' concert can never be called dull,' noted *Irish Echo* reviewer Leonard Doyle. 'The six members of The Chieftains, each in his own inimitable way contributed to the special Christmas flavour of the evening. Paddy Moloney, the driving force behind The Chieftains, rightfully believes that the presence of dancers, and other entertainers on the stage, with the group, brings a fullness to their concerts.'

A few months later Burgess Meredith brought Moloney to film director John Huston's 80th birthday party at his house in Los Angeles. The director, who was nearing the end of his life, was then hard at work on his final film *The Dead*, starring his daughter Anjelica and scripted by his son Tony.

'Burgess and I went and knocked on the door,' remembers Moloney. 'We could hear John inside speaking very loudly. He was full of beans and he was giving instructions. We decided to let him cool down for ten minutes and then we came back and knocked on the door again. This time it opened.'

Moloney and Meredith went in and found the craggy-faced director of such classics as *The African Queen* and *The Treasure of the Sierra Madre* in excellent spirits.

'I played him Happy Birthday on my tin whistle,' says Moloney. 'And then I played him a slow air called *An Chuilfhionn* and a big tear came down from his eye. I remember that so well. That was the last time I ever saw John and he died a year later.'

*   *   *

At the dawn of 1986 Paddy Moloney embarked on the next phase of the development of The Chieftains where they would collaborate with the world's leading pop and classical musicians. Their first full musical collaboration with James Galway was made possible when The Chieftains changed record labels from Columbia to RCA.

'I had fairly good ideas for the album,' said Paddy, 'and with James Galway's manager Michael Emerson chipping in with some tunes, we were back in Windmill Lane Studio in January 1986. We had been talking about doing an album for about three years and when it finally came together I knew there would be some difficulties.

'If you're doing a Chieftains' album you can get stuck in. As you know the capabilities of each musician so you won't be asking for the impossible. This was the first time I'd come together with a major artist like James and had to sort out a lot of problems. But there was a great sense of humour about the whole thing. And it did turn out to be a great record.'

The musical interaction between Galway and The Chieftains was captured by a BBC-TV crew for a documentary and video on the making of the album. In the studio there was a warmth and rapport between the musicians as they honed each piece to perfection before it was recorded.

Musically Galway's golden flute added a new texture to The Chieftains' music and his duets with Matt Molloy were a delight.

'I enjoyed playing with Jimmy Galway but that's maybe because I'm a flute player,' says Molloy. 'He's very easy to work with and a pleasure. He's a man to be around after-hours. Oh yeah.'

As The Chieftains and Galway got down to work they got into a rhythm and recorded the tracks for the album in under a week.

'Well we were always working on getting things better,' says Galway. 'The rehearsals, when we actually got down to them, were very professional. Well organized and of course with a sense of humour. Something that the boys don't lose. It's built in.'

During the week of the sessions Galway and The Chieftains traveled to Belfast to record a concert at the Grand Opera House to be included on the video. The highlight of the performance was a stunning set of Carolan music including *Fanny Power, Mabel Kelly* and the inimitable *Carolan's Concerto*.

'What I like about The Chieftains is their integrated style,' says Galway. 'They're like an old music group who play baroque music. Well, they play with the same dedication.'

Seán Keane believes that The Chieftains' collaboration with Galway was a major step forward in the group's development.

'That project was a milestone for us,' says Keane. 'Jimmy Galway is a very professional musician.'

Eighteen months later Galway went out on a US tour with The Chieftains to promote the release of their album *James Galway and The Chieftains In Ireland* when their appearance together at the Hollywood Bowl was declared a triumph by *Variety*.

Wrote *Variety*: 'Celtic traditionalists The Chieftains and classical flutist James Galway, two of Ireland's best-known musical exports, joined forces at the Hollywood Bowl recently, delighting a capacity crowd with a soulful, evocative program of old Irish jigs, reels and airs.

'Galway, one of the world's greatest classical players, blended beautifully with the group, participating more as a kind of seventh Chieftain than a featured soloist.'

At the Aspen concert Galway decided to play a practical joke on Paddy Moloney on stage.

Remembers Galway: 'My son Patrick was with me and he had bought a plastic hand in a joke shop in New York. So when Paddy was announcing the air we were going to do called *Give me Your Hand* I reached over and shook hands with him. Only I had the plastic hand which I let go. He literally took my hand away. It was so funny. I thought Paddy was going to fall down dead laughing.'

Galway remembers the tour as being very subdued with very little socializing after concerts.

'There wasn't a lot of the partying which people seem to think goes with an Irish group,' he says. 'If you look at the tour schedule it's just murder. You can't indulge every night in wild parties and stay up all night for the crack of it. I mean you've got to realize that Derek Bell is a Buddhist and sometimes he and Paddy would take off to a Thai restaurant like a couple of old cronies. A couple of old Buddhists.'

21

Irish Heartbeat

Since his teens Derek Bell has studied Eastern mysticism and the Buddhist religion under many masters including Krishnamurti and Yogananda. The Chieftains' multi-instrumentalist believes in the power of music to counteract evil and tries to spend at least two and a half hours a day in meditation.

'Before I took human form I had eight million incarnations in plant and animal form,' declares Bell matter-of-factly. 'That's an average for what everybody has. It also takes about a million years of disease-free evolution before your magnetism is so magnetized that you can express Christ consciousness. It may take a good few more before you can express cosmic consciousness.'

The other Chieftains respect Derek's beliefs, although even they find his habit of changing ties according to ascending cosmic rays a little eccentric.

'It's the red ray today,' explains Bell, who is also a Druid, pointing to his bright red tie. 'It was violet yesterday and it'll be yellow tomorrow. Every day of the week has got a different planet and therefore a different colour and the eighth ray is the diamond Christ ray which is in force every day or we'd be gone.'

Many of Bell's solo classical works have been directly influenced by his religious beliefs and he is widely read on the subject. So when Van Morrison began his own personal pilgrimage into the mystic, he turned to Derek Bell for guidance after hearing the Chieftain's recording of a waltz by the English occult composer Cyril Scott.

'At that time Van was deeply searching for an answer,' recalls Bell. 'A friend of his had threatened to commit suicide and for two years he'd done no work and just gone into his shell reading and studying theosophy; the Rosicrucians, Scientology. Every bloody thing he could think of.

'Van was very interested in my recording of Cyril Scott, who had written a treatise on how music could influence future history, and how all the great composers like Handel, Chopin and Schumann had done so. Van knew that I must be up to my neck in all this so we became friends.'

In September 1987 Morrison organized a conference at Loughborough University called *The Secret Heart of Music*, and invited Derek Bell to participate. The symposium, described in its catalogue as 'an exploration into the power of music to change consciousness', included lectures on such esoteric subjects as 'Music, Magic and Mysticism' and 'Music as a Force in Spiritual Development.' But Morrison, who has a notoriously short attention span, had soon moved on in his spiritual quest to become a born-again Christian.

'Van wanted teachings at the time but he didn't want to do any work,' explains Derek Bell. 'He was in a hurry. He wanted them now and if you didn't have them you could fuck off.'

The troubled singer was also trying to reconcile his Celtic roots to his unique vision of blues and soul music. Having already touched upon traditional music on earlier records, Van decided that he wanted to pursue his Celtic roots further so in the autumn of 1987 he telephoned Paddy Moloney.

'Van called up from London and asked me to do an album,' remembers Moloney. 'In his brusque way he said, "Oh we'll meet. Yeah. Yeah. OK come and see me. Great. Will you come and see me?" I said, "Of course I will. I'll be over Saturday." '

Morrison had not realized that Moloney was in Dublin so when the Chieftain leader flew into London for the meeting he was surprised.

'Van couldn't believe it when I met him at the London Hilton,' says Moloney. "What, you came over all the way from Dublin?" '

Morrison then announced they would have lunch and Moloney, who was hoping for a good meal washed down with a bottle of wine, was somewhat disappointed when the singer took him to his favourite greasy cafe in Notting Hill Gate where he regularly breakfasted.

'He got stuck in,' says Moloney. 'Nobody came near him and that's why he went there because he wasn't pestered. Over lunch we had a bit of a chat about doing the album together. Not about the content but basically about just doing it and "that'll be great, that'll be terrific." There was great agreement between us.

'I think at that time Van was searching for his Irish roots. It was this man of blues, of rock 'n' roll, jazz and more importantly soul, coming home to his Irishness with The Chieftains and the music we'd been playing for so many years. Musically we were going to meet each other half way.'

As Van Morrison saw Moloney off in a taxi back to the airport he agreed to come to Dublin soon for further discussions on making the album.

'This was a very important transition time for The Chieftains,' says Moloney. 'We had done an album with James Galway, and I had played on a lot of people's albums, but I'd never done a full-blown collaboration as we would do with Van. This was very important in the field of popular music.'

A month later Morrison flew to Dublin to discuss the mechanics of making *Irish Heartbeat*. Collecting Van at Dublin Airport, Moloney drove him to Wicklow in his green Mercedes where he had booked him a room in the Roundwood Inn. Run by Moloney's friends Jürgen and Áine, the Roundwood Inn is a favourite haunt of the Wicklow set which includes film directors Jim Sheridan and John Boorman, Garech Browne and actor John Hurt.

When Moloney arrived at the Roundwood Inn the following morning to collect Van he was told that the singer had eaten breakfast and was upstairs taking a shower.

Remembers Moloney: 'When I went upstairs Van was screaming that he couldn't get the hot water to work. I said, "Oh my God." And I went to get help. Then Jürgen came running upstairs. "What's the matter Mr Morrison? What's wrong?" Van screamed out, "Well, I can't get the hot water to work."

'So Jürgen tells him to try the red tap. "Oh yeah. It's OK now. It's OK." '

Highly relieved that everything was all right, Moloney and Áine went downstairs for a coffee to let Morrison take a shower and get dressed. But their peace was short-lived when suddenly there was loud banging coming from the ceiling.

'We went back upstairs and Van was screaming, "I'm locked in the bathroom. I can't get out." Oh Jesus almighty. So we tried everything to open the door without success. Then Áine said, "But Mr Morrison, why did you lock the bathroom because there's no one up there but yourself?"

' "I had to lock it. I had to have a shower. I couldn't leave the bloody thing open." Then she asked him what he had locked it with. "The bedroom key."

'We tried everything to open that door and all through this Van was getting more frustrated,' laughs Moloney.

Half an hour later, after failing to find a locksmith who made home calls, Jürgen finally resorted to bashing in the door with a crowbar.

'And out came the boyo with his wet hair pulled across this way, and wanders back into his bedroom smiling,' says Moloney. 'We later found out that he could easily have opened the door if he'd only used the little latch. I was mortified.'

An hour later Morrison was in decidedly better spirits when he and Moloney left for the drive to Dublin.

'We were walking along the street when I suddenly started to break up laughing,' says Moloney. 'I mean what else could you do but laugh? And then Van went into convulsions. He was falling around all over the place laughing, it was incredible. I've never seen Van laugh like that before.'

After the bathroom incident all the tension between Moloney and Morrison disappeared as they both relaxed and got to know each other.

'It was a friendship and trust,' says Moloney. 'Very important to him I think is trust. But I doubt it was the other way around. But until we got that album finished that's the way it was. It was good and I think it was a great album.

'Van was at a funny stage in his career. I just felt that he was going through something. And he would drink pots of coffee and that was it. No alcohol, smoking, whatever.'

For the rest of the day the two musicians walked around Dublin deep in conversation, eventually winding up at St Stephen's Green.

'We talked and talked,' says the piper. 'Most of it had nothing to do with Irish music or songs or whatever. And then he said we'd do the album. He'd do this. We'd do that. No you do that with The Chieftains. No that doesn't suit me. Then we hit on a programme and fixed up to go into the studio.'

At the end of 1987 Paddy Moloney, who was to co-produce and arrange the music, called two rehearsal sessions at the Clarence Hotel. Morrison turned up for the second one but left after an hour. Earlier it had been agreed that the album would be called *Irish Heartbeat*, named after one of Van's compositions on his album,

Inarticulate Speech of the Heart. It would consist of seven traditional tunes, one Scottish one and two of Morrison's own. The superstar also used his clout to insist that the album come out on his Polygram Record label.

In January 1988 Van Morrison went into the Windmill Lane Studios with The Chieftains to start work on *Irish Heartbeat*. In preparation for the sessions Moloney found Morrison a set of drums, which he wanted to play on *Raglan Road* and the bassist of Clannad, Cíaran Ó Braonain was recruited to play on a number of tracks.

With the exception of Derek Bell and Paddy Moloney, who by now had had Morrison over to his house in Annamoe for one of Rita's delicious curries, none of the other Chieftains knew much about Van Morrison. And there was much speculation about how well the two factions would gel.

'It was strange to begin with,' says Seán Keane. 'But we weren't phased out as many people had expected us to be. Maybe the fact that I didn't know much about the man helped. I'd never met him. I'd just heard him on the radio. My eldest son was crazy about him. Knew every note Van ever recorded.'

Morrison's genius was immediately apparent to all in the studio. Effortlessly pulling inspiration out from the depths of his soul, the Belfast singer was in top form delivering his trademark scat phrasing to perfection. It was an ideal musical marriage.

'I admired the fact that Van just goes in and does it,' says Conneff. 'There's no fiddling around with trying things out or whatever. If it went past take three he would lose interest. He'd say, "You're wasting your time. Go onto something else. And if you do a hundred takes you'll go back and find that take one or two is the best. So why waste time? Get on to something else."

'And I like that. OK, there may be a few skidmarks or a few bumps or maybe a knock on the microphone but what the hell. You're not in a glass case.'

Moloney admits that a couple of planned tracks didn't work out and had to be dropped but says he and Van Morrison were delighted with the results.

'He rang me up one night and left a message on my answering machine,' says Moloney. ' "Great shapes, Paddy. Wonderful shapes. It's great. It's going to work." Van was very happy.

'He's such a musician. When he'd go off into one of his cadenzas at the end of a song, it would be like he'd entered a world of his own.'

Even Derek Bell, usually restrained in his musical praise, loves *Irish Heartbeat* and says he has no time for the purists who disliked it.

'It's a classic,' says Bell. 'An absolute classic. In a sense from the purist's folk point of view it's grotesque, to put it at its most kind. Some critics didn't think the collaboration came off at all.

'I mean no purist is going to sing things like *She Moved Through the Fair* repeating "Our wedding day" three times. That's an element of soul music. The repetition and jazz-like style of words for the sake of emphasis. That belongs to soul. It has nothing to do with our tradition at all.

'What Van does with *My Lagan Love* is even more grotesque. He virtually makes a Hindu chant out of it in the last note. And the folkies don't like it.'

*   *   *

A month later Van Morrison helped The Chieftains officially celebrate their milestone 25th anniversary in Dublin. The singer agreed to make a rare television appearance on a special edition of RTE's *The Late Late Show's Tribute to The Chieftains* and play live with the group.

The day before the programme was recorded Paddy Moloney was honoured by Trinity College who awarded him a doctorate of music. Morrison and the other Chieftains attended the ceremony at Trinity where Moloney, wearing a flowing academic black gown and cap, received his doctorate. And after the award a celebratory party for Moloney went on late into the night.

Morrison was in great form the following night for the tribute to The Chieftains recorded at the RTE television studios in Dublin. Introduced by Irish television talk show host Gay Byrne, the often emotional two-hour show was virtually a Chieftains' *This is Your Life*, with assorted friends and family reminiscencing about the group.

In his introduction Byrne called The Chieftains 'one of the grandest little bands in the world' and congratulated them on their 25th anniversary and their unwavering devotion to traditional music.

Then, turning to Paddy Moloney, who was sitting with the rest of The Chieftains around him in a half circle, Byrne began, 'Good evening to you doctor. It has been said of you, doctor, that you operate constantly non-stop like a man with a mission and little time to complete it. Why?

'It's mainly the money,' joked Byrne prompting howls from the audience, to which Moloney conceded, 'You have to keep the pot boiling anyway. We rate music first; places and people we play for second and then the few bob that may roll in. That's our priorities.'

Among the guests who played musical tribute to The Chieftains were The Dublin City Ballet, Mary Black, Dolores Keane, Christy Moore and Van Morrison. During the show Byrne read out congratulatory telegrams from Jackson Browne, Paul McCartney and Art Garfunkel.

And the real sense of family was strengthened even further when Martin Fay's wife Gráinne McCormack, a former world champion step dancer, led their son Feargal and daughter Dervla in a breathtaking demonstration of Irish dancing.

For the show's finale a smiling Van Morrison brought his guitar up on stage to lead a rousing session of *Star of the County Down*, which he had just recorded with The Chieftains.

* * *

Yet the honeymoon between Van Morrison and The Chieftains would be short-lived when they embarked on a month-long European tour together in Aberdeen on April 30th. The sometimes temperamental singer disliked touring and it did not take The Chieftains long to learn that being around Van was like walking on egg shells.

'There were some almost unpleasant instances on tour with Van,' remembers Kevin Conneff. 'There were times where he would get into a mood, usually alcohol was involved, and I didn't want to be near him. He could be quite unpleasant. He was never particularly unpleasant to me but you could get this vibe around him that things were not quite right for him so everybody around him had to suffer. That happened once or twice on tour.'

In spite of his eruptions, by the time the tour had reached London in mid-May the music was transcendent with *Melody Maker* going as far as declaring it a life-altering experience.

'You have just watched genius culminate, pass the utmost. A wondrous sight,' said the music paper.

On stage Morrison appeared relaxed as he cracked jokes with Paddy Moloney and laughed at Derek Bell's stage antics.

Kevin Conneff sees similarities between Morrison and a lot of traditional musicians whose personality traits may leave a lot to be desired, but are ultimately forgiven because of their brilliance as musicians.

Says Conneff: 'I found Van a very curious person coming obviously from a Protestant background in Belfast but singing in such a broad scope of understanding. And yet one wondered, in as much as one got to know him, how he had that broader understanding because he stayed very much in a box to himself. He didn't really socialize. But he obviously has a pair of eyes and a pair of ears that are very sensitive and he certainly has soul.'

When the tour reached the Dutch capital of The Hague a young teenage fan called Joanie turned up at the stage door with her collection of Chieftain records.

'This wee girl came backstage during the sound-check and she wanted us to sign her albums,' remembers Moloney. 'She didn't have a ticket as it was sold out so I told her to come backstage and I'd get her in. She came in before the concert started and I introduced her to the band. Once she met Kevin it was pop goes the weasel.'

The following week when the tour played Rotterdam, Joanie returned and went backstage after the show where she renewed her acquaintance with Kevin Conneff. They had a lot to talk about. An art student in The Hague, Joanie loved Ireland and Celtic culture and her dream was to study at Trinity College, Dublin.

Four months later Joanie happened to be London doing some art research when she saw a poster for the upcoming Van Morrison and The Chieftains' concert at the Royal Albert Hall and went along.

'After the show Joanie came to the stage door,' says Conneff. 'Our tour manager Mick O'Gorman recognized her and brought her backstage. And that was it really.'

The two fell deeply in love and Joanie came to Ireland for two week-long visits before they got married.

'Me, I thought I was going to be the bachelor and now suddenly I'm very much a family man and a home man,' jokes Conneff who now has a seven-year-old daughter Pegí and a three-year-old son Ruari.

* * *

When *Irish Heartbeat* was released in the summer of 1988 Paddy Moloney, a strong believer in the value of good publicity, wanted Van Morrison to promote the record. Morrison, who harbours an intense dislike for journalists and shies away from interviews, was not enthusiastic.

Remembers Moloney. 'I was saying to Van, "Look, when are we going to advertise the album? People will want to know about it." We had these arguments about it . . . "Jeez, we're making this record but if you're not going to publicize it." '

Eventually Moloney persuaded Van to spend a day with him at the Aer Lingus-owned Tara Hotel in London, where he always stayed, meeting journalists in the lounge to promote the album. Unfortunately Morrison was uncooperative and to Moloney's embarrassment made each writer run the gauntlet.

'I could see there was a glint in Van's eye,' says Moloney. 'I figured that he'd obviously made up his mind that this wasn't going to happen. And I'd come all the way over from Dublin to do it.'

The first writer up was Liam Mackey from Dublin's *Hot Press* who was immediately accused of dirt-digging by Morrison.

'I tried to open things up and talk about the album,' remembers Moloney. 'When he was asked how this song came about, Van started to get angry. "Well, what are you after? It's obvious how the bloody thing happened. There's no point in asking." Only Van was using slightly stronger language. So bang, that was the end of that fellow.'

As each journalist came up to the crease to bowl questions, Morrison would attack each in turn and actually seemed to be enjoying himself as he either feigned boredom or ripped into the poor writers.

'I thought, there goes two opportunities down the drain,' sighs Moloney. 'There was only one newspaper who eventually got any kind of hearing. Well he can be very very difficult with interviews. He says he's been misquoted so many times so I don't blame him. Van's attitude is, "Look, there's my music. Just listen to it. What do you want to talk to me for?" There's an awful lot of sense in what he's saying.'

Derek Bell says Paddy's love/hate relationship with Van Morrison came to a head later that summer when tempers flared on their European tour.

'Well it went along very nicely at first until we had some real differences,' says Bell. 'Then it was very prickly for the rest of the time. But I think that's fairly common with Van.'

The incident Bell referred to happened in a Copenhagen hotel when Moloney and Morrison got into a little wine-throwing disagreement.

'It was basically just the culmination of a bit of tour fever,' Paddy later told *Irish Independent* writer George Byrne.

'You know yourself, a group of people sitting around in a hotel after a show, a certain type of conversation starts up, there's a bit of drink involved and before you know where you are there's glasses of wine being thrown. I honestly thought that would have been the last of working with Van but I got a call about three or four months later asking if we'd do a couple of shows with him and that put things back on track.'

Derek Bell says that Morrison's on-stage sensitivity is often mistaken for him being difficult.

'If he plays some concerts and one of the audience shouts, "Boo" at him, he has been known to turn his back on the audience for the next four numbers. And if somebody says "Boo" again, he's been known to walk off home and let the band finish the concert without him. So I don't think that's difficult. I think if the audience is out to be insulting, I can quite understand that he can be easily insulted.'

* * *

The release of *Irish Heartbeat* in August 1988 catapulted The Chieftains into the realm of rock stars. Acclaimed by the critics, the collaboration with Van Morrison introduced the traditional group to a new audience as well as bringing them to the attention of other musicians who also decided they wanted to integrate The Chieftains' sound into their records. The Chieftains even ventured into the world of cartoons by doing the music for children's story *The Tailor of Gloucester*, which was narrated by Meryl Streep.

'I got my meows in for Simpkins the Cat,' says Moloney proudly. 'That was great fun.'

Rolling Stone magazine was ecstatic about *Irish Heartbeat* and applauded The Chieftains for rejuvenating Van Morrison's career.

'It would be hard to imagine a more natural merger of pop and folk than this collaboration between Van Morrison and Ireland's pre-eminent old-wave traditional band, The Chieftains,' wrote reviewer David Browne.

'Yet even those expectations don't prepare one for the splendor and intense beauty of *Irish Heartbeat*, a collection of ballads that finds both acts at the top of their form.

'Never hokey and always affecting, *Irish Heartbeat* taps into the melancholy, deeply spiritual side of the Irish heritage.'

22

A Chieftains' Celebration

In July 1988 Dublin celebrated its millennium and Paddy Moloney wanted The Chieftains to play a major part in the celebrations. A year earlier he had approached the Dublin Millennium Committee with a corporate sponsor and offered to organize a Celtic week to help mark the occasion. But there was so much red tape involved that his plans had fallen through.

Refusing to give up Moloney went ahead and composed his own *Millennium Celtic Suite* and booked the Gaiety Theatre for its premiere, which was to be recorded live for the upcoming *A Chieftains' Celebration* album. But tragedy struck the day before the first show when he had a head-on collision as he was driving his green Mercedes into Dublin.

'It was a massive crash,' remembers Moloney. 'I skidded right across the road into somebody. It was terrible.'

Moloney was rushed to hospital where he was treated for injuries to his rib cage and leg but insisted on going to the Gaiety Theatre for rehearsals. 'I was assisted on-stage each night and suffered great pain. But the show had to go on – there were Galicians and Bretons there, and Gabriel Byrne was M.C.

'But when I crashed I did it right,' chuckled the piper. 'They wrote the car off but I wouldn't let them. I had got the left-hand drive car which belonged to the Iranian ambassador before he was recalled in 1986. It only had 25,000 miles on the clock at the time. I made the insurance company rebuild the whole car.'

A Chieftains' Celebration, the group's 20th album, featured an array of special guests including Van Morrison, performing his *Boffyflow and Spike* instrumental, and Nashville singer Nanci Griffith, making her first appearance with The Chieftains. A long-time fan of the traditional group, the country singer was staying in a Dublin hotel on a tour when she was told that Paddy Moloney was waiting for her downstairs in the lobby.

Remembers Nanci: 'I thought, "Wow, Paddy Moloney from The Chieftains. Why would he want to talk to me?" And I went down and Paddy said he was in the middle of an album and wanted me to sing this 16th century Christmas Carol. Would I be willing to come into the studio and sing on this?

'And I thought I was going to be singing harmony. I didn't have a clue that Paddy wanted me to come in and make it a Nanci Griffith vocal. I was honoured.'

The next day Griffith went into Windmill Studios and laid down *The Wexford Carol* in just two takes.

'I remember Paddy said, "OK, here's your part" and I was overwhelmed. I think we maybe spent half an hour at the most recording it. It just went that fast.'

All the Chieftains had a hand in arranging different tracks of the *Celebration* album. Kevin Conneff arranged the drinking song *Here's a Health to The Company*, which he performed a cappella with the rest of The Chieftains joining in on the chorus. Matt Molloy came up with the hauntingly beautiful *The Strayaway Child*. Seán Keane delivered a rousing medley of Scottish dance tunes called *The Iron Man* and Martin brought his beautifully sensitive feel to an air called *Gaftaí Baile Buí*.

But the major work on the album was the live version of Moloney's *Millennium Celtic Suite*, featuring The Chieftains on stage during their week-long *Celtic Celebration* at the Gaiety Theatre. For the special shows The Chieftains appeared with an assortment of Celtic musicians, dancers and singers from Brittany and Galicia.

During their week of Dublin concerts The Chieftains also found time to make a guest appearance on a new album by the chart-topping English rock group Ultravox, who were best known for the chart-topping single *Vienna*.

'I came up with the song *All Fall Down* which was a very Celtic kind of protest song,' explains Ultravox's leader Midge Ure. 'It screamed for some Celtic playing and the idea of Ultravox, the so-called kings of the synthesizer, collaborating with The Chieftains, the kings of the non-synthesizer, appealed to my sense of humour.'

Ultravox flew into Dublin for a day's recording with The Chieftains at Windmill Lane Studios but when the traditional musicians arrived some of them appeared a little the worse for wear.

'I think they turned up with a serious combined hangover,' remembers Ure. 'Paddy came in as fresh and bright as a daisy and went straight into the control room but the rest of the guys went straight into the backroom and crashed out in various states.'

For the next couple of hours Moloney talked through the song with Ure and together they worked out the different parts.

'Paddy had it all down in his head by the time he got the rest of the guys in and sat them down,' says Ure. 'He told them exactly what he wanted them to do and everyone just kind of created their own parts. The fuzziness seemed to be slipping away and they were all getting into it. It's just a natural organic thing for them. It's in the blood.'

A few weeks later The Chieftains flew to London to appear in the video for *All Fall Down*, which was directed by the prize-winning video team of Kevin Godley and Lol Creme. The gory apocalyptic video featured The Chieftains performing with Ultravox. During the song people start dropping dead with their blood eventually forming a map of the world. Unfortunately the record flopped and the video was never shown.

On August 1 Paddy Moloney celebrated his 50th birthday while in Brittany. When Pádraic Larkin, owner of the Galway Inn in Lorient, heard of this, he insisted on throwing Moloney a party he'd never forget.

'The owner had lined up 50 pints of Guinness on the bar,' laughs the Chieftain. 'I had about five of them during the course of the evening, and fortunately some other people came by to help me with the rest of them, mostly musicians, of course, which led to a wonderful music session. I never had such a fantastic birthday.'

* * *

In January 1989 The Chieftains were appointed official musical ambassadors to Ireland. It was the highest honour ever accorded to a group of musicians by any government and they were given an official mission to promote Irish tourism at their concerts abroad. At a special presentation the six Chieftains and Charles Comer, who had become almost a seventh member of the band, were given special leather briefcases with the words 'Ambassador for Ireland' embossed on them in gold.

'When people ask us about our music we tell them about Ireland,'

Paddy Moloney told journalists at a reception at the Irish Tourism headquarters. A few days later a pinstriped Kevin Conneff also made the papers with a party at the Guinness Brewery to celebrate the release of his first solo album, *The Week Before Easter*.

In February The Chieftains celebrated the 250th anniversary of the great Irish harper Turlough O' Carolan by teaming up with a 26-piece harp orchestra for a joint celebratory show at Dublin's National Concert Hall, part of which was recorded for the album *Celtic Harp*.

At the beginning of March The Chieftains flew to the States to begin an exhaustive 34 city tour which would culminate in their annual St Patrick's Day concert at Carnegie Hall with a special guest appearance by actor Richard Harris. Jean Butler, still only 18, made her first solo appearance. When they arrived in the States, New York-based Charles Comer launched them on a tidal wave of publicity highlighting the two Grammy nominations for *Celtic Wedding* and *Irish Heartbeat*. But it would be another three years before The Chieftains would finally win a Grammy at their sixth attempt.

At Carnegie Hall Richard Harris knelt on the stage, looking like a medieval preacher with his long white hair and flowing robes, as he sang Irish songs with The Chieftains and recited some of his favourite stories. He later joined The Chieftains for their traditional St Patrick's Day celebration party at Eamonn Doran's bar on Second Avenue in Manhattan.

'The Chieftains have been coming here every St Patrick's Day since we opened,' says Doran, whose birthday happens to fall on the day after St Patrick's Day.

'It's become a tradition that Paddy will get out his tin whistle as soon as he walks into the bar and play me Happy Birthday. A few years ago it was very crowded and there was all sorts of stuff going on with people singing. And the next thing was Paddy let out a roar. "Will you shut that thing up. I want to play Eamonn Happy Birthday." Everybody got a big kick out of that.'

In May Matt Molloy became a publican himself, realizing a long-held ambition to open his own bar and make it a haven for traditional music. Molloy and his wife Geraldine, who had no previous experience of the pub business, bought a 19th century pub and grocer's shop on Bridge Street in the centre of Westport. Retaining the original frontage and fixtures of the shop, which has a preservation order on it, Matt converted it into what it is today – Matt Molloy's.

'I finally decided to exploit the bald head and the beard,' laughs Matt. 'I suppose that I'm reasonably well known in the traditional music scene and I thought there was a need for a place where musicians can meet up and play together.'

Christy Hyland, who is a garda in Westport, says there was much excitement when the locals heard a Chieftain was moving into town.

'We were all waiting to see what Matt Molloy was going to do,' says Hyland, who has since become good friends with the flute player. 'Since he bought the pub it has greatly enhanced the commerce and social profile of the town.'

All The Chieftains loyally travelled to Westport, Co. Mayo for the official opening of Matt Molloy's on May 17th where they gave a special open-air performance on a flat roof overlooking the back of the pub.

'They were supposed to play inside but there was so many people it was crazy,' says Mags Staunton, who now runs The Killary House Bed and Breakfast. Paddy was officially appointed to open the bar, but after cutting the ribbon was unable to get inside. So Matt loyally passed a pint through the back window.

Paddy Moloney still makes it a point to mention Matt Molloy's at all Chieftains' concerts and fans come from around the world to sample, what Matt boasts is, the best pint of Guinness in Ireland.

'Matt's name attracts customers from all over the place,' says Geraldine, who used to work 60 hours a week behind the bar during the first couple of years. 'I'm very proud of Matt and that his music has spread so far.'

A month later in Dublin Paddy Moloney was mobbed by fans when he gave an impromptu concert on his pipes in Grafton Street to promote *A Chieftains' Celebration*.

'The crowd is getting younger all the time,' quipped the beaming piper to a Dublin evening newspaper. 'They seem to be impressed by the fact that we've played with so many famous people.'

In an enthusiastic review in *Folk Roots*, Colin Irwin wrote that although the group could easily be resting on their laurels after a triumphant collaboration with Van Morrison. the new album was 'positively inspired'.

Wrote Irwin: 'Martin Fay still looks like a kindly undertaker and

Derek Bell still looks like the nutter on the bus. The most wretched sleeves known to mankind and the most divine music. The anomaly is that the older they get the more intent they become on creating ever more complex and stimulating patterns, and pushing back those musical barriers just that little bit further.'

On June 20th The Chieftains were officially honoured for their contribution to traditional music by the Lord Mayor of Dublin, Ben Briscoe at a ceremony at the Mansion House.

In his address the Lord Mayor presented the group with Waterford Crystal and a sculpture, saying: 'We are extremely fortunate that our traditional music has been taken into the custody of The Chieftains.'

* * *

In January 1990 The Chieftains began their second major collaboration with James Galway. As his next step in his exploration of Celtic music Moloney focused on Scotland to record an album with Galway of Scottish and Irish tunes he called *Over The Sea to Skye – The Celtic Connection.*

'Do you realize we're only 14 miles apart,' pointed out Moloney. 'That's how far Fair Head in Antrim is from the Mull of Kintyre.'

After the success of their first joint album, James Galway flew to Australia with The Chieftains to tour and a new album was recorded live at the Queensland Performing Arts Center in Brisbane and completed at the Studios 301 in Sydney.

Their Australian tour was a sell-out and Galway says that The Chieftains and other Irish artists have a loyal audience wherever they play.

'There's an awful lot of Irish scattered around the world you know,' notes Galway. 'People think the British were a great colonizer but in fact the Irish were even better and they did it peacefully too. I mean any big town you go to that has been colonized by the British you will see some street named after an Irish hero like Michael Collins. There's just millions of Irish people all over the place so there you've got an audience.'

Over the Sea to Skye features a marvellous duet between Galway and Matt Molloy in the stirringly beautiful *Dark Ireland.*

'It's a success because Matt plays the first flute and I play second to him,' says Galway. 'So that works out.'

As on *Celebration* all The Chieftains, with the exception of Kevin Conneff, did arrangements with Martin Fay doing a rare composition for his piece *A Fanfare*.

The final track *Solo Salute* gets increasingly rowdy as each member of The Chieftains in turn struts their musical stuff, with Derek Bell playing his patented Scott Joplin rags that have endeared him to audiences the world over.

To celebrate the June release of the album, The Chieftains and Galway did an extensive tour of Ireland and Great Britain in support.

'Far from hogging the limelight, Galway takes a seat with the group, coming forward occasionally to shine with his flute,' wrote reviewer Pete Clark who saw the show at the Fairfield Halls in Croydon.

'There are times when rock 'n' roll just will not do and this was one.'

That spring Paddy Moloney was commissioned to write the music for a new version of *Treasure Island* starring Charlton Heston and Oliver Reed. He was given just ten days' notice before he had to go into the studio with The Chieftains and a 36-piece orchestra to record the completed score.

'It was madness,' says Moloney. 'At one stage we fell out with the production team during the filming of the cable TV movie. I had to come up with 72 different cuts of music in ten days. Some of them were done in the studio. I'd be thinking about them the night before and just go in and do them.

'There was a short cut with tin whistle and tiompán and it turned out to be a super little piece. Often little things like that can turn out better than the ones you might be working on strenuously for weeks. You might come up with something, BANG. That's what I want. And it just happens like that.'

Treasure Island also marked the beginning of Moloney's on-going collaboration with the young Galician piper Carlos Nunez, who was brought in to play on the recording. As a young boy growing up in the ancient port of Vigo, in the South of Galicia, Nunez had idolized The Chieftains. He began playing the Galician pipes, which are similar to the Scottish bagpipes, when he was eight and bought all The Chieftains' albums.

'I copied a lot of things from Paddy when I was learning as a child,' says Carlos. 'I looked up to him. He was my musical hero.'

When Carlos was 13 he telephoned Moloney in Dublin to tell him how much he admired his style of piping.

'I said Mr Moloney I like your music,' recalls Carlos. 'You are a real piper.'

Three years later Carlos finally met his hero when The Chieftains paid a visit to the conservatory of music where he was studying in France during the Lorient Festival.

'It was Paddy's birthday and my teacher asked me to play him some Galician music,' remembers Carlos, who was then 16.

'It was a big responsibility and I was very shy but Paddy seemed to like my playing.'

Soon afterwards The Chieftains played at an open-air music festival in Galicia and Carlos went backstage before the concert to say hello. Moloney was delighted to see him and immediately asked him if he wanted to join the group on stage and play a tune.

'This was my dream,' says Carlos. 'I only had five minutes to learn the tune but I improvised and it was one of the biggest thrills of my life to play live with The Chieftains.'

When Moloney decided to feature Galician pipes on his score for *Treasure Island* he remembered the Galician teenager and invited him to Dublin for the recording.

'That was my first serious experience with The Chieftains,' says Nunez, who has become almost a musical son to Moloney.

'This was the first time that anybody had ever used Galician pipes with a symphony orchestra for a big film.'

Moloney also incorporated an Australian didgeridoo into the music played by guitarist Steve Cooney. Cooney, who was unhappy about the tone of the ancient Aboriginal instrument, used a length of waving pipe to get the correct pitch.

American film critic Leonard Maltin would later single out Moloney's 'sea-worthy' musical contribution to *Treasure Island* success in his movie review in his best-selling *Movie and Video Guide*.

23

The Bells of Dublin

On November 9th, 1989 the world order changed dramatically when the Berlin Wall came down and Germany was unified for the first time in almost 50 years. As East met West in a head-on cultural collision anything seemed possible as Communism crumbled and history was made on a daily basis. Ex-Pink Floyd leader Roger Waters decided to celebrate the end of the Berlin Wall by performing his concept album *The Wall* by the Brandenburg Gate. To stage the superstar concert, which was to be broadcast live around the world and recorded for a double album, Waters recruited English rock entrepreneur Tony Hollingsworth and former Chieftains' manager Pete Smith. Now working for the London-based E.G. Management Smith was given the task of pulling together a high calibre guest list of performers.

'There was a need to have as cultural a mix as possible,' explains Smith. 'I literally just called a number that I had in my book from many years before and found Paddy Moloney.'

Although the July 21st concert fell in the middle of The Chieftains' summer holidays, Moloney immediately agreed to perform when he heard that other artists included Van Morrison, Marianne Faithfull, Sinéad O'Connor, Bryan Adams and James Galway.

Tony Hollingsworth had first met Moloney in the early 1980s when he hired The Chieftains to perform at the main stage at the Glastonbury Festival.

'He's a card is Paddy,' says Hollingsworth. 'A real character. I remember at Glastonbury there was some question about whether they needed to pay VAT or not. He would have been happier if I hadn't made him pay it.'

Hollingsworth was delighted to renew their friendship in the lavish backstage area and remembers Moloney being very gregarious and constantly entertaining the other artists with his tin whistle.

'There was everybody in the world backstage,' says Moloney, who had brought along Rita and Pádraig. 'That was a great get-together. A great session. And when I say backstage I don't mean for an hour or two. For an event it's usually two or three days and that's when you really get to know people and you get to talk.'

The Chieftains played the opening sequence to *The Wall* in front of a huge audience of 350,000. Afterwards the piper was having such a good time that he stayed on until the end.

'It was like a big happy family,' he remembers fondly. 'I didn't bother to leave for two days. The fact that we were there at the Wall was just fabulous.'

A few weeks after the concert Moloney telephoned Pete Smith and invited him to take a second shot at managing The Chieftains. Since the departure of Maurice Cassidy in 1983, Paddy Moloney had been at the management helm, barring a couple of years when his solicitor Joe Whitston had taken over temporarily, mainly working from his office.

At this point Moloney realized that The Chieftains needed a strong management push if they were to break through to greater success. When Smith took over, BMG were about to bring out a compilation of Moloney's film themes called *Reel Music*, but there were no new studio albums in production.

Smith then called a meeting in New York with Steve Vining of BMG Classics to analyse the situation. They both agreed that there was a particular phenomenon occurring with The Chieftains that could be utilized to great advantage.

With this in mind The Chieftains set off to make a conceptual Christmas record with universal appeal through a collection of popular guest artists. For the last three years Paddy Moloney had wanted to make a Chieftains' Christmas album since he met the singer Paul Anka in Los Angeles.

'We were talking and Paul was telling me about the show he does every Christmas,' says Moloney. 'I told him that we also did a Christmas show and so we decided to do one together. It seemed a brilliant idea. Then we came up with the idea of a Christmas album and it developed from there.'

Over the next year Moloney and Anka discussed the Christmas project by telephone but eventually it fell apart as their two schedules never met. When Moloney and Smith first took the idea of doing a celebrity Christmas album to BMG, the record company were not over-enthusiastic. But they finally agreed granting a limited budget for the record, to be called *The Bells of Dublin*.

'I was really impressed by Paddy's ability to put our ideas into action,' says Pete Smith. 'It was intriguing because I sat down with him and said I've thought about this record and it doesn't necessarily have to go against the integrity and tradition of everything The Chieftains stand for. Immediately Paddy came back with a musical plan for the record. He had everything that he was going to do laid out in his mind.'

Moloney decided to start and finish *The Bells of Dublin* using the bells from the 12th century Christchurch Cathedral in Dublin, which he fondly remembered from his childhood.

'It was always a great time around Christmas,' remembers Moloney. 'I loved to go into town to see Santa Claus and the carol singers all dressed up. Most of all I loved to hear the Christchurch bells.'

The 12 bells of Christchurch date back to 1738 with the largest, named 'The People's Bell' a full five foot three inches in diameter and weighing more than two and a half tons. Moloney realized that the logistics of recording the bells would be awesome so he decided to pay an evening reconnaissance visit. Leaving Rita in the car he went in to meet the bell ringers and discover how he could use the bells to best advantage.

'I went up into the belfry,' remembers Moloney. 'It was very scary especially because I'm scared of heights. You have to go out on the parapets overlooking the City of Dublin then go into this big room with bell ringing charts on the wall.'

Moloney got so carried away learning about ringing the bells that he forgot about Rita being in the car and stayed for two hours.

'She was none too pleased to be left waiting outside,' he says.

A few days later intrepid sound engineer Brian Masterson crawled out onto the roof of Christchurch and set up various microphones to record the majestic peels of the bells. For the recording Moloney joined the bell ringers in the belfry to play his part.

Explains Moloney: 'For my bell sequence at the beginning of the album I fade from the big bells of Christchurch into the small handheld bells and finally into Derek Bell, who's playing bells sounds on the tiompán.'

Moloney had a clear plan in his head when he started inviting his celebrity friends to be on the record.

'He wasn't shopping blind,' says Smith. 'We were going to particular artists because they suited the conceptual flow of the record.'

The artists who agreed to appear on *Bells of Dublin* were Elvis Costello, who had recently featured Derek Bell on his Celtic-flavoured *Spike* album, Ricky Lee Jones, Anna and Kate McGarrigle, Marianne Faithfull and Nanci Griffith.

American rocker Jackson Browne, who had last appeared with the group a decade earlier, was delighted when he got the call from Moloney.

'It's so prestigious to work with The Chieftains as they're a national treasure in Ireland,' explains Browne, who'd been asked by Moloney to select a carol to sing.

'As I began singing these Christmas carols I realized that it's one thing to sing a carol with your friends or to yourself, but it's quite another to perform it. There weren't too many Christmas carols that I wanted to do. I felt weird about it.'

The plan was to record Browne's contribution in the Topanga Skyline Studios in California during The Chieftains' US tour in May 1991. But with the session only days away Browne was worried as he still had not found a carol he felt happy with.

Finally the singer confided his dilemma to a friend during an intense conversation about religion.

Recalls Browne: 'He said, "Well, you're a songwriter, write one." Normally I go to great lengths to tell people that I can't do that but in this case I said, "Well, maybe I can."

'I just wrote this song *The Rebel Jesus* which came out very close to my innermost feelings about Christmas. It really is the only time in my year that my family comes together and that we remember our connection to one another. It always breaks my heart that the world is in the shape that it's in.'

Moloney loved Jackson's carol, which imagined how, if Jesus were alive today and could see the modern exploitation of Christmas, he would become an outlaw.

'The night before we went into the studio he said, "What do you think of these words I just tossed off?," ' says Moloney. 'I thought it was great and he was actually composing it the night before we recorded. It's totally different from all the other songs on the album. To me this is the new Christmas carol.'

While they were in the studio Moloney put together *Jackson's Jig* as a thank you to his friend but it was mysteriously misnamed *Skyline Jig* on the album.

The piper also recruited Burgess Meredith to recite the moving seventh-century Irish hymn, *Don Oiche Úd I mBeithil* or *One Night in Bethlehem*.

'I first heard it when my young son Pádraig sang it at midnight mass,' says Moloney. 'I thought, "Oh God, that's brilliant." '

Moloney had it translated by Seán Mac Réamoinn and Meredith came into the studio to recite it with a Chieftains' accompaniment.

'Luckily I didn't have to read it in Gaelic so I got away with it,' laughs Meredith. 'I think the integrity of that group is remarkable. The way they've held up the quality of their playing and singing. It's a very rare thing to see that in a group.'

After the recording they went straight to Venice Beach with a video crew to film the actor pretending to panhandle on the beach while Moloney played his tin whistle.

'Would you believe he collected $10,' says Paddy. 'He was a really good sport.'

While in Los Angeles Moloney also managed to recruit Rickie Lee Jones to lay down her own unique version of the carol *O Holy Night*, which at first some members of The Chieftains were doubtful about.

'I thought Rickie did a great job,' said Moloney. 'To me it was like going into the pub across the road on a Christmas Eve and somebody singing a carol after drinking a few ports.'

Back in Dublin, Moloney asked the iconoclastic Elvis Costello to do something for the album. The rock star agreed to write words to Moloney's music.

'Elvis reminds me of James Joyce since he's moved to Dublin,' declares the piper. 'I sent him an old cassette where I was banging out the music on a piano.'

The acerbic songwriter came up with lyrics for a tune called *The St Stephen's Day Murders* which in fact had nothing to do with killing.

'Anybody would think, "Ireland. Murders. Oh my God," ' says Moloney. 'It is about a typical family celebrating Christmas together in the old Dublin-style. Everything in the garden is sweet and rosy but things can get pretty hot around St Stephen's Day. Maybe there might be a bit of an old argument, a schimozzle, that could lead to a blow or two.'

When Marianne Faithfull came into the Windmill Studios to record one of her favourite childhood Christmas carols *I Saw Three Ships A Sailing*, she seemed very nervous. It was the first time that the singer, who now lived outside Dublin, had sung with Paddy since their impromptu performance at the Ritz Hotel in the early 1980s.

'Paddy was really great,' remembers Marianne. 'He told me, "Don't worry, stick with me, Marianne, and I'll make you into a star." And when I feel that I have become a star I will say, "Well, there you are Paddy, you did it." '

For the *Bells of Dublin* video Paddy Moloney rented out a country cottage near his home in Annamoe and invited his neighbours and the group of Strawboys and girl dancers, friends of Kevin's, to perform to the previously recorded 'Wren' medley, which was mimed by The Chieftains and Northumberland piper Kathryn Tickell.

'We reenacted the whole Wren celebration,' says Moloney.

When the *Bells of Dublin* was released in October it struck an immediate nerve with both critics and the public alike. *Rolling Stone* applauded the album, calling it 'Magnificent . . . exactly what you might expect from The Chieftains' and *People* magazine declared, 'It's a lovely collection. The Chieftains, a sextet that has been together 28 years, haven't compromised their style. They've just added some star power to help them deck the halls.'

By Christmas 1995 *The Bells of Dublin* had been certified gold selling 500,000 copies in America alone.

* * *

The weekend before leaving to perform at the Berlin Wall concert Paddy Moloney and Derek Bell had gone into a Belfast studio to record a couple of tracks for Van Morrison. Since *Irish Heartbeat*, Morrison and Bell had become great friends, with the singer always visiting Derek's house whenever he came to Belfast.

Eventually Van Morrison decided that he wanted Derek Bell in his band and launched a relentless campaign to entice him away from The Chieftains. When Bell refused, telling Morrison that he didn't have the necessary jazz background, the temperamental singer blew up.

'We had a row about the way I was ruining my life,' remembers Bell. 'Van said that I was too much under Moloney's apron strings. He told me that it was no good reading all these books about masters and then not living the life. And of course for the sake of peace I had to agree with him. Indeed that is no good.

'But then he said that worse still, I was under Moloney's thumb and so was Matt and so was Seán. Van said I just hadn't got the guts to break out, stand up on my own and do something. So I said, "Well, I suppose that's an acceptable viewpoint Mr Morrison."

'Then he says, "Look, where do you think I am? I've got to the top of the tree here. Where do you think you are? You're down here. And that's why I can't hold a conversation with you." '

With that Morrison stormed out, banging the door behind him, leaving Bell to walk the two miles back to his home. But the very next day Morrison was back on the phone as if nothing had happened, asking Derek him to take part in a W. B. Yeats' concert he was doing at Dublin's Abbey Theatre.

'Van doesn't hold any kind of grudges,' explained Bell. 'So I went down to Dublin in good faith but unfortunately when I got there found that he had cancelled the concert.'

Paddy Moloney says that he was well aware that Van Morrison wanted Derek to join his band.

'At one stage Van thought Derek should forget about The Chieftains and join up with him, earn more money and all that sort of thing,' says Moloney.

* * *

In August 1991 model Jerry Hall invited Paddy Moloney and his daughter Aedín to be her guests at the annual Rolling Stones' birthday party in London's Hyde Park. Since the Slane Castle concert Moloney had seen Mick Jagger intermittently when their paths happened to cross. A few years earlier in New York, Moloney and Derek Bell had played Happy Birthday for Jagger's daughter Jade as a special favour. And in 1987 Moloney had laid down a track of uilleann pipes for the *Party Doll* cut on the rock star's second solo album, *Primitive Cool*.

The party was still going strong at 2:00 a.m. when Moloney decided he ought to leave to catch the first flight back to Dublin.

'As I was leaving Jerry said, "You don't happen to have a tin whistle?" ' remembers Moloney. ' "Would you play a tune before you go?" As it happened of course I had one, but I said, "I can't compete with the disco let's go into the park."

'So we went and some of the band came out, Elton John and everybody. We all sat around in this circle, and I played a few tunes. We had a great bit of fun. At five o'clock I left to go home. Back to Ireland.'

24

An Irish Evening

In July 1991 The Chieftains stormed into London with their own week-long music festival. Booking themselves for two nights each in the London Palladium and the Royal Festival Hall, plus a night in the Brixton Academy, Moloney invited a host of music celebrities to guest in what was billed as the First Annual Chieftains' Music Festival.

One London Palladium show saw The Chieftains performing with Roger Daltrey of the Who and Roddy Frame of Aztec Camera while the next night they played the Festival Hall with Kate and Anna McGarrigle. But even Derek Bell reached for his earplugs when they found themselves on stage with The Pogues south of the Thames in Brixton.

'I think it's a terrible thing when rock stars deafen themselves on stage with loud sound apparatus,' says Bell. 'It was far too loud, and even dangerous, when we played with The Pogues. I had to put in ear plugs first.'

When Irish singer Feargal Sharkey got a call from Moloney to appear at one of the more sedate Palladium shows he was delighted to get back to the traditional music he'd grown up with in Derry.

'That's the genre of music that I started out playing,' says Sharkey, who made his name as lead singer of The Undertones in the 1970s. 'It was quite an intriguing thing to go back and dip my big toe in traditional music again.'

Sharkey says there was little rehearsal before the concert where he was to join The Chieftains for *She Moved Through the Fair* and a couple of other tunes.

'We sort of loitered around a rehearsal room talking nonsense for an hour or two,' recalls Sharkey. 'Playing on stage with musicians of that calibre was great. An amazing experience. Although I'd had a reasonably successful career as a musician for 15 years with number one records, my father never saw me as successful until I played with The Chieftains. To him I'd finally made it and he came back from Spain especially for the show.'

Midge Ure appeared at The Chieftains' second Palladium show where he performed *All Fall Down* and joined them in the grand finale for *Rachamíd a Bhean Bheag*, where everyone does an individual solo.

'It was hysterical,' laughs Ure. 'I sang *Marie's Wedding* and I'd never sang stuff like that in my life.'

On the same bill that night was Roger Daltrey who did a mesmerizing version of The Who's *Behind Blue Eyes* with The Chieftains. Initially the idea of the lead singer of one of rock music's loudest and hardest rock bands, with a predilection for smashing up their instruments, working with a traditional music ensemble seemed preposterous. But the end results were astounding.

'Everyone was wondering if it would work or not,' says Pete Smith. 'It was almost an unplugged item. I mean here was the lead singer with The Who singing live with The Chieftains performing a Who number, which had only ever been done as rock 'n' roll, now doing it in a completely acoustic traditional context.'

After the success of the London festival Ulster Television offered The Chieftains their own television special. The idea was to perform two performances at the Belfast Opera House with special guest stars and televise the show.

'I cut a very good deal there with the expert legal assistance of lawyer and friend James Hickey,' says Moloney proudly. 'We were very canny. I said if we're going to do concerts and a television show we might as well get an album and a video out of it.'

Ulster Television agreed and coupled with BMG's record and video advance, The Chieftains received four different payments before they even played a note of what became *An Irish Evening*, to be broadcast by America's PBS station the following year at the Cannes TV festival.

Flushed from their successful collaboration at the Palladium, Moloney immediately asked Roger Daltrey to guest star in the show with the bill being completed by American-born champion step dancer Jean Butler and country singer Nanci Griffith.

'There was a bomb scare at the Opera House on the afternoon of the show as we were going into rehearsals,' remembers Griffith. 'It was like a bad "B" movie. The Chieftains, Roger Daltrey and me were all evacuated to a bingo parlour down the street. We walked in and it was full of old ladies playing bingo. It was surreal and so hilarious. Then the old ladies recognized Roger Daltrey and started coming up asking him for his autograph.'

When the police finally allowed the Opera Hall to re-open there was no time for a sound check or any rehearsals before the evening performance.

'It was massive bedlam,' says Griffith. 'But it was fun and so fresh because it was all totally unrehearsed.'

In her featured spot with The Chieftains, Nanci Griffith sang *Red is the Rose* for the very first time in her life using a lyric sheet.

'It was a real experience,' she says. 'It was Paddy's idea. He wanted me to do something traditional.'

Matt Molloy gave a standout version of his set flute solo *The Mason's Apron*, in which he becomes the traditional equivalent of jazz great Roland Kirk by playing two tunes simultaneously on his flute. As he finished to a standing ovation Paddy Moloney raised a laugh by quipping, 'Not bad, Matt. Not bad at all.'

Ever since the London Palladium show Moloney had been hard at work on a new arrangement for *Behind Blue Eyes* for Roger Daltrey.

Explained Moloney: 'If somebody visits you who does rock 'n' roll music while you're a traditional musician, you won't ask them to do reels and jigs. Besides, I like to experiment with the band and *Behind Blue Eyes* has a nice air to it. It has a lovely touch and it's quite a sad song in a way that fits in perfectly with the band. And just in the middle, where the guy has a high point, I go into a reel – you won't find that on a Who record. But I see that as The Chieftains' contribution to the singer's story; you know, the idea that things weren't always sad. He had a good stage at some time of his life.'

When Moloney announced Roger Daltrey the blond-haired singer strolled up to the microphone to address the audience.

'What can you say about these guys?' he began, pointing to The Chieftains. 'It's been a very interesting time for me because singing rock 'n' roll is one thing but singing traditional Irish music is another. And I was thinking maybe one day in the future they'll be guys on stage like this playing antique guitars. In a few hundred years time they'll be playing Who songs as traditional rock 'n' roll songs. And I'm just hoping they don't look like these guys.'

Daltrey then launched into a Van Morrison-inspired version of *Raglan Road* before calling his friend Billy Nichols to the stage to join him on *Behind Blue Eyes*.

'Roger was great and he loved it,' says Moloney. 'He wanted to come out on the road with The Chieftains for the rest of his life.'

25

Another Country

After the stunning success of *The Bells of Dublin*, BMG's whole attitude towards The Chieftains changed radically. Now a proven record-selling force, BMG ironically began to look at the group's long-term career potential, almost 30 years after the first Chieftains' record was released. When *An Irish Evening* shipped 250,000 advance, with *Behind Blue Eyes* getting heavy radio play as a single, The Chieftains suddenly found themselves plunged into an exciting new phase of their career. Finally the years of hard work and non-stop tramping around the world looked like paying off as they knocked on the doors of superstardom.

Looking to capitalize on his newfound success Paddy Moloney turned to country music, which had always fascinated him, to realize his long-held ambition of recording an album in Nashville. Country music was on the brink of exploding into the American mass market to become the hottest new segment in the music industry. The Chieftains' timing could not have been better.

Yet *Another Country* had its roots more than 30 years earlier when Moloney had presented a radio series on RTE exploring the relationship between traditional music and American country and western music.

'A friend of mine had given me a book by the folklorist Alan Lomax that had a lot of North American songs and music,' explains Moloney. 'I used some of them in the radio series with me playing and somebody else singing. Since then I had it in the back of my mind to do a country record as I recognized how close our two musics were. For instance, a tune like *Did You Ever Go A-Courtin, Uncle Joe* is a very popular reel in Ireland where it is called *Miss McLeod's Reel*.'

In March 1992 The Chieftains were on tour in the United States to promote *An Irish Evening* when everything fell into place to make a country album. During their Nashville appearance at the Tennessee Performing Arts Center The Chieftains were invited to guest-host the top-rated *American Music Shop* for The Nashville Network. The show's producer Brian O'Neill said he had spent years trying to get The Chieftains on his show playing with different country musicians.

'It was my dream show,' says O'Neill, who had been a fan of The Chieftains since childhood. 'I wanted to show the similarities between traditional American folk, Bluegrass and country music with traditional Irish music. The ideal situation was to bring in The Chieftains and pair them up with some Nashville pickers, singers and players. I finally managed to do it when they played Nashville that year.'

The one-hour show, featuring The Chieftains playing with Ricky Skaggs, Chet Atkins and The Nitty Gritty Dirt Band, was so successful that O'Neill very kindly offered Paddy all his contacts to put together The Chieftains' country album.

'I thought, "Gee it would be nice if people could listen to this music on a CD," ' says O'Neill. 'Then Paddy told me that he had always wanted to come to Nashville and make a country album.'

From there things moved at lightning speed as The Nitty Gritty Dirt Band enthusiastically agreed to go into the studio the following day to record *Killibegs*.

'To me the opening track was the getting together,' explains Moloney. 'The merging of our sounds with the sounds of Nashville and country music. Call it country music meets its Irish roots.'

Jimmy Ibbotson of The Nitty Gritty Dirt Band says he was delighted when he got a call from Moloney, as he had been a Chieftains' fan since the 1970s when some Irish relations first played him their music.

'In 1972 I read an interview which described The Chieftains as an Irish Nitty Gritty Dirt Band,' remembers Ibbotson. 'I thought that was a wonderful compliment to us.'

When The Nitty Gritty Dirt Band first went into the studio with The Chieftains, Ibbotson was immediately struck by Moloney's knowledge of studio technique and his diplomacy.

'Paddy just ran the session with great humour but he was very much in charge,' said Ibbotson. 'I remember our drummer Jimmie Fadden wanted to play a full drum kit and Paddy wanted him to just play his harmonica.

'The two were soon at loggerheads and I could see that there was going to be an argument. I was trying to explain to our drummer that Paddy only wanted the sound of the bodhrán and not rock 'n' roll drums, but he really did want to play his drums. Paddy just let Jimmie do what he wanted behind a soundproof barrier but after the take he got Jimmie to do it again the way he wanted in an overdub. It was all very pleasant. But on the record you don't hear anything of Jimmie's drums. Paddy really handled him very well.'

During the six weeks The Chieftains were away from Nashville, Moloney sent back cassette tapes with a traditional version of his song *Killibegs*, written about the Irish village where Ibbotson's family had originally come from.

'Paddy's cassette was absolutely thrilling,' recalls Ibbotson. 'He was just humming the parts and singing along. He's got a very quick rapid mind and I thought this is absolutely the finest musician I've ever met. He went way over my head I'll tell you.'

On the tape Moloney had suggested incorporating a slip jig into *Killibegs*, which totally transformed the whole piece.

'When I play the song it sounds like a country or folk song,' says Ibbotson. 'But when The Chieftains played along it sounded magic. To me it sounded like leprechauns dancing at a wedding.'

Working flat out on the project Pete Smith booked a week at the Javelina studios in Nashville, where Elvis Presley had recorded a couple of records, for the end of April. And using his contacts Brian O'Neill began helping Moloney recruit country stars for the sessions.

'What I normally do is just get onto the artists themselves,' explains Moloney. 'It's the best way. Get the buzz, get the feel, get their number and just get on with it.'

A week later The Chieftains were in Toronto on St Patrick's Day playing the Roy Thomson Hall with Canadian blues star Colin James as their special guest. James, who had listened to his uncle's Chieftain records as a child, had grown up in the prairies of Saskatchewan playing traditional music on his tin whistle.

The day after the concert, at Moloney's invitation, James went into the Sounds Interchange Studios with The Chieftains to record *Cúnla* on which he sang and played mandolin.

'It was a real whirlwind of a session,' remembers James. 'They all sat down in a circle and played at once and I joined in. Paddy's so hard-working and always so excited about the music that it's infectious.'

Back in Ireland Moloney went backstage at the Point Depot after a Highwayman show to enlist the help of Willie Nelson, Waylon Jennings and Kris Kristofferson to record *Goodnight Irene* two days later in the Windmill Studios. The session was arranged by Brian Masterson at short notice for Good Friday, the only day of the year where bars are closed in Dublin.

'I told the lads not to worry if they wanted a pint of Guinness or something as I'd organize it,' laughs Moloney. 'We did it in two takes. I had the arrangements made out for the song including a new introduction piece. Willie Nelson told me that my introduction was the best version of the song he'd ever heard.'

Matt Molloy was thrilled to play with Willie Nelson, who was one of his favourite singers and proudly displays a photograph of himself with the singer from the session in the music room at Matt Molloy's.

'To watch him deliver a song was really something,' says Molloy. 'It was all done very quickly. He sang it twice and that was it. And to boot he brought in Kris Kristofferson to do backing vocals which was an unexpected pleasure. They were just dead on.'

After the session, which featured Aedín Moloney's musical debut as a back-up singer, Moloney took the country musicians to a nearby bar which had agreed to open its doors on Good Friday especially for the occasion.

When The Chieftains arrived back in Nashville to begin recording on April 28th Moloney was in a panic as all the sessions had to be completed in a week.

'I had the whole thing on my shoulders,' he remembers. 'I had to coordinate everything but once we got to the studio it turned out to be great.'

In Nashville The Chieftains found themselves the talk of the town with a number of stars wanting to be on the record. Long-time country fan Matt Molloy says he was amazed by their reception.

'There was great rapport between us and the country players,' says Molloy. 'We were surprised and delighted that a lot of musicians and singers knew about us and were closet Chieftain fans. It was great. They were very interested in placing their music against a Chieftains' backdrop.'

For Ricky Scaggs, whose family hailed from Donegal, Co. Derry, playing on *Another Country* was the beginning of an on-going friendship and collaboration with The Chieftains.

'When we got together we really hit it off,' says Skaggs who sang *The Wabash Cannonball* and *Cotton-Eyed Joe* on the album. 'Musically we had a gel. It was like we'd been playing together forever.'

Skaggs personally showed The Chieftains around Nashville and arranged for them to realize Moloney's dream of playing the legendary Grand Ole Opry.

'I told the general manager of the Opry that The Chieftains were in town and it was a perfect time for them to be on my show,' says Skaggs. 'He said no problem and Paddy was so delighted. They played there twice in one week.'

The country star also introduced Derek Bell to Dairy Queen ice cream and unleashed a monster.

'He went nuts,' laughs Skaggs. 'We got him hooked on those big Ol' Blizzards with oreo cookies and vanilla ice cream with a long spoon sticking out of it. From then on he just had to have them.'

When country legend Don Williams coolly strolled into the studio smoking a cigarette, he knew exactly how he wanted the Ray Charles' classic hit *I Can't Stop Loving You* to sound. As Paddy Moloney did the run through, the bearded star gently called a halt, insisting on slowing the rhythm down to waltz time resulting in a fine version of the song.

One of the week's most memorable sessions was for Keane's version of *Heartbreak Hotel*, which featured guitarist Chet Atkins, who had played on the original Elvis Presley recording on January 10th, 1956. Seán Keane, who used to listen to Atkins as a teenager, was overawed by playing with his musical hero.

'It suddenly hits you, "Jesus, this is a legend you're playing with," ' says Keane. 'The same as a lot of artists on that record.'

In a break during the recording of *Heartbreak Hotel*, Keane asked Chet Atkins what it had been like to work with Elvis on the original version.

'Chet just started to get into it,' says Keane. 'He really loved the subject. He said that when Elvis would come in to do a recording session he was full of tricks. It took a while for him to get serious and do the recording. He sounded like a really nice man.'

A couple of months later Moloney met the song's composer Mae Hoyt Axton in a television studio when they were both being interviewed for the show *Nashville Now.*

'It was a total coincidence,' says Moloney. 'I thought she'd give me a clout for what we did to the song but she thought it was great.'

For the grand finale of *Another Country*, Moloney had 27 musicians in the studio to record a 12-minute stomping medley of *Did you Ever Go A-Courtin'* and *Will the Circle Be Unbroken*.

'I can still picture everybody sitting in a circle,' says Jimmy Ibbotson. 'There was Ricky Skaggs, Emmy Lou Harris and Chet Atkins. Paddy was laughing and directing everything. He had these big sheets of posterboard on the wall because the songs were all very complicated and it had to be cut in three sections.'

Moloney says that he wanted the last track to be like a big Irish Hooley with everyone doing their own solo.

'There was great atmosphere in the studio,' remembers Moloney. 'We were belting away. The likes of Bela Fleck, Jerry Douglas and Sam Bush. Wonderful musicians. I remember in the middle of my solo Bela Fleck came flying in on the banjo. He just got taken away. And down at the other end Emmy Lou was doing her clog dancing. That's how she works out with the music. The next thing she ran up to the mike to do *Love Will You Marry Me* with Kevin.

'There were 27 of us in a circle and almost as many again in the control-room. A lot of the great musicians from Nashville came to hear what was going on. Some of the biggest names in the country world.'

Kevin Conneff remembers the Nashville recordings for *Another Country* as being the best time he ever had in the studio with The Chieftains.

'They were magical days,' he says. 'It was just a pleasure playing real music. It was so relaxed that we pretty much forgot about the recording and just got on with it. I still listen to that album with a great amount of joy and pride.'

* * *

By early 1992 director Ron Howard had finally moved his long-dreamed-of Irish project called *Far and Away* off the back burner and into production. And keeping his promise to Moloney, made almost ten years earlier on their night out in Hollywood, The Chieftains were to perform the theme music for the big budget movie starring Tom Cruise and his new wife Nicole Kidman.

The film, which also featured a cameo performance from Aedín Moloney as a prostitute, told the story of Irish emigration to America through the eyes of a young Irish couple in the 19th century. Ron Howard credits The Chieftains for giving him the inspiration after seeing them in concert in Pasadena.

'There was one song they played about an emigrant going off to America that was bittersweet, romantic and very Irish,' he says. 'You know how music somehow sets you thinking and I was day-dreaming all the way home in the car about that song.

'Then I started making a few notes and plot ideas. That concert was point of origin for the movie, so it seemed fairly logical when John Williams was doing the music that we should bring The Chieftains in to play the main themes.'

Film composer John Williams, who did the music for *Star Wars*, had been hired to compose the score. Moloney first received the orchestrations in Philadelphia in the middle of their annual American tour in March, just three days before they were due to go into the studios in Hollywood for the recording session with a full symphony orchestra. After going through Williams' music Moloney briefed the rest of the group on the bus from Baltimore to Philadelphia.

Three days later The Chieftains were at Sony Studios to rehearse with Williams under a giant screen showing a black and white print of the film. Paddy Moloney had made his own changes to the score to make it more Chieftains-friendly and Williams was delighted with the results.

'We needed Irish music played by Irish artistes,' explained Williams. 'These men are the best in the world – they're uniquely great. There's no side to them. They just turn up, play their instruments and get on with it.'

Williams, who would later collaborate with The Chieftains with his Boston Pops Orchestra, sees the group as the globe-trotting 20th century equivalent of medieval travelling musicians.

'In a way they remind me of Mozart as a child, always traveling on from one job to another,' says Williams. 'They're unpretentious, down to earth, and that's part of why they are so great.'

The following day Tom Cruise and Nicole Kidman were in the sound booth to see The Chieftains record the score with the orchestra under Williams' direction. During the session the film star was instantly smitten with The Chieftains.

'It's marvellous,' Cruise told writer Joe Steeples from the English *You* magazine. 'Listening to them conjures up all the sights, sounds and flavours of Ireland. They're great musicians and the sound they make is perfect for the movie.'

The following January The Chieftains were at the Royal Charity premiere of *Far and Away* in London, which was attended by Princess Diana, British prime minister John Major and Tom Cruise and Nicole Kidman. The troubled princess was big news as a new book had come out that very day detailing her suicide attempts and bulimia. Derek Bell was curious to see how the Princess would handle the pressure.

'I was very keyed up with interest as to what she'd be like,' remembers Bell. 'I thought with the book coming out she would have cancelled the whole thing but not at all. There were no bloody flies on her, bulimia or no bulimia. She was lovely and far taller than she appears on television. You would really want to take her home for Sunday dinner and she'd appear to your granny as balanced, with a good head on her.'

*   *   *

That summer The Chieftains got a chance to preview their up-and-coming release *Another Country* when they were invited to guest star on *The Tom Jones Show*. The Welsh singer was making six 30-minute programmes, each one featuring a different style of music. He decided The Chieftains would be perfect to demonstrate the influence of Irish traditional music on American country.

'I'd first seen them on television and they struck me as a very authentic Celtic band,' remembers Tom Jones. 'And then I'd heard Van Morrison talking about working with them so I was aware of them again. When we did a show exploring the connection between Celtic music and country we felt that The Chieftains would be the band to demonstrate this better than anybody else.'

At rehearsals Paddy Moloney suggested they play *Heartbreak Hotel*, which they just recorded with Chet Atkins in Nashville.

'*Heartbreak Hotel* is basically an Irish tune,' explained Jones. 'We also did *Danny Boy* of course because that's a typical Irish song.'

Prior to the filming in the Nottingham studio Tom Jones downed a few beers with The Chieftains to get to know them.

'I mean he can put away his beer,' says Matt Molloy admiringly.

'We knocked back a couple of pints and were chatting away about nothing in general. And then we went up and we did the show.'

Jones remembers that he, Molloy and Martin Fay were grabbing the odd beer between takes when the producer came over and suggested putting the beer on the set to add to the atmosphere.

'But Paddy didn't want to do that,' says Tom Jones. In his mobile dressing room outside the studio, Paddy sat and discussed his ideas for the programme with the Welsh star. It was to be a medley of songs – *The Green, Green Grass of Home, Danny Boy, The Tennessee Waltz* (later on *The Long Black Veil* album) and finishing with *Cotton-Eye Joe*. Then Tom joined Jean Butler for a rousing dance finish. Pints of Guinness were enjoyed by everyone after the show.

'Tom was very pleased with our performance,' says Molloy. 'He said, "That's great lads, ok" and we all started knocking back the pints and having great fun. About an hour later when we had drunk about three or four pints the producer came in and clapped his hands, "Gentlemen, please would you consider doing that again?"

'We said, "What, another drink?"

' "Oh no the show. . . ." ' I thought, 'Ahhh for fuck's sake.'

'Jones knew that this was coming. He had a glint in his eye and he was smirking at me. Just laughing. Anyway we went back in and I suppose it loosened up a bit. It was definitely loose, there was no question about it. I don't know whether it was better than the first time but it was more fun and more relaxed. And then it was off to the bar again.'

* * *

On June 22nd The Chieftains moved *An Irish Evening* six thousand miles west to the Universal Amphitheater to restage the concert with Roger Daltrey and Nanci Griffith. Against all the odds *Behind Blue Eyes* looked like becoming a hit single and was getting heavy airplay on American radio. The Chieftains and Daltrey were also booked to perform it live to a nationwide audience on the inaugural week of NBC's *Tonight Show With Jay Leno*.

'I now know what it feels like to be a pork chop at a synagogue,' joked Daltrey as he self-consciously strutted out on stage past The Chieftains at the Universal Amphitheater.

But the American audience loved the pairing of Daltrey with

The Chieftains and were even more enthusiastic than the Belfast audience had been as they danced in the aisles for *Behind Blue Eyes*.

'The mix is unique,' wrote *Variety* reviewer Rich Martini. 'Doing mike swinging rock star moves, Daltrey belted out a traditional *Carrickfergus* and a soulful version of *Raglan Road*.' But although *Los Angeles Times* critic Steve Hochman agreed 'the improbable pairing worked', he warned against taking things too far.

'The peril is that it can appear a bit gimmickry,' wrote Hochman. 'Who next? Ozzy Osbourne? Still, gimmicks or not, Tuesday's joint ventures gave more proof of the versatility of The Chieftains' accomplished music.'

Indeed, BMG's senior director of sales and marketing, Steve Vining, who then handled The Chieftains, was so delighted with the success of the collaboration that he wanted to record a studio album with Roger Daltrey and try to emulate the success of *Irish Heartbeat*.

'Roger was also really keen to make a proper album with The Chieftains as an extension of the live thing they'd been doing,' remembers Pete Smith. 'The Universal Amphitheater concert had been so phenomenally successful that BMG thought there was enough momentum to make the album.'

Ironically part of the next Chieftains' album was recorded almost by accident two days later when the group were invited to visit the then ailing rock legend Frank Zappa. The unpredictable musician had first met The Chieftains in 1988 when they had appeared together on a radio programme in London for the BBC World Service. Zappa had been fascinated by The Chieftains and traditional music and had told Paddy Moloney to call him when he was next in Los Angeles.

Says Pete Smith: 'I remember Frank Zappa saying to me that he couldn't actually tell whether this Chieftain or that Chieftain or the other Chieftain were the best exponents of their instruments in the traditional Irish idiom. But when he heard them all play together there was no combination to match it.

'I think Frank had that understanding of what Paddy had achieved by bringing together this phenomenal talent. Whether or not you'd point to them individually as being the best in the world, the sum is definitely greater than its parts. And that includes Paddy.'

When Moloney finally made the telephone call Zappa was

delighted and told him to bring The Chieftains straight over with their instruments for some recording.

'It was like an informal experiment,' remembers Zappa's recording engineer Spencer Chrislau, who still runs the Zappa studio, which is known as the Utility Muffin Research Kitchen. 'Frank wanted to try out some recording techniques that we were inventing.'

Zappa placed The Chieftains around a gigantic hoop, four feet in diameter, which was covered in microphones. He then had the group play some new music he had written.

'Frank Zappa's a genius,' declares Paddy Moloney. 'To me he's a hundred years ahead of his time. I think his music is incredible.'

By midnight they had finished the experimental recording but Zappa was having such a great time working with The Chieftains that he wanted to continue.

Remembers Moloney, 'He said, "Look lads, I'm not spending two days setting up this studio for you. Why don't you use it?" '

The Chieftains were already working on some pieces for *Celtic Harp*, their projected 200th anniversary tribute to the traditional music collector Edward Bunting. Now Moloney saw the perfect opportunity to start recording and save expensive studio time. When the other Chieftains said they were too tired and wanted to go back to the hotel Zappa and Moloney rallied them into action.

Zappa was particularly insistent that Kevin Conneff record the difficult a cappella song *The Green Fields of America*.

'Kevin really didn't want to,' says Moloney. 'He said, "Paddy, my voice is gone. It's 12 o'clock for god's sake." '

Conneff had already recorded the song three times but had never been satisfied with his performance but Zappa had Spencer Chrislau set up a microphone in the back room of the studio, which had a natural vibrato, and persuaded him to give it another go.

'Frank suggested I sing,' remembers Conneff. 'After a couple of false starts – because I had a slight sore throat and was totally exhausted and couldn't think straight – I sang *The Green Fields of America*. And apparently it floored him.'

Gail Zappa says that Kevin's recording of *The Green Fields of America* became Frank's favourite song during the last months of his life when they would often listen to it together. It was later played at his cremation.

'It's still very hard for me to listen to it,' says Gail. 'Because it was recorded in our studio and Frank loved it so much. Frank and I used to listen to it together and the two of us were just in tears. I will never forget that. It was so extraordinary.'

After the recording Kevin Conneff was still not happy with the take and tried to do it again.

Says Gail: 'Frank had said, "No, no. I really like the first take. I think it's great." And that's the one they ended up using on the record. It is the song but it's not the song. It was the whole experience of working with them and hanging around with those guys and having them over.'

By two o'clock in the morning The Chieftains had managed to record five tracks representing more than half *The Celtic Harp* album and Moloney was delighted.

'We just went for it and to hell you know,' says the piper. 'That's how it can happen sometimes.'

Two months later The Chieftains completed *The Celtic Harp* in the Windmill Lane Studios with The Belfast Harp Orchestra under the direction of Janet Harbison. The group had first collaborated with the harp orchestra a few months earlier when The Chieftains had played London's new Barbican Centre for the first time. The show was so successful that the orchestra flew to Dublin in August to appear as guests of The Chieftains at the National Concert Hall and lay down five tracks for *The Celtic Harp*.

* * *

If The Chieftains were exhausted after their hectic US tour they had only a couple of weeks' breather before they were to start a 23-city European tour, including an appearance at the World Fair in Seville, Spain. Then it was straight back to the States for the release of *Another Country* and to perform *Sgt. Early's Dream* with the Houston Ballet, for which Moloney had put together the music.

Now they were hotter than ever the band had agreed to work flat out for two years in order to take advantage of their new earnings' potential. Mostly in their 50s, The Chieftains' tough schedule would tax a group half their ages.

'We're a joke among the hard-core rock 'n' roll people that we've been meeting in the last few years,' says Matt Molloy. 'They can't believe the amount of work that we've loaded on ourselves. They think we're crazy and sometimes I think they're right.

'I mean they've all said it. The Stones, Frank Zappa, Sting. There are loads to musicians who have said to us, "How do you create anything? How do you charge and recharge your batteries? How do you survive?" These fellows work intensely for maybe 18 months or whatever but then they'll disappear for a year. We never stop.'

Paddy Moloney's amazing drive and single-mindedness knows no limits and his part in the success of The Chieftains can never be underestimated. He loves to go beyond the call of duty to protect his baby and this was demonstrated when *Another Country* was released to great reviews in September. Moloney didn't consider RCA was giving the record adequate promotion and quietly visited Nashville to personally investigate.

'I found they hadn't even heard of the album,' Moloney told Dublin writer Joe Jackson at the time. 'RCA sold the album but didn't push it, partly because we're still on their classical label. They are still trying to break beyond those barriers but this has always been an uphill struggle for The Chieftains. *That's* where a lot of my drive comes from, the energy I've needed to fight this kind of battle for the past 30 years.'

The American critics loved *Another Country*, declaring it 'magic.'

Wrote syndicated reviewer Larry Nager: 'The relationship between Celtic music and American bluegrass and country has been well documented. But it's never been explored with such passion, virtuosity and such sheer delight.'

26

A Pilgrimage to the Grammys

A full 30 years after their formation The Chieftains soared to new heights when the Grammy nominations were announced in the first week of 1993. For the traditional group had been nominated for no less than five Grammy awards, music's equivalent of an Oscar.

Another Country was competing in three separate categories: best contemporary folk album; best pop instrumental performance with Chet Atkins; and, best country vocal collaboration with The Nitty Gritty Dirt Band. Additionally, *An Irish Evening* was nominated for best traditional folk album. With six previously unsuccessful nominations in the last few years, the traditional group were now up against Eric Clapton, who had nine nominations for *Unplugged* and fellow Dublin band U2 with *Achtung Baby.*

Bono of U2 had grown up listening to Chieftains' music and was a hard-core fan.

'My dream was for Johnny Lydon (formerly Johnny Rotten of the Sex Pistols) to make a record with them,' Bono told the author. 'Now there's a set of pipes . . . what a smash hit that would be . . . keening all the way to the bank.'

When the nominations were announced The Chieftains were in Los Angeles to perform at the annual BMG conference of distributors at the Beverly Hilton. With *Celtic Harp* due to be released in March, no firm decision had been taken on the next Chieftains' album.

Moloney had set his sights on a second country album using the new Nashville talent while RCA's Steve Vining wanted the collaborative album with Roger Daltrey.

'No one was seeing eye to eye about what the record should be,' says Pete Smith, who would soon be replaced as the group's manager. 'It was obviously a turning point because they'd had these three collaborative records followed by a traditional one.'

After The Chieftains' performance at the conference, Steve Vining found himself in the unfortunate position of having to announce the next Chieftains' blockbuster without knowing what it would be. Trying to hedge his bets, Vining promised his sales force that the next Chieftains' record would make everyone proud without being more specific.

*   *   *

When they were in Los Angeles Gail Zappa invited The Chieftains over to her house to take part in a BBC-TV *Late Show* documentary being made on her husband, who by then was terminally ill. In an effort to cheer Frank up, every Friday night Gail organized social salons of musicians to come over, talk, play music and generally boost his morale.

'We called them the margarita hour,' says Gail. 'I remember the night The Chieftains came over Frank was very ill and did not feel well at all.'

Among the guests that night at the salon was blues man Johnny 'Guitar' Watson, The Chieftains, Terry Bosio and some Russian musicians.

'Frank wanted to get them all into the studio and see what would happen,' says Gail. 'He liked to give people certain parameters and establish some control over the event to make it work. But he didn't really have the energy to get into it any more.'

As the cameras rolled The Chieftains played some rousing traditional music for the music legend which brought a smile to his face.

'Frank loved the sound of Paddy's slide whistle and the drone pipes that he played,' says Spencer Chrislau. 'He just thought they were wonderfully weird sounds and he was into that.'

*   *   *

'I woke up one morning with a calling to go to India,' explains Moloney. 'I used to keep telling Derek about this and he finally said, "Well, I might come with you." But The Chieftains' hectic schedule took over and it took six years for us to get there.'

Bell wanted to go in 1993 as it was the centenary year of the birth of his master Babajee. So a deal was struck where Moloney would accompany him on a pilgrimage to Babajee's Himalayan cave in return for Bell coming with him to visit Mother Theresa in Calcutta. Once a date had been set the piper found a travel agent and planned an itinerary while Derek wrote off to his Indian contacts for advice.

Arriving in Delhi the party moved into the luxurious Oberoi Hotel, which was owned by one of Garech Browne's friends Prince Oberoi. As well as sightseeing, Moloney began setting up meetings to plan a benefit concert he wanted to do later in the year at the Taj Mahal. His idea was to raise funds to build a hospital in Bhopal as a tribute to those lost in the tragic Bhopal factory disaster.

A few days later night was falling when the Irish party arrived to stay at a monastery ten thousand feet up in the Himalayas. It was their first stop on the way to Babajee's cave and they found themselves ill-prepared for the freezing weather. There was a full-scale blizzard blowing and when the head monk came out to greet them he broke into fits of laughter.

Moloney remembers: 'Here we were, these dirty old gob shites of Irishmen and women with suitcases. He said, "Come on in. You're not dressed for the mountain, are you?" We didn't know where we were going. Of course Derek never checks anything out. He was wearing his usual thing; jumper, suit, no coat, no hat, no case. Just a Marks and Spencer plastic bag. That was it. The same as he goes on tour. I think he brings that plastic bag to bed with him.

'Anyway we went into this place and we were shown up stone steps. Talk about going to jail. I mean we walked into this room that was just concrete. There was this very old-fashioned brown glass in the window that went out in the 1930s but I was surprised there was an electricity light bulb hanging from the ceiling.'

They sat down with the monks for a meal of hot soup, which was heartily devoured by the frozen visitors. Then the head monk told them he would pray and meditate for a change in the weather or they would never reach Babajee's cave which was still 23 kilometres away.

'We heard that the road up the mountain was blocked with snow,' says Bell. 'We prayed to Babajee that he would allow us to see the caves because we had come so far.'

Pádraig shared a bed in one damp room with Derek while Paddy and Rita took the other one. It was so cold in the room that

Paddy and Rita put on every article of clothing in their suitcases and huddled up together to stop shivering. When at two o'clock in the morning they still couldn't sleep, Rita and Paddy prayed to all the Catholic saints to keep them warm.

Incredibly, their prayers were answered when they awoke at six o'clock the next morning to find the sun shining down on the mountain and melting the snow.

'It was magnificent,' says Moloney. 'The sun was out and the birds were in the trees singing. It was perfect conditions to go to the cave.'

After breakfasting on the monastery roof, where a simple soup was served, their guide arrived to drive them the 17 kilometres up the mountain to where the road finished. He would then help guide them the remaining six kilometres to the cave. As they began their arduous three-hour ascent up the mountain, Moloney could see that the overweight and out-of-condition Derek Bell was having trouble keeping up.

'I was afraid that Derek's big dream of reaching the cave wasn't going to happen,' says Moloney. 'He was totally out of breath and I was very afraid that he would collapse.'

At one point Rita agreed to stay behind with Derek while Moloney and Pádraig went on ahead to see what conditions were like up ahead. As they were walking up the mountain they passed a young shepherd boy who was singing a beautiful air to his sheep. Moloney stopped, captivated by the tune.

'I learned the air immediately,' says Moloney. 'As I didn't have a whistle I started to sing it back to him after each verse. And then he'd start the next one and so on. Now my singing was something dreadful. Eventually the young fellow let a few remarks out and the guide broke up laughing. He was not very complimentary about my singing.'

Eventually Moloney sang the air into Pádraig's video recorder, to ensure it wouldn't be lost, and determined to use it in his upcoming symphony to commemorate the Great Famine in 1995. Going back to meet Derek, Moloney was alarmed to see that his friend was gallantly soldiering on although he was red in the face and was having trouble breathing perhaps because of the altitude.

'I asked him if he wanted to go back, but he insisted on carrying on. For him this was a dream coming true. Having reached the cave I shouted to Derek that five more minutes would get him there, and he finally made it, to his great delight.'

Reflecting back on his tortuous walk up the mountain, Derek Bell plays it down by saying: 'It's a little more difficult if you've got short legs when everyone else has got longer ones.'

Finally achieving his dream of going to Babajee's cave, Bell was a happy man when he went in to meditate. Later he joined his friends in a circle where they all prayed that Rita's ageing father Faley, who was very ill in Dublin, would survive until she could return to say good-bye. A couple of days later Rita decided to fly back to Ireland to be with her father but she insisted that Paddy, Derek and Pádraig continue their trip.

During the three-week tour they travelled to the temple on the banks of the River Ganges where Babajee had studied and journeyed far into Nepal. In Calcutta they visited Mother Theresa's hospital and were shown around by some Irish nurses in an emotional afternoon where they met the sick children. There was so much to see in India that music, for once, took second place.

'It was our intention to play more music,' says Moloney. 'I had a whistle but I hadn't brought my pipes and Derek didn't have his harp. But we got so wrapped up in our visits that we didn't get around to it.'

Back in Ireland, Moloney continued his discussion about the projected album. He then flew to Hamburg to join the rest of the group where they were filming a television special.

While they were in Germany, Rita's father died and Moloney found himself torn between his commitments to The Chieftains and to his family. In an agonizing decision he decided to stay and do the show which was televised, and therefore miss his beloved father-in-law's funeral by one day. Two weeks later the piper would cathartically explain his reasoning to *Hot Press* writer Joe Jackson.

'I really should have come home to console Rita,' he told Jackson. 'And the whole thing left me feeling very torn and disturbed. But we really had this important show in Hamburg, which was being televised and though we tried to move the gig we couldn't. But apart from the fact that he was my father-in-law, Felix, or Faley O'Reilly as we called him, was a great friend and had asked me to play his favourite song, *Boolavogue*, at his funeral. Once again, I called on my good friend Seán Potts to play it, but I know it's not the same thing. But *that* is the extent of my commitment to

The Chieftains, right or wrong. And I knew Faley would have insisted.'

* * *

Before leaving for the Grammys, Paddy Moloney, now 54, spent a day at the Shelbourne Hotel in Dublin promoting his new album *Celtic Harp*. Looking back over his epic career the piper attempted to articulate his vision for The Chieftains, to which he had devoted his life.

'More than 30 years ago I had a dream like Martin Luther King,' he began. 'And that was a dream to spread the gospel about Irish music and what it really was. Because a lot of people in America thought it all started and ended with *When Irish Eyes are Smiling* and *Did Your Mother Come from Ireland?* – all those tearjerkers. But there's more to it than that. It's great, great music and The Chieftains have their own magical way of putting it across.

'The band uses the full range of traditional instruments, and we remain unique in this respect.'

When The Chieftains arrived at the $800 a plate pre-Grammy party, held in Paramount Studios the night before the ceremony, they found themselves in the company of the likes of Mariah Carey and Billy Ray Cyrus who were both holding court.

Coming off the plane from Dublin, a weary Matt Molloy joined the other Chieftains and Rita Moloney at the party where all nominees were presented with special medals with red ribbons.

Paddy Moloney had previously met Welsh singer Tom Jones at his Bel Air mansion to discuss recording *The Tennessee Waltz* the morning after the Grammys. Not having seen The Chieftains in the six months since they guested on his television show, Jones was delighted with the upcoming project.

'We get on really well together,' says the singer. 'Welsh people and Irish are very similar. We love to talk and have a few pints.'

The following afternoon The Chieftains and publicity man Charles Comer, decked out in gleaming tuxedos, arrived with Rita at the Shrine Auditorium for the Grammy ceremony. Finding their seats in the huge theatre they sat through mountains of presentations until it was time for the five categories for which they had been nominated.

First off Moloney saw his *Tahitian Skies* collaboration with Chet

Atkins, in the 'Best Pop Instrumental' category, lose to *Beauty and the Beast*. Then *Killibegs* got beaten by *The Whiskey Ain't Workin'* by Marty Stuart and Travis Tritt in the 'Best Country Vocal Collaboration'. By the time that *Cotton-Eyed Joe* was knocked out of the 'Best Country Instrumental Performance' to Chet Akins and Jerry Reeds' *Sneakin' Around* it looked another year of Grammy failure for The Chieftains.

A visibly despondent Moloney peered through his glasses at the programme saying, 'I hadn't realized who we were up against in each of these categories. Joan Baez, T-Bone Burnett, Michelle Shocked, The Indigo Girls! We haven't a chance.' Then addressing the other Chieftains Moloney tried to make the best of it by cracking a joke, 'Hey lads maybe we should do a rap album next year!'

But then everything changed. Suddenly the Best Traditional Folk album envelope was opened and they all perked up as they heard, 'And the winner is: The Chieftains for *An Irish Evening*.' As if in disbelief Moloney slowly rose to his feet and led the other group members onto the stage to accept the Grammy Award.

At the microphone Paddy went into his concert schick and began thanking the audience in Gaelic. Stopping himself with a laugh he started again in English, 'That was just our way of saying "thank you" from Ireland.'

Before they could even leave the stage for the obligatory meeting with the press the announcer called them back again to receive a second Grammy in the 'Best Contemporary Folk album' category for *Another Country*.

During the break before the main telecast The Chieftains were swamped by well-wishers congratulating the group on their success. One young man accosted Kevin Conneff saying, 'We love The Chieftains. We listen to them a lot.' Turning around to only see one person Conneff inquired who the 'We' was. 'Me and Michael,' came the reply.

An hour later the penny dropped when Kevin saw the man go up to receive an award when Michael Jackson's *Dangerous* won best engineered album of the year.

During the break in the ceremony Paddy met a number of stars like singer Gloria Estafan, *Star Trek* actor Patrick Stewart and tenor Placido Domingo.

'I did more business in the jax in that one hour,' he said. 'The whole event was great. I made more connections at the Grammy's than you can imagine.'

Later at the Grammy's press conference Moloney told the *New York Daily News* that winning two Grammys was the ultimate recognition for The Chieftains from the recording industry.

'In the last ten years we have had very solid success in the States,' he announced. 'The Grammy's have added another notch, so to speak. It is just a culmination of our work.'

After the ceremony they went to a disappointing celebration buffet at the Biltmore Hotel complete with plastic knives and forks. But there was very little celebrating because, as Moloney reminded them on the way back to the Hyatt Hotel, 'We all have to be up bright and early to do that session with Tom, in Zappa's house.'

'Paddy discourages drinking before a gig,' says Kevin Conneff. 'When I first joined The Chieftains I was a nervous wreck playing on stage in an ensemble so I used to have a couple of whiskies as Dutch courage. But then I realized that I did much better without any at all. It's just a question of building up confidence.'

Conneff says that today there is little drinking, if any, before going on stage and not much more afterwards.

'Paddy doesn't rule us with an armed guard or anything,' explains Kevin. 'But he obviously doesn't want us too much under the influence when we are performing. That's fair enough in my book.'

Moloney says that Chieftains' music is a careful blend of structured arrangements and improvisation and if one member was drunk it would throw everybody.

'For any one of us to go on even half-locked would ruin everything,' he explains. 'Once or twice it did happen and the rest of us can hear how the flow and the rhythms are being broken and that can really upend a show.

'That's not to say the lads don't have one or two bottles before going on but the drinking is always controlled. And though they can drink beer I really do have to say no to spirits.'

Although he admits to some drinking in his time, Moloney says that he now only has the occasional social drink so it doesn't interfere with his music. And he never drinks before a show. In fact the band never accept pre-show drinks receptions from sponsors.

'Anyway I've had my great party years,' he says. 'I always enjoyed a drink, but drank in moderation, and in the last two years

I decided to cut out beer and spirits entirely. Now I enjoy wine. Maybe because I see a better future ahead for The Chieftains than I ever could have dreamed of. And I don't want anyone to blow that because of drink. And over-drinking really is becoming a mug's game, don't you think?'

27

Chieftains and Friends

When The Chieftains arrived at Frank Zappa's house to set up to record *The Tennessee Waltz* at the Utility Muffin Research Kitchen, the ailing musician was having a bad day as he prepared to go into hospital for cancer treatment. A couple of days earlier when Paddy Moloney had telephoned to ask if he could use his studio to record with Tom Jones, Zappa had agreed. But now it was an inconvenience.

'Frank wasn't too enthused about the whole thing,' remembers Spencer Chrislau who engineered the session. 'It was an outside project and Frank didn't really have a lot of input. So he said it was no big deal and stayed away leaving me on my own with Paddy to record it.'

Back in the control room Frank Zappa was chatting to Irish journalist Joe Jackson when he suddenly said he wanted to 'set on record' his feelings about The Chieftains and their rightful place in modern music.

Said Zappa: 'U2 is maybe the most popular and successful musical export coming from Ireland today, but there's no comparison between the musical quality of what they do and what The Chieftains do.

'We play together here nearly every time they're in town and I love the sounds these guys make. I love the melodies and the chord changes, and especially the way their music is performed. Each member of the group is an expert on his instrument, not just in terms of technique, but in terms of the concept they have of what the final ensemble product is supposed to sound like.

'That is something you are only going to get with a group that has been together 30 years. People describe U2 as "post-modern rockers", but what does that mean? Do they themselves know? And which would you rather have? Mediocre invention, or a direct linear descent from Celtic culture, which is what I hear in the music of The Chieftains? The Chieftains are their own culture and I hear traces of not only Celtic history but global history in their work, echoing back to the beginning of time. I've noticed that when they play here in my home with ethnic musicians from all over the world.'

After expressing his feelings to Joe Jackson, Zappa felt better and started to take more interest in what was happening outside in the studio. When Tom Jones arrived at 2:00 p.m. the studio came to life as The Chieftains practised the little *Tennessee Mazurka* that Moloney had composed two days earlier. On hearing the beautiful sounds emanating from the studio, Frank Zappa suddenly came to life and strolled into his studio to listen. He suggested a number of alterations to the arrangement for which Paddy was very grateful.

'He started changing the parts,' says Chrislau. 'He came up with a new intro for the bass player and a whole different way of phrasing the whole song. He was just doing an arrangement. It was really funny because although he had said he was not interested, it turned out that in fact he was very interested and very instrumental in the end result.'

Tom Jones said he had been shocked to see the terminally ill Zappa at the session.

'He was on his last legs,' says the singer. 'That wasn't funny. He left in the middle of the session to go to the hospital to have another check up. You could see he wasn't well.'

Tom Jones gave the *Tennessee Waltz* three distinctly different treatments in the studio, impressing all The Chieftains with his sheer brilliance and professionalism.

'I sang it straight ahead at the beginning,' recalls the Welshman. 'I didn't know how to treat it and whether to sing it a little lighter because of the instrumentation. But when I listened back to it I thought, "No, I can give it some more. I can give more bite on it." Then I listened back to the retake and I felt, "No. I can give it a little bluesy effect. A gospel effect." I knew the instruments would take it. Then I thought maybe I should sing it more like an Irish thing. But because of the way they played I felt I could put some more weight onto it. So I did.'

That third and final Irish-flavoured take was the one that made the album. After the session wound down Tom Jones and The Chieftains went off to the pool-room where they discovered a large fridge full of German beer that Gail Zappa had thoughtfully provided. Finally The Chieftains could relax and celebrate winning two Grammys.

'It was like being in a pub,' says Gail, who had invited her friend actress Beverley D'Angelo, who immediately struck up quite a rapport with the Welshman. 'Everyone was standing around telling stories and getting more and more carried away. It was rather alarming.'

Tom Jones, who was supposed to catch a plane back to New York as he was booked on *The Late Show With David Letterman*, was having such a good time that he missed his plane and had to dash out to make the last red-eye east.

'I almost missed the bloody plane,' laughs Jones. 'We were drinking and talking and telling stories. It was tremendous. It was a great night. It's wonderful when you can record like that rather than be too business-like or serious.'

* * *

A month after their triumph at the Grammys Paddy Moloney decided he needed a North American-based management team to reflect The Chieftains' new stature in the music business. Pete Smith, their previous manager, who is still on good terms with The Chieftains, saw the practical reasoning behind the decision and bore no grudges.

'They were selling hundreds of thousands of records mostly in America, and that's not where I was at,' says Smith who is based outside London. 'We were at a crossroads and as managers we tend to find our contracts come up for renewal.'

On the suggestion of publicist Charles Comer, Moloney met with the Vancouver-based Mind Over Management and was highly impressed with partners Steve Macklam, Sam Feldman and Bruce Allen. The three managers had been involved variously in the careers of Bryan Adams, k.d. lang and Colin James and a three-year management deal was hammered out in meetings all over the world.

On signing, Steve Macklam, who had started his career as a London-based freelance rock writer, began working closely with Moloney on lining up sessions for what would become *The Long*

Black Veil. But at the top of their list of priorities was the re-nego-tiation of The Chieftains' record contract with BMG's Steve Vining.

In July The Chieftains headlined sell-out two nights at the Holly-wood Bowl, where they performed a programme of Paddy's film score music with the 95-piece Hollywood Bowl Orchestra under the direction of John Mauceri. Paddy Moloney was instrumental in selecting guest performers for the show, which played to 25,000 people over the two nights. A couple of days before the shows he called up his friend Anjelica Huston to ask her to reprise *Mrs McGrath*, which she had sang at Paddy's New Year's Eve party so many years before.

'Paddy asked me to do a repeat performance of *Mrs McGrath* for what he described as a small intimate gathering,' laughs Anjelica. 'After I agreed he informed me that I would be singing at the Hollywood Bowl, one of the more terrifying venues in Los Angeles, if not the world.

'So I went along with a bunch of friends and we took a picnic with a fair amount of booze. I wanted to be loose for the event. By the second half of course we were pretty raucous and all the usual classical music aficionados around us were looking at us askance.'

When Moloney introduced Anjelica to the huge Hollywood Bowl audience she was so nervous she could hardly sing.

'It was like I was going into a vortex,' she remembers. 'I knew there were thousands of people in front of me but you couldn't see them because the lights were so bright. I was totally hoarse but I didn't know it until I sang a couple of verses with The Chieftains. I was in total terror. But Paddy has a way of making you feel as though you are in his living room.'

After the show Moloney invited Anjelica back the next night to sing again.

'God no,' says the actress. 'I thought I'd spare the audience that pleasure.'

For the grand finale of the show Moloney had lined up Michael Flatley to lead the Patricia Kennelly Dancers in a thrilling display of pre-*Riverdance* step dancing acrobatics.

'Michael was a flyer,' says Moloney. 'He was unbelievable. I had all these Irish dancers come out on the apron of the Hollywood Bowl and then an entire Scottish pipe and drum corps marched through the middle of the crowd and onto the stage for a massive finale. It was brilliant.'

*   *   *

Following their Hollywood triumph, The Chieftains flew straight to London to play, by special request, at the Rolling Stones' 30th birthday party which doubled as Mick Jagger's 50th. In their thrilling 90-minute set The Chieftains rocked the French Revolution-themed costume party which was full of celebrity friends of the Rolling Stones and their families.

'It was brilliant,' declared Moloney. 'There were all sorts of funny people there – royalty and such. It was a great party.'

Jagger and the Stones were so delighted with The Chieftains' performance that they agreed to repay the favour by appearing on the next Chieftains' album.

A month later Paddy Moloney visited Jagger at the beautiful old Georgian mansion he had rented for the summer in Co. Kildare, while he was recording the new Rolling Stones' album *Voodoo Lounge*, to discuss his contribution to the album, which had been given the working title *Chieftains and Friends*.

'I tried to persuade Mick to sing an Irish rebel song,' laughs Moloney. 'He said, "Ah come on now, Paddy. You can't ask me to do that, you'll get me in terrible trouble." I thought he would because he already played Ned Kelly, but no. We finally settled on *The Long Black Veil*.'

The tragic song, about a man who goes to the gallows for a murder he didn't commit rather than reveal he was in the arms of his best friend's wife, was a long-time favourite of Mick Jagger. He had first heard it with Marianne Faithfull in the late 1960s when it had been covered by The Band on their first *Music From Big Pink* album.

'We played it all the time,' says Marianne. 'That was the song of the moment in Mick's and my lives. I remember Mick and Keith were mixing *Let it Bleed* in Los Angeles and we had a lot of fun. When we weren't too busy we would go out to the desert at Joshua Tree and play *Long Black Veil*. It never came off the turntable.'

At the beginning of September Mick Jagger came into Windmill Lane to record the song with The Chieftains and Rolling Stones' engineer Chris Kimsey.

'There was no big hassle,' says Moloney. 'No big rehearsals. Just into the studio. I sorted it out, in advance, the shapes, as Van

Morrison calls it. We got an old piano in and Mick played and sang. Steve Cooney played the didgeridoo which fascinated Mick.'

The following day the rest of the Rolling Stones were due at Windmill Lane to join forces with The Chieftains to record *The Rocky Road to Dublin*. Although Moloney had sent them a tape of the song no one had bothered to listen to it and learn the words or music.

'I knew it was going to be a go-for-it,' laughs Moloney. 'Was it rocky? – good lord. They brought their own bar and we provided the Guinness or whatever. There's always a party atmosphere.'

Mick Jagger was the first to arrive at 5:00 p.m. and two hours later, when the other Stones failed to turn up, a worried Paddy Moloney sent a bus to collect them from Ron Wood's house outside Dublin. At the last minute Moloney had decided he wanted Jean Butler to lay down a step dancing track on the recording so he sent out an SOS for her. Sound engineer Brian Masterson finally tracked her down at a reception and drove her to the studio.

'They were having a full-scale party when I arrived,' says Masterson, who was later recruited to sing back-up vocals with Mick and Keith on either side of him. 'I'd never seen anything like it at a recording session.'

By midnight hardly a note had been laid down and the inscrutable Derek Bell was beginning to wonder if the recording was ever going to happen.

'Suddenly at midnight everything came together,' says Bell. 'I went into the studio and got the only bloody thing I did all day down. That was apparently it.'

As no one else knew the words of the verses, Kevin sang them, and everyone else joined in on the choruses. On Paddy's instructions, Keith played his immortal riff from *Satisfaction*.

'Keith at first couldn't understand,' remembers Moloney. 'He was saying, "How could that work in a ballad?" Yet it did, I think.'

Moloney freely admits that for once he wasn't fully in control of the session.

'We just went soaring into it,' says Moloney. 'At first I thought I was in command, "OK lads, when it comes to this section I'll give you the nod. That's when we wind down after the playout." I thought the boys were following me. Lovely lads. Not at all. They weren't listening to me at all. So I just let them go on and I did a fade away. It was the only thing I could do.'

At about two in the morning The Chieftains and Garech Browne took the Rolling Stones out on the town to a club called Lillie's Bordello. There they found the traditional group Altan in the midst of a release party for their new album *Island Angel* and various members of The Chieftains and Stones joined Altan in an impromptu jam on stage.

Remembers Moloney: 'At three in the morning Keith had his arm around me, smoking a cigarette, he'd forgotten that I'm allergic to them, and said, "You know, Paddy at the end of the day you know music is music and musicians are musicians and that's what it's all about." '

It was coming up to sunrise when all three groups of musicians rolled out of Lillie's Bordello to head for the traditional music bar The Ferryman, which Moloney had called ahead to request an extension for the party which was still going strong.

'The wrinkly rockers showed admirable stamina for their age,' reported *The Sunday Press* two days later. 'And the night continued well into Friday.'

Looking back on the *Rocky Road to Dublin* session, Keith Richards had nothing but admiration for Paddy Moloney.

'What about that Paddy Moloney,' Richards told the author. 'What a piece of work! And the rest of them, Oh Lord.'

*   *   *

In November, on their way to Japan, The Chieftains stopped off in London to record *Lily of the West* with Dire Straits' leader Mark Knopfler. A year earlier the English guitarist had been booked to record a track for The Chieftains' projected second country album, but BMG had cancelled the session when the album had been abandoned.

'I had a big falling out with the record company over that,' explained Moloney. 'They weren't sure where I was at because I wanted to do a second country record. I'd already booked Mark Knopfler so I said, "Right, I want you to tell him." And they had to do it.'

With good relations restored with BMG, Moloney met Knopfler to discuss his contribution to the still unnamed *Long Black Veil*. The original plan was to record an instrumental but when Moloney played him an old version of *Lily of the West*, Knopfler immediately remembered the song from his early days playing in the folk clubs of London.

'It was really natural,' remembers Knopfler, who came to Dublin for the recording session. 'I grew up in folk clubs and I'd heard a lot of that music. I suppose it's in there somewhere and it just comes out. I think because it's quite a tough song I found myself singing in a way I never have before. I didn't know whether it was ridiculous or not. I just did it.'

Knopfler's friend the Irish guitarist Paul Brady sat in on the session and contributed the air *The Lakes of Pontchartrain*, that Knopfler played on the record.

'Mark was more familiar with that air so we swapped it into the original *Lily of the West* song,' says Moloney. 'He did a great job and you'd be easily mistaken thinking it was some guy down in the west of Ireland having a *craic* in a pub.'

Kevin Conneff applauded Knopfler for managing to capture the authentic flavour of the song.

'You'd think Mark Knopfler was a born ballad singer,' says Conneff. 'The way he approached it was wonderful.'

At the session Knopfler was impressed by Paddy Moloney's energy and musical creativity.

'You have to hand it to Paddy, he certainly gets all these ideas,' says Knopfler. ' "Hey Mark, I've got a great idea. Would you like to go and play in front of the Taj Mahal?" 'Oh not really, I was thinking of the pyramids.'

'You never know what's he's going to come up with next. It's amazing that he wasn't actually standing playing on the Berlin Wall when that came down.'

In December, while The Chieftains were in Los Angeles on their 13-city US Christmas tour, Paddy Moloney called Gail Zappa to arrange to see Frank. Gail told him that Zappa was very ill but invited The Chieftains over for Sunday lunch.

'Frank died the day before,' says Moloney. 'We heard the sad news and decided we would still go.'

When they arrived Moloney commiserated with Gail and her two sons Dweezil and Ahmet and later they all went into Frank's studio to record a special tribute which is due out on a future album.

'I had a little tune that I wanted to do for Frank,' says Moloney.

'We recorded it and I had Derek play a little bit of Frank's music in the middle of it on piano.'

Looking back, Gail Zappa says The Chieftains had a profound impact on Frank Zappa's final months.

'I'll be eternally grateful to all of them for that beyond anything else,' she said. 'It's something that transcends everything to have a friendship that starts through music and then moves beyond that. It's amazing.'

On Frank's instructions Kevin Conneff's *The Green Fields of America* was played at his funeral.

'It's one of the biggest compliments I was ever paid,' says Conneff. 'Gail told me that in his dying weeks he often listened to this particular song and it was one of the tracks that was used for his cremation ceremony. The three highest compliments of my entire life were Frank Zappa and those great Irish musicians Willie Clancy and Seamus Ennis, who all said favourable things about my singing. They must have got me on a good night.'

* * *

In February 1994 The Chieftains reunited with Van Morrison at Windmill Lane Studios to record a new version of his song *Have I Told You Lately That I Love You?* Moloney had a particular traditional tune in mind for Morrison, but the singer, still fuming that Rod Stewart's version of the song had been a bigger hit than his original version, insisted on re-recording it.

To give the song a traditional flavour Moloney had written a beautiful new introduction featuring harp and tin whistle and Van was delighted.

'The introduction has a whole traditional feel about it and then it's straight into the song,' says Moloney. 'People seem to like it so it must be all right.'

Morrison was in top form for the session and the song was recorded in a couple of takes leaving enough time over for The Chieftains to record a track for Van's next album.

'I think Van did a brilliant job on it,' says Moloney. 'It was amazing.'

Moloney admits a love-hate relationship with Morrison but says he'd never want the singer to change.

'Van Morrison is a great friend and a great enemy too,' says

Moloney. 'We've had our ups and downs but we're too close not to be friends. He's eccentric, but whatever makes the man tick, let him be, because it brings out the genius. When he goes into some of those long ending songs he could be a Connemara man singing a sean-nós song.'

For his track on *The Long Black Veil*, Van Morrison arranged an exchange licensing deal with The Chieftains. 'So,' explains Moloney, 'he owns the recording of *Have I Told You Lately That I Love You?* that is on the album. We had to give him the recording. But, he does that with everything now, since he did get ripped off. And I can't blame him for that.'

A couple of days after the Van Morrison session, Marianne Faithfull came into Windmill Lane to record the sadly moving song *Love Is Teasin'*. Marianne had first heard the Dolly MacMahon version of the song 30 years earlier on an album Moloney had produced for Claddagh.

'Paddy and I had talked about doing *Love is Teasin'* for years,' says Marianne. 'It wasn't until *The Long Black Veil* that Paddy had the right context for the song. It's about heartbreak and it's about love and loss. I think it's the most beautiful thing on the album. It's just perfect for this very sort of deep, heartbreak record.'

During rehearsals Marianne wanted to make the song slightly more upbeat than Moloney had in mind so he hunted down the original Dolly MacMahon tape to show her what he wanted.

'She still wasn't convinced,' says Moloney. 'But the day before we went into the studio she said, "Paddy, I was thinking about that and I think you're right." So we compromised. At the end I put in a slow waltz as if she got up and started to dance with somebody. I added an accordion to give it that kind of sad feeling.'

Marianne says that Moloney has a knack for relaxing her in the studio so she can deliver her best performance.

'Paddy's very casual,' explains Marianne. 'Which is a very good thing for me because it doesn't give me time to get het up and nervous. He just calls me up and says, "I want to do this thing, could we knock it out? Could you come to the studio at 2:00 o'clock?"

'I just say, "OK man" and I go in. The Chieftains are all my dear friends. You know I'm very fond of them, Particularly Derek. There's never any big fuss. Just professional to professional. I think that's what works with musicians. Paddy takes it completely for granted that any good musician will do very good work with The Chieftains.'

The Long Black Veil

On February 23rd The Chieftains took their places among the elite of rock 'n' roll to celebrate The Who's 25th anniversary at Carnegie Hall. Joining a galaxy of rock stars including Bruce Springsteen, Sinéad O'Connor and Pearl Jam's Eddie Vedder, who were playing musical tributes to The Who, Paddy Moloney had especially composed a special middle and end section for the Pete Townsend's classic, *Baba O'Riley*.

'We start off with 64 bars of Chieftains' music with a big orchestra,' Moloney explained to Dublin *Evening News'* rock writer Dermot Hayes.

'And then a Turkish bit before the band come in and then it all goes back to The Who and I've written a polka for the end. It finishes with Roger singing *Teenage Wasteland*.'

The respected American film composer Michael Kamen was in rehearsals for the show, where he was conducting the Juilliard Orchestra, when he first met Paddy Moloney.

'Frankly I'd heard of The Chieftains but I didn't know who Paddy was,' remembers Kamen, who wrote the score for the film *Robin Hood*. 'And he walked into the studio and he was enchanting. Within 50 seconds he said, "And I could do it this way." And he pulled a little tin whistle out of his pocket and started playing. Suddenly I heard some real music for the first time since the rehearsals had started.'

Kamen and Moloney discovered an instant musical rapport and agreed to work together in the future, but the person who made the biggest impression on the Chieftain was Pearl Jam's Eddie Vedder. The intense long-haired grunge singer, who delivered riveting solo versions of *The Kids Are All Right* and *My Generation*, met the piper at the party after the show and found a common bond in music.

'Eddie and I just hit it off,' says Moloney. 'He was one of the best guests on the show and I think he'd be one hell of a guest for The Chieftains. Musically we got on very well and we spoke the same language. I know that if we sat down in the studio with Pearl Jam and started jamming we'd come up with something very interesting. Eddie even told me his secret code so I can always get in touch with him.'

Before Christmas Moloney had met Sinéad O'Connor in Dublin, where she had agreed to guest on The Chieftains' St Patrick's Day Show at Carnegie Hall and record two tracks for *The Long Black Veil*. During their meeting Moloney played her some tapes he'd made of various songs he thought might be suitable.

'We were together for about four hours going over songs and playing tapes,' remembers Moloney. 'I was showing her this and that and playing her tunes on the whistle. She became really emotional and loved getting back to the traditional songs that she'd forgotten. She used to sing *She Moved Through the Fair*, which was one of her favourite songs, but the old *Foggy Dew* was the one I turned her onto. She remembered it from her schooldays. She got so excited that we even discussed doing a whole album together.'

Sinéad, who was still trying to get her career back on track after the uproar when she tore up the Pope's picture on NBC's *Saturday Night Live*, was very moved when Paddy told her about the Symphony he was composing to commemorate the upcoming 150th anniversary of the Irish Potato Famine.

'She later wrote me a letter in Gaelic about her feelings for the famine,' says Moloney. 'She even recorded a song about it on her album *Universal Mother*. Sinéad is like my daughter. She's very talented musically and although she puts on an act to deal with the world, when it's time to sing the song she's always ready to do it.'

On March 15th, the morning after her appearance with The Chieftains on the *Late Show With David Letterman*, Sinéad walked up the stairs of Clinton Studios on New York's West Side escorted by Chieftain manager Steve Macklam and publicist Charles Comer. The session was to be engineered by Jeffrey Lesser, who had worked with Barbra Streisand and Lou Reed, and he went to great lengths to make Sinéad feel at home.

'I built a little environment in the studio for her,' explained Lesser.

'I actually went out before the session and got her a vase of flowers and she was very touched. It seemed to put her at ease.'

The legendary guitarist Ry Cooder, who was in New York to record with The Chieftains the following day, played slide guitar on the session and observed Sinéad working to give her best possible performance.

'As much of a star figure that Sinéad is, poor thing, she has to deal with the fact that here is her uncle Paddy,' Ry Cooder told the author. 'How much of a job are you going to do on Paddy? You're going to make it work for his sake because you want to please him. And I think Sinéad took off on that a little bit.'

Cooder watched Sinéad carefully psyche herself up to perform *Foggy Dew* and *She Moved Through the Fair*.

'She's like a method actor,' says Ry. 'She had to search to find herself dramatically in the part. That's how she seems to approach things and that's what I hear coming through her music. Sinéad enacts the whole thing and gets into character to achieve a dramatic presentation. And then you say, "OK, when this person gets themselves up to speed, we'll hit it." '

The Dublin-born singer delivered two stand-out performances and impressed Matt Molloy with her professionalism and vocal delivery.

'Well she's one of us,' says Molloy. 'Great lady apart from all the wild things you hear but that didn't surface as far as we were concerned. She just launched into it and held nothing back.'

Kevin Conneff said Sinéad's singing on *Foggy Dew* was mesmerizing.

'She really made the hairs stand up on the back of my neck,' he says. 'She's one hell of a voice.'

Also in the studio to witness the session was Tony Hollingsworth, who hadn't seen Moloney since The Wall concert in Berlin. Hollingsworth told Paddy Moloney about a major music event he was planning in Japan that May called The Great Music Experience, which was similar to Moloney's postponed idea for the Taj Mahal concert the previous year. Hearing about Hollingsworth's plan, to feature every kind of music from Japanese monks to the hard Australian rock band INXS, Moloney and Ry Cooder asked to take part.

'Paddy has his antenna out all the time,' says Matt Molloy, who was in on the conversation. 'He doesn't miss anything, he's incredible. If somebody says, "yeah, we'll go to Japan." He'll immediately try and work out how it can be done and get it in perspective.

'An idea will take him over and he'll work at it 24 hours a day. If he gets the ball he keeps it under his arm until he's right in front of the goal. And then he scores. That's the way he does things. That's why The Chieftains are where they are.'

The following day Ry Cooder returned to the studio to record *The Coast of Malabar* and *Dunmore Lassies* with The Chieftains. Moloney had first met Ry the previous December in Los Angeles after cold-calling him to appear on the album.

'I found out right away that Paddy's such a knowledgeable and crazed manic little dude,' says Ry Cooder. 'You get to cover a lot of territory in a hurry. He's so speedy and so expert that you can whip through your outline of topics in a split second. Paddy wants to cut to the chase as they say around here. I really appreciate that as we've only got a little time.'

But when they began recording *Coast of Malabar*, Ry Cooder was not comfortable with the song's rhythm. And the more he tried playing it the more frustrated he got.

'I could see the whole thing falling apart,' recalls Moloney. 'We were getting in deep water. So I went off to the jax, where I go to get fresh ideas, and thought about it for a while.'

In the toilet Moloney cast his mind back 50 years to his grandmother singing the tune to him as a young boy. He thought about the storyline of the sailor going away and landing on a faraway island called Malabar and falling in love with a young maiden. And his heartbreak of leaving her to go home, knowing he'd never see her again.

'So I thought about giving it a south sea islands' kind of feel. A calypso rhythm,' says Moloney. 'And then I went out to tell Ry. He said, "Oh man, that's great." So we went tearing into it from a different approach and he became much more comfortable.'

Ry Cooder said it was just a question of finding a common meeting point between his and The Chieftains' music.

'I'm not a traditional player,' explains Cooder. 'So it's just a matter of finding a groove. These guys play with a very Irish kind of lilt. It's a different bag. So once you find a rhythmic middle point everything else will fall into place. The real thing is to find the inside groove we can all use.'

Kevin Conneff was delighted to be working with Ry Cooder,

whose concerts he had always made a point of seeing when he played Dublin.

'I've idolized Ry Cooder for years,' says Conneff. 'He was a joy to work with and he definitely put his own stamp on the song.'

On March 1st The Chieftains were just about to go on stage in Savannah, Georgia, when an excited Charles Comer telephoned with the news that they had won their third Grammy for *The Celtic Harp* in the 'Best Traditional Folk Album category'. The group had been at the Pre-Grammy party the night before at New York's Metropolitan Museum of Art but had flown to Georgia as they didn't expect to win.

'It was a huge surprise,' Moloney told *Hot Press*. 'Charlie rang up and said, "You've got it, you've done it, you've won!" And I just said, "You must be joking Charlie!" It took me totally by surprise. One can't be too greedy after all.'

* * *

Back in Dublin, just five days before she was due to appear at Carnegie Hall at The Chieftains' St Patrick's Day concert, Sinéad O'Connor discovered that her American visa had run out. When Moloney heard, he was livid and telephoned all the friends he knew in high places. Finally, three days later, everything was sorted out thanks to the personal intervention of Senator Ted Kennedy, and Sinéad got to New York.

On St Patrick's Day a sea of green-clad Chieftain fans paid $45 each for the Carnegie Hall tickets to see their musical heroes. The high point of the show came when Moloney introduced Sinéad O'Connor, who shyly walked out on stage wearing a long green velvet dress with her trademark crew cut. It was her first New York performance since the humiliation of being booed off stage at Bob Dylan's 30th birthday concert a year earlier.

'She's a great girl and a fabulous singer,' Moloney told the audience as Sinéad looked uneasy and embarrassed by the applause.

After singing emotionally-charged versions of *She Moved Through the Fair* and *The Foggy Dew*, Sinéad sat down on Kevin Conneff's rostrum to clap along to The Chieftains' next few songs before Paddy called her back for the encore.

In her concert review, Helena Mulkerns of *The Irish Times* summed up the evening saying: 'If Irish visibility is at its apex on St Patrick's

Day in New York, then thank God for The Chieftains at Carnegie Hall who eclipsed all "Kiss Me. I'm Irish" buttons with a splendid presentation of Irish culture in Manhattan's most prestigious setting.'

* * *

At the beginning of May, The Chieftains flew from Dublin to London to record a track with Dolores O'Riordan and The Cranberries, who were presently at the top of the English and American charts. But the morning of the session The Cranberries, who Paddy Moloney had nicknamed The Dingleberries, abruptly cancelled the recording session when they were offered an appearance on BBC-TV's *Top of the Pops*.

'The bone of contention was that we had paid our fares over there and it wasn't going to happen,' explains Derek Bell. 'They just called up and said it's off. The only redeeming grace was that they brought Paddy and me to dinner the night before so I would have thought it was going to take place. I was never told the reason why they cancelled.'

A week later The Chieftains flew to Nara City, Japan, to take part in Tony Hollingsworth's Great Music Experience to be broadcast to an estimated 200 million television viewers in over 30 countries. Funded from a grant from UNESCO the project was the first in a projected series of concerts challenging the world's leading musicians to explore different cultures.

The site of this monumental event, more than three years in the making, was the 1,200-year-old Todaiji temple in Nara City – the world's largest wooden building. It featured artists ranging from western stars like Bob Dylan, Bon Jovi, Inxs, Ry Cooder and Joni Mitchell to the Japanese rock band Hotel Tomoyasu to groups of Okinawan folk musicians and Buddhist monks.

'The Chieftains played an enormous role,' explained organizer Hollingsworth. 'They were the musical glue that held it all together. They play traditional instruments that are not unlike the instruments played in Japan in the sixth century.'

The musicians arrived two weeks before the three-day event to start rehearsals. Michael Kamen was conducting the shows and composing an overture for the event which would involve all the musicians.

'At one point I had 500 people up on stage in front of me,' said Kamen. 'And I was trying to conduct them. I suddenly realized that the real homogenizer in that group were The Chieftains. They were the great unifying ingredient.'

At one point in rehearsals Moloney suggested a particular Irish jig for the overture which was immediately incorporated. The ancient Japanese orchestra quietly learned the jig and everything seemed fine until Hollingsworth received a visit from the orchestra's anxious director at two in the morning.

Remembers Hollingsworth: 'He said, "I'm very sorry to disturb you but I have something very serious to say." I thought, "Oh gracious, they're pulling out of the show." But the problem was that Paddy's Irish jig had the same melody as a lot of Japanese pinball machines. He said, "We can't possibly play that, everyone will laugh." So we had to find another jig that sounded different.'

Far more difficult, from some of The Chieftains' religious points of view, was their collaboration with Joni Mitchell, who was performing a new song she'd written about the shame of the Irish Magdalen laundries. The laundries were the Catholic Church refuge for unmarried pregnant women in Ireland in the last century and most major towns had one. Joni was so moved when she read the story about the discovery of 130 young women's graves, found in the grounds of a Dublin convent in 1970, that she wrote the song for her album *Violent Indigo*, which would later win a Grammy.

Ry Cooder, who also performed with The Chieftains at the event, said the Magdalen laundry song was his musical highlight of the whole three days.

'The Chieftains backing up Joni Mitchell when she did that song was bone-chilling,' said Cooder. 'It was the zenith of that whole thing and most of it was junk, including my performance.'

During The Chieftains' medley dancer Cara Butler brought the audience to their feet when she step danced with a life-sized Bunruki puppet to the Kerry Slides. Paddy Moloney says his high spot was meeting the Okinawan musicians and discovering how much their two musics had in common.

'One of the things of the Great Music Experience was to break down the barriers, which we did,' explains Moloney. 'We played with Chinese and Japanese musicians and it was very interesting behind the scenes. I remember we went into a room with the

285

Okinawans and we just started playing and they joined in. It was totally incredible. You wouldn't believe how we all gelled together.'

Ry Cooder, who had previously written a song called *I'm Going Back to Okinawa*, saw Moloney's talent for spotting connections in music from different countries and then bridging the gap.

'They are all connected up and Paddy won't miss a beat,' explains Cooder. 'He's hearing the connection wherever he goes. And the connection's there. If you are looking at diatonic music, which probably half the world is into historically, Irish music is as deep as any of it, and it fits. Somehow it will link up with just about everything because of the scales and the melodies. You can play it with Chinese people, you can play it with Okinawans. Paddy's got really good at it. He's put a lot of time into practising that craft and that approach and finding that pathway.'

A few months later The Chieftains visited Okinawa during a Japanese tour where they played some concerts and met the President. They even brought Okinawan singer Shokichi Kina across to mainland Japan as their musical guest for some shows.

Back in Ireland, Derek Bell would later sum up the Great Music Experience in his own inimitable manner, saying: 'There were so many colourful artists there but I think the Japanese women were the best. They looked so nice. The flute player in the orchestra was very beautiful and so was the harpist and for that matter so was the tiompánist. It was a tremendous spectacle.'

* * *

On a Thursday afternoon at the beginning of June, Paddy Moloney telephoned Sting at his estate in Wiltshire, England, to invite him to appear on what was still being called *Chieftains and Friends*. The rock superstar immediately agreed but said they would have to record at his home studio the following Tuesday, as he was very busy writing songs for his new album. Sting also insisted on singing in Gaelic.

'I was delighted by the idea,' said Sting. 'Except that I really didn't have time to leave home because I was trying to write some music. So I said I'd do it if you come to England.'

Seizing his opportunity Moloney swung into action and asked his old friend Seán Mac Réamoinn, the veteran Radio Éireann broadcaster who had penned the liner notes to the first Chieftains' record, to translate the 18th century Jacobite song about Bonnie Prince Charlie, *Mo Ghile Mear* or *Our Hero*.

'I had to act very quickly to get everything together in time,' says Moloney. 'Sting wanted to sing the whole lot in Irish but at the end of the day we compromised. He sang the choruses in Gaelic and the verses in English.'

Over the next few days Moloney worked flat out coordinating the recording session, asking Brian Masterson to engineer and lining up a crew to film the session for a video.

It was a sweltering hot June day when The Chieftains and crew arrived from Dublin *en masse* at Sting's beautiful country house on the banks of the River Avon.

'Of course the first thing Sting did was show us the house and the whole estate,' remembers Moloney. 'And it's just an incredible place. Unfortunately Derek walked into the lily pond by mistake.'

Moloney wanted to begin the session immediately but Sting insisted on serving them a fantastic lunch by the swimming pool prepared by his personal chef.

'That was more important than getting on with the song,' says Moloney. 'And of course I couldn't eat at all. I was pretending to be relaxed but underneath my smile I was very worried about how it was going to go. Because you never know, you could lose it.'

After lunch at about 2:30 p.m. Moloney sat down with Sting at the piano in his 72-track library recording studio to go over the Irish words of *Mo Ghile Mear*. Singing phonetically, Sting easily mastered singing the Gaelic words and Moloney relaxed.

'He was a school teacher and he's into languages in a big way,' explains Moloney. 'I was a bit nervous about him wanting to have a crack at it in Irish. But he did a day's work on it and he seemed to have quite a grip on the whole thing.'

Sting says his lack of Gaelic did not detract from his performance in any way.

'Lyrics can communicate without necessarily being understood,' he said. 'The feeling and mood that the writer puts in are already there whether you understand it or not. I mean, I sing my own words and I don't think about what I'm singing. It's not just about words, it's about words and music. It's a different medium. It's a conversation.'

Matt Molloy thoroughly enjoyed the session with Sting and was delighted with the results.

'It's trial and error and you hope for the best,' says Molloy. 'Sting's a very informed man, very smart and a great musician. He was interested in what we were doing. He had a go. Good for him.' It only took a couple of hours to record *Mo Ghile Mear*, and this left time for the band to record Leonard Cohen's song *Sisters of Mercy* with Sting for a future project.

By the time the session had finished at about 8:00 p.m., Sting and The Chieftains had become very friendly and were already discussing future projects together.

'We had a great day,' says Sting. 'The Chieftains are an excellent band and I think they are an attractive band to work with because it's a long tradition. They're also a great bunch of guys to be hanging out with. It seemed to be very prestigious for me to sing with them.'

Not easily impressed by the musical abilities of rock stars, Derek Bell thought Sting was excellent.

'I like Sting,' says Bell. 'He had brains and musicianship and whatnot. He sang very well.'

On hearing the finished recording Seán Mac Reamoinn was also pleasantly surprised by how well Sting had sung the Gaelic words.

'I could understand every word of him singing Irish,' laughed Mac Réamoinn. 'But I couldn't understand a word of his English verses.'

* * *

The Chieftains were all looking forward to playing *The Soldier's Song* on the pitch at New York's Giants Stadium, in front of 75,000 soccer fans for the Ireland-Italy World Cup opening round match in June. The group had been invited to perform by the Irish football association (FAI) but at the last minute the World Cup USA committee decided not to go ahead with this plan.

'There were a lot of politics involved in the decision,' Moloney complained to *The Cork Examiner*. 'They decided we could not be allowed to play the anthem. Instead the anthems for both teams were played by a regular military band.'

The following week Paddy Moloney paid a special visit to Quebec to discuss plans for his long-planned Famine Symphony to be performed in May 1995. Irish actor Richard Harris had expressed interest in narrating the story of the famine and Michael Kamen had agreed to conduct the Quebec Symphony Orchestra who would perform with The Chieftains.

In Quebec Moloney met with Canadian politicians to try and get funding for the ambitious concert, which would involve musicians and performers from all over the world and be filmed for a documentary. He also paid a heartfelt visit to Gross Île, the small island on the St Lawrence River that housed a quarantine centre where 15,000 Irish immigrants died, and played a lament on his pipes over their graves. A month later Moloney met Irish president Mary Robinson in Vancouver and discussed the event, which would benefit the charity, Concern, with her.

'The whole question of underprivileged children and countries facing famine is close to her heart,' Moloney told the Irish *Sunday Independent*.

Unfortunately the following year the delicate international negotiations needed to get the famine symphony off the ground fell apart and Moloney had to put it on hold indefinitely.

After winding up their American tour, The Chieftains flew back to Ireland exhausted and looking forward to relaxing for their summer holidays. But while the other Chieftains went home, Paddy Moloney began the arduous job of mixing tracks from the new album at Westland Studios.

One night U2's Bono came into the studio to overdub a vocal track on Mick Jagger's vocals for *The Long Black Veil*. Bono had listened to The Chieftains while he was growing up in Dublin and was a long-time fan with a huge admiration for the group.

Says Bono: 'I heard a story that in Nigeria (I think it was Nigeria) during one of their many coups, rebel forces took over one of the national radio stations and were playing The Chieftains along with various other African artists. Whether this is true or not, it is this connection between Irish and African music that makes Paddy Moloney's minstrels so vital to me, so un-northern European, so ancient, primeval – yet still the sound of the future. Six very dangerous men. East of Eden. It's no wonder they're popular in China – they scare the shit out of the Anglo Saxon.'

But when Moloney heard Bono's singing his duet with Mick Jagger he felt it did not work and mixed it right down although the Irish singer's voice is still there faintly.

'I think what he'd been doing that night had been fairly experimental,' said U2 manager Paul McGuinness. 'It was an elaborate form of humming and we certainly didn't feel that it was fair to describe it as a duet with Mick. So we preferred not to take the credit. I felt that it certainly wouldn't have been fair to U2's fans to tell them Bono was on the track.'

Paddy Moloney said Bono's voice added texture although it was barely audible.

'Bono wasn't mad about it and I agreed,' said Moloney. 'When us Irishmen get together we know what's good and what's bad.'

On June 26th The Chieftains abruptly pulled out of performing at the Newry Music Festival, due to be broadcast live on BBC Radio 2, leading to press speculation that they had received death threats from the outlawed loyalist group UFF. Calling a press conference Moloney denied the reports and cited the group's heavy workload as the reason.

'A lot of circumstances, including personal reasons, made it impossible to do yesterday's gig,' Moloney told *The Irish Press*.

On August 5th Seán Keane was rushed to hospital with a suspected heart attack just hours before The Chieftains were due to headline the International Celtic Festival at Lorient. Keane was soon given the all-clear and released from hospital a day later but Seán Potts flew to Lorient to take his place.

'We panicked at first, but thankfully, it's not serious,' Chieftains' manager Steve Macklam told *The Evening Press* in Dublin the next day.

'He is out of hospital but will sit out this performance.'

Keane says that stress, caused by The Chieftains' punishing schedule, was the problem and he was now taking things easier.

'Some reports said that I had a heart attack but I didn't,' he said. 'It was stress and I am learning not to let things get on top of me. I've looked after it and it's behind me now.'

After Seán's health scare the rest of The Chieftains, some of whom were approaching 60 years of age, were forced to take a good long look at their workload which seemed to be growing geometrically with each new success.

* * *

In November BMG finally decided to name the new Chieftains' album *The Long Black Veil*. In an interview with the *Sunday Indepen-*

dent Paddy Moloney criticized the record company for the new title and for delaying its release until after Christmas.

'There is apparently enormous interest in the album,' Moloney told the *Sunday Independent*. 'But in their wisdom they have decided not to release it until January, thus missing the big selling Christmas-time market. They have also changed the title from *The Chieftains and Friends* to *The Long Black Veil* because that's the name of one of the songs. It doesn't make sense.'

29

A Pilgrimage to Galicia

The Long Black Veil was finally released on January 24th, 1995 to ecstatic reviews all over the world. The group's 31st album was acclaimed as a true crossover from the eclectic World Music segment to mainstream pop.

In a four-star review in *Rolling Stone*, respected rock critic John Swenson lavished praise on Paddy Moloney:

'The Chieftains, inadvertent prophets of the world-music boom for more than 30 years, have travelled the globe, emphasizing the compatibility of traditional Irish music with local sounds from Nashville to Beijing. Fittingly, this sonic circumnavigation ends up with the world beating a path to The Chieftains on *The Long Black Veil*, an album of traditional music performed with the help of some of the biggest names in the business.

'But the overall success of the album rests in the skilled hands of Chieftains' leader Paddy Moloney. A sonic *auteur* of the highest order, Moloney has devoted much of his career to exploring the forces that unite seemingly disparate musical traditions and has developed a specific genius for designing arrangements tailored to the strength of his subjects.'

Awarding the album four stars, *New York Post* critic Dan Aquilante, who would later select it as his best CD of 1995, wrote: 'I can't even begin to guess the magic that chief Chieftain Paddy Moloney and his band use to bring out the best in people who play with them, but they do.'

USA TODAY's Edna Gunderson declared *The Long Black Veil* 'sublime'. She wrote that the band 'blends its folk traditions with top pop talents, who enhance but never overwhelm the haunting, playful and gorgeous musicianship'.

New York Times' music critic Neil Strauss saw a cinematic quality to the songs on the album, writing: 'The droning pipes, chirping tin whistles, floating flute melodies, slow harp glissandos and resonant bodhrán frame-drum thumps are extremely evocative, working in perfect tandem with the lyrics to create a picture with substance and depth.'

But perhaps the most meaningful review of all came from Marijohn Wilkin who wrote *The Long Black Veil* in 1959. The Nashville-based song writer admitted she never before understood the song's mystery until she heard Mick Jagger sing it with The Chieftains.

'I didn't want anyone with me when I listened to it,' Wilkin told *R&R* magazine. 'I'm a strange person. When I heard it beside Sting doing an ancient Celtic melody, I just sat here and cried because every ounce of my heritage came through in that melody. Listening to that Chieftains' album, I thought, "And they wonder where country music comes from." '

Within two weeks *The Long Black Veil* had entered the *Billboard* album charts at No. 24 with a bullet, selling 20,000 copies in England and 10,000 copies in Japan. Describing The Chieftains as 'musicians' musicians', Paddy Moloney was jubilant as he chronicled his litany of successes for England's *Daily Express*.

'I wanted to spread the gospel of Irish music,' he said. 'Like Martin Luther King, I had a dream and that dream has come off.'

But back in Ireland, some of the purists were more reserved in their judgment, feeling that The Chieftains were taking a backseat to visiting pop stars.

'I think there was a backlash against them after *The Long Black Veil*,' says Ciarán Mac Mathúna. 'But I say more power to them. We've had enough censorship in this country. I have said publicly that if the core music can't survive without being protected and insulated, or put into intensive care, it won't. It has to be able to weather the storm out there in the open market and I trust that The Chieftains would never desert it.'

Peter O'Toole, a life-long lover of traditional music, said he was delighted that the masses were now embracing *The Long Black Veil*.

'We've known in Paddy's lifetime what his contribution is because we can hear it and see it,' says O'Toole. 'But when the history of these times is written it is going to be remarkable that this gentleman, who has cleaved firmly to his beloved instrument, has never budged an inch in his integrity or the quality of his musicianship. They have brought Paddy in and it's not the other way round. Paddy has been taken up and rightly so, deservedly so. It's a superb sound and he's a superb musician. He doesn't know the meaning of the word compromise.

'He is prepared to play his uilleann pipes be it for the hooley, be it for a requiem mass. It doesn't matter so long as he's let play his pipes. And let him play in his own way without compromising himself one little scrap.'

* * *

On March 10th The Chieftains were made honorary chiefs of the Oklahoma Choctaw Nation at a special ceremony at SMU in Dallas, Texas. The award, never before been given to a non-American Indian group, continued a unique relationship going back 150 years to when the tribe sent $175 to Ireland to relieve suffering in the potato famine. When Paddy Moloney first heard the story of the Choctaw gift he had contacted the tribe to thank them.

'Even Queen Victoria wouldn't lift a finger to help but the Choctaws did,' said Moloney. 'It was a great honour for them to make me an honorary chief.'

When President Bill Clinton invited The Chieftains to entertain at the White House on St Patrick's Day they declined as they were already booked into New York's Avery Fisher Hall with special guest Marianne Faithfull. Amazingly, although Marianne had known The Chieftains almost 30 years, this would be their first concert together.

'It was a great show and I loved it,' said Marianne whose performance of *Love is Teasin'* received a standing ovation.

'Although it was Avery Fisher The Chieftains were far more relaxed than I have ever seen them,' said Marianne. 'Their music has become much more popular than when they were first playing it. It's the same music as it was then. Paddy hasn't made any changes but it used to be a much more specialist side road or musical by way. But to have a popular base he had to broaden it. I think it's fantastic now and much more entertaining.'

After the concert Marianne joined The Chieftains for their annual St Patrick's Day celebrations at Eamonn Doran's. And the singer also joined the group on their 20-city Spring tour for dates in Boston and Washington D.C. as well as appearing with them on the CBS networked *Late Show with David Letterman*.

That month also saw The Chieftains venture into cyberspace

when RCA Victor opened a web site for them on the Internet giving fans tour information, discography and audio excerpts from *The Long Black Veil*.

In a press release Steve Vining proudly trumpeted the news saying, 'We think it's appropriate for a band that weds the past and present so beautifully in their music to lead us into the next frontier.'

The Chieftains were also active on the big screen with Moloney supplying a new version of *O'Sullivan's March* for *Rob Roy*, starring Liam Neeson and music for Maeve Binchy's *Circle of Friends* starring Chris O'Donnell and Minnie Driver.

By April *The Long Black Veil* had gone gold in America, selling a staggering 650,000 copies and seemed on the way to selling a million prompting a delighted Steve Vining to tell United Press International that they were still only in the initial stages of marketing the record.

'It's like selling a soap powder or anything else,' explained Matt Molloy. 'I mean we try to hold true to the music but you do have to broaden your base. We're selling a product. Recognition of the band has come very slowly and there's been a lot of leg work.'

Paddy Moloney was taking it all in his stride when he told *Time* magazine that, 'We are not going off our rocker. And we are not going to *become* rockers.'

Admitting that 'The diehards don't like us,' Moloney boasted that they had made a million more friends than they had lost. He also gave *Time* his recipe for world peace, saying: 'The great leaders of the world should learn the tin whistle and have a party. And the world will be a happier place.' This prompted *Time* writer James Greenberg to add: 'Listening to this timeless music, you can almost believe that a song could save the world.'

Even before the release of *The Long Black Veil*, Paddy Moloney had began work on his next Chieftains' project which would be an album of Galician music. As the next step on from *Celtic Wedding*, Moloney embarked on an ambitious project to follow the threads of Celtic music through Galicia, in north west Spain, onto Cuba and South America recording local musicians for an album tentatively called *The Chieftains' Pilgrimage to Galicia*.

In November 1994 The Chieftains flew to Bilbao to play a concert and then spend three days in the studio with local musicians. Tragedy struck when British Airways managed to lose Derek Bell's

Harp. A Basque harpist kindly lent Derek her instrument for the concert but needed it back afterwards.

'I arrived at the studio harpless and just had to sit and listen and write out things I could add later,' remembers Bell.

On the second day British Airways called the studio to say they'd found the harp and were bringing it straight round.

'It was completely smashed,' says Derek. 'It was a total wreck and both the case and the harp were write-offs. It must have fallen out of the airplane and landed on a metal spike because the case is sturdy.' The Chieftains had to arrange to have a replacement harp flown out from England. A couple of months later Martin Fay would leave his fiddle on his fish tank as he was changing a string and forget about it. Two days later he came in to find it floating with the fish. Not wanting to pay for the instrument to be repaired Fay revarnished it himself.

'It was a good instrument worth a fortune,' says Moloney. 'He's a terrible man.'

After the recording in Bilbao The Chieftains headed west to Santiago De Compostela in Galicia, where they were to perform Paddy Moloney's newly written Galician Overture with The Santiago Symphony Orchestra. The overture, which is dedicated to Polig Monjarret, began life as a 30-second introduction but took on a life of its own.

'My plan was to give it little overtones of Irish, Scottish, Breton and Galician music but it just got bigger and bigger,' says Moloney.

As usual Brian Masterson was with The Chieftains to record the sessions for orchestra and choir at Convent Cathedral, and he says that setting up the microphones and placing the group and male choir in the huge cathedral was a real challenge.

'The acoustic in that cathedral was beyond belief,' remembers Masterson. 'The sound went up into the roof and just flowed back. It was magic. I had The Chieftains all spread out sitting in the pews and the choir up on the altar rails.

'But behind us there was what I can only describe as a huge dungeon with big bars. And behind these bars were a closed order of nuns who had a vow of silence. I had set up my equipment at the back and when The Chieftains started playing I just felt the hairs on the back of my neck stand up. I looked around and there were all these nuns, whom you could barely make out, peering through the bars to see what was happening.'

From Santiago The Chieftains headed 50 miles south to Carlos Nunez's hometown of Vigo. The young piper, who had helped Moloney select Galician music for the album, had recruited musicians to come to the Dublin bar for the live recording of the album's grand finale.

'We only invited 20 musicians and 150 turned up in this tiny little bar,' laughed Moloney. 'We just let loose and it was really wild. I've left all the screams and claps on the track to give a real party feeling.'

Two months later in Los Angeles The Chieftains recorded a track with Los Lobos and Linda Ronstadt, called *The Mexican Connection*, later to become *Guadalupe*.

* * *

After an eight-city British tour The Chieftains arrived in London on Wednesday May 17th to appear on their second *Late Show with David Letterman* in just three months. For the show, which had an Irish theme, The Chieftains played a song from *The Long Black Veil* with Sinéad O'Connor and a 'jovial' Van Morrison, on *Have I Told You Lately That I Love You?* The show, which was being produced from London that week, also had Peter O'Toole as a guest, who was delighted to see Moloney again and try to play his uilleann pipes.

After the show Van Morrison failed to find any humour in David Letterman, and was actively hostile when he was summoned to meet with the American talk show host ten minutes after end of the show.

'There's more *craic* in a morgue,' Morrison remarked to his fiancée, the former Miss Ireland, Michelle Rocca. 'He looks like Bugs Bunny.'

The next morning The Chieftains flew straight to Los Angeles to play at Don Henley's wedding and at the star-studded premiere of Mel Gibson's new film *Braveheart*. On the flight over from London, Moloney, who had been composing his Famine Symphony into a micro cassette recorder, managed to lose the tape going through customs. After a two-hour panic tour manager and soundman Danny Cleland found the tape and averted a disaster.

Staying at the plush Wyndham Bel Age Hotel, Paddy Moloney was visibly jet-lagged on Friday morning as he met manager Steve

Macklam for breakfast to finalize logistics for the busy weekend ahead. Asked about Morrison's performance on the Letterman Show, Moloney said: 'Van took off on his own. He started singing Sinéad's harmonies.'

At 4:30 that afternoon The Chieftains assembled in the hotel lobby for the short drive to Paramount Studios in Melrose Place for the *Braveheart* premiere. Kevin Conneff's wife Joanie, who was over for a vacation, sat at the back of the bus which was driven by Steve Macklam. Publicist Charles Comer sat up front cheerfully handing out the latest concert reviews to each member of the band.

On their arrival at the Paramount lot they found that work has just started to construct a 13th century Scottish village around the small stage where The Chieftains would perform. After a sound check the group retired to their dressing room where they were joined by dancers Cara Butler and Donny Golden for a buffet meal.

At the far end of the long table Paddy Moloney sat alone drawing up his set list for the evening on a small sheet of paper. In a bid to liven things up Charles Comer started an impromptu sing-song before the call to take their places in the huge cinema to watch the screening of *Braveheart*.

Asked if the group perform at many private parties Derek Bell smiles, saying: 'There must be a lot of money in it. I personally can't wait to get home to feed my tabby.'

After the film, The Chieftains took the stage to perform a set for the VIP audience which included Mel Gibson and Jodie Foster. But the group found themselves having to compete with an undercurrent of conversation through the music, leading Bell to shrug his shoulders and say, 'I look at it from the churchly point of view. If you can make one person pay attention, it's a success.'

But The Chieftains got a standing ovation, and as they left the stage after an encore, a smiling Mel Gibson rushed up to congratulate them on their performance. Since being introduced to their music by Roger Daltrey a couple of years earlier at the *Irish Evening* concert at the Hollywood Bowl, the Australian film star had become a big fan. Now backstage Gibson picked up a tin whistle and played a duet with Moloney as they posed for press photographs.

'Mel loves The Chieftains,' says Paddy. 'And he's not a bad whistle player either.'

On the way back to the hotel The Chieftains were in good spirits as Macklam navigated the bus down Sunset Boulevard past corners of colourful West Hollywood hookers and transvestites. In a great mood Moloney cracked jokes and recounted the time that Derek Bell tried to chat up what he thought was a woman in a dress only to discover it was a long-haired man in drag.

Next day Don Henley's $2 million wedding had almost presidential security. Secret maps showing the wedding location deep in the Malibu mountains at Saddlerock Ranch had been sent to guests and The Chieftains all had to sign a secrecy form forbidding them to talk to the press.

Don Henley, who had flown in The Chieftains especially to perform straight after he exchanged wedding vows with model Sharon Summerall, said he specifically wanted their music at the ceremony.

Explained Henley: 'We invited The Chieftains to play at our wedding because both my wife and I have Scottish-Irish blood on at least one side of our respective families.'

After the early evening outdoor ceremony, in a tree-lined grove covered with roses, the 500 guests were directed along a candle-lit path to where The Chieftains were waiting to start playing.

'We thought that having The Chieftains play would be a beautiful and appropriate gesture,' said Henley. 'And we were right.'

But before they could begin Jack Nicholson suddenly spotted Moloney and came running up on stage to say hello.

'Great to see you Paddy,' Nicholson told Moloney. 'I often think about that party you threw in Wicklow. It's about time you had another one.'

After The Chieftains played the guests moved into a huge marquee for the wedding reception where they were entertained by an array of superstars including Tony Bennett, Sting, Billy Joel, Jackson Browne, John Fogerty, Bruce Springsteen and The Eagles.

'It was great to see The Chieftains play at Don Henley's wedding,' said Jackson Browne, who also served as one of the bridegroom's ushers. 'Their music was quite a momentous affair at that big wedding and they were the first on the bill of great artists and orchestras who played.'

Later Don Henley said that The Chieftains were the perfect start for the evening's festivities, getting everyone in a great mood for the champagne reception.

'The simple up-tempo Irish jigs can wash all of one's cares away,' said Henley. 'There is something primal in this music and it touches people deeply. Indeed, I think The Chieftains have survived for so long because of the quality and the timelessness of the music they play. Also, I think the energy and tenacity of Paddy "The Operator" Moloney has certainly been a factor. Blarney, indeed.'

The following afternoon on the bus to the House of Blues on Sunset Boulevard, to tape Dan Aykroyd's *Live at the House of Blues* TV show, several of The Chieftains still nursed sore heads from the Henley wedding which had lasted until daylight. In the dressing room before the sound check, Paddy Moloney met Sarah McLachlan, the 27-year-old singer-songwriter from Halifax, Nova Scotia, who would sing *Foggy Dew* on stage that night and guest on their upcoming US summer tour.

'My dad got a Chieftains record in about 1965 so I first heard them when I was very young,' said McLachlan. 'When I heard about *The Long Black Veil* I actually listened to it and became really familiar with them again. When I was asked to do summer dates with The Chieftains I immediately said yes. I thought it was an amazing opportunity.'

The young singer ran through *Foggy Dew* twice with The Chieftains during soundcheck and performed a stunning version which was seen by millions when the show was broadcast the following month.

'It was very loose on my part,' said Sarah. 'I didn't want to know the song that well as I just wanted to get up there and wing it. It was pretty terrifying.'

After the show The Chieftains held court in their dressing room to Hollywood producers from Disney, Paramount and Morgan Creek. That night Chieftains' managers Steve Macklam and Sam Feldman sealed a deal with Morgan Creek for Paddy to write the score for the new Sandra Bullock, Dennis Leary comedy *Two if By Sea*. They also met with the producers of Disney's *Winnie the Pooh* for which Moloney had been commissioned to give *Winnie the Pooh's Song* a Chieftains feel.

'Film scores are becoming more and more important for The Chieftains,' explained Macklam. 'Their music is so visually stimulating and evocative and it is very popular with directors.'

* * *

On July 4th The Chieftains played on the lawn of the Capitol

Building at the official *A Capitol Fourth* concert which was broadcast live on PBS. Rita Moloney, Aedín and Pádraig were in Washington and the following day the Moloneys would fly to Boston to help their youngest son settle into MIT, where he had been accepted for an engineering course.

While The Chieftains waited in their caravan with country star Ricky Skaggs, who was to join them on stage, there was a heavy thunderstorm. But as Stacy Keach announced the Chieftains the skies suddenly cleared up as they casually strolled onto the stage. Two songs later, when Skaggs came on to perform the *Wabash Cannonball* and *Cotton-Eyed Joe*, Moloney had the audience on their feet as he led a Washington hooley with an estimated audience of 400,000 plus millions of television viewers.

Two weeks later The Chieftains weren't quite so lucky with the weather when they opened their summer tour with Sarah McLachlan at the Jones Beach Theater. It was near 100 degrees and humid when they took the stage after Sarah MacLachlan's set. Everybody was sweating with the exception of Derek Bell who was still wearing his red sweater which never seemed to come off for the entire tour.

Forty minutes into the set, during Matt Molloy's flute solo on *The Mason's Apron*, there was a fierce lightning storm. The first The Chieftains knew about the storm was when a union representative rushed on stage and ordered the band to stop the show. It was the first show in the group's 32-year history not to have gone the distance.

'Look,' said Molloy proudly pointing to the constant barrage of lightning over Long Island Sound. 'I invoked the heavens.'

Later that night The Chieftains retired to Fitzer's Bar at the Fitzpatrick Hotel in New York's Lexington Avenue to celebrate Carlos Nunez's 24th birthday. The party was still going strong at 3 a.m. when Paddy Moloney led a conga line through the bar.

The Summer 'Shed' tour with Sarah McLachlan played 16 cities through America winding up at Red Rocks in Denver on August 3rd, where the singer's crew decided to play a practical joke on Derek Bell.

'You know how Derek always wears the same red sweater?' said Sarah. 'About 20 people in my crew all put on red sweaters and went out to his piano during his solo and started dancing. Derek looked up and he just laughed his head off. He played his very best solo of the whole tour that night.'

On the tour Sarah, who sang *Foggy Dew* and joined in their rousing finale *Did you ever Go A' Courtin' Uncle Joe*, witnessed the tremendous pace that The Chieftains work under.

'They're crazy,' she said. 'I'm only 27 and it tired me out. They're very hardy but I couldn't tell you what they're doing to themselves. I think ultimately what keeps them in such good shape is that they really love playing music so much. Their energy is incredible.'

On August 1st Paddy Moloney celebrated his 57th birthday on the road in Austin Texas. He was about to become a grandfather, thanks to his eldest son Aonghus, but showed no signs of slowing down. Among the many projects he was juggling was a piece of music he'd composed as a theme song for Ireland's new world middle-weight boxing champion Steve Collins called *The Celtic Warrior*; his Famine Symphony, assorted movie offers; as well as plans for an all-female Chieftains collaboration; and, a second country album.

'I don't know why I do it,' admitted Moloney in a rare moment of personal reflection. 'I've always been known as a workaholic. The band will tell you that they want me to slow down sometimes. But I have this urge all the time. I wake up in the morning and if the phone isn't ringing I worry. The band is my baby and I have to keep the whole thing ticking on. It's crazy.'

Moloney is so busy with the Chieftains that he is the only member of the band who has not yet made a solo record. Rita has nagged him to do a solo record for more than 20 years and two years ago at their 30th anniversary party Moloney finally got up and promised he would.

'But I didn't say when,' he laughed. 'And I just don't have the time as there are always Chieftains projects on the go.'

His daughter Aedín believes that Moloney's relentless drive comes from a need to succeed.

'My dad still doesn't believe that he's made it,' says Aedín. 'He still doesn't realize that he's one of these legends that people talk about. I don't mean that in a critical way, and I think that where his freshness comes from. That's a real Irish thing as well. It's almost like an insecurity thing as well.

'I think that it's evident that he's always asking guest celebrities on his records. My father doesn't think of himself as a celebrity at all. It's incredible.'

* * *

At the beginning of August Paddy Moloney called up Grateful Dead lead guitarist Jerry Garcia to invite him to appear on the Galician album. This was now called *Santiago* and went on to win a Grammy for Best World Music CD in 1997. Many years earlier Garcia had told Moloney that his father was of Galician descent and his mother Irish. Moloney considered this was the perfect combination for the album.

'Jerry was in the Betty Ford Clinic at the time I was looking for him and it was agreed that he would call me the following Saturday night,' remembers Moloney. 'That evening I started composing the music for a song I wanted him to do. Then something very strange happened. Two hours later I got a call telling me Jerry had died. Weird. Anyway I'm calling it *Jerry's Tune* and we've done it as part of the score on the Galician album as a tribute.'

By the end of August *The Long Black Veil* had sold more than 1.2 million copies worldwide, fast approaching platinum status in the US It had also hit gold in Australia, New Zealand and Canada and double-platinum in Ireland.

On September 9th Paddy Moloney's *Celtic Warror* theme became the Irish battle anthem when Steve Collins retained his WBO super-middleweight crown by beating Englishman Chris Eubank in Cork.

'Steve made his entrance to the ring to the stirring anthem recorded for him by The Chieftains,' wrote *The Irish Sun*, who were offering readers the chance to win a copy of *Celtic Warrior*. 'They said it would send Eubank reeling and they were right.'

The following day Bell joined the rest of The Chieftains to fly to Modena to take part in famed Italian tenor Luciano Pavarotti's annual charity concert to raise money for the children of Bosnia. Princess Diana was the guest of honour and other performers included U2, Michael Bolton and the Cranberries.

'I tried to get Pavarotti to sing *Danny Boy* with us but I didn't quite succeed,' laughs Moloney. 'Eventually we ended up doing *Funiculi, Funicula* which everybody loved. Backstage was like a star's emporium.'

Composer Michael Kamen was rehearsing with The Chieftains

when Martin Fay came running in, stuck a piece of music in front of Derek bell, and asked him to play it.

'It was some impossibly difficult piece of Paganini,' remembers Kamen. 'And Derek looked at it for less than a second and started rattling it off on the keyboard of the piano. Not only with the right hand, as written in the Paganini but he also added an accompaniment with the left. It was one of those mind-blowing pieces that Paganini used to do to entertain the courts of Europe. It was really fast and you could barely play it on a fiddle much less a piano. I mean five fingers and a bow are no match for ten fingers. Derek's unbelievable. That's the first time in my life that I've ever seen that kind of virtuosity. Absolutely stunning and quite scary.'

Kamen, who watched all the stars come up on stage in turn to play with Pavarotti and perform their own sets, says The Chieftains were the one group not trying to out-do everyone else.

'Everyone was working hard to impress and astound,' says Kamen. 'Then The Chieftains walked on stage and they played old Irish tunes and within seconds the audience was eating out of their hands. They just went wild. That music absolutely transforms an audience from observers to participants.'

After their performance Princess Diana came into the backstage area to meet The Chieftains and congratulate them on their performance.

'She was delighted,' says Moloney. 'I spoke to her later at the banquet that night which went on until four in the morning.'

From the banquet The Chieftains got straight on a plane to fly to Oviedo in the north west of Spain to perform with Van Morrison the next night in front of 10,000 fans at an open air concert in the city's bull ring.

'There was a little bit of a party afterwards with our old friend Van,' says Moloney. 'It went on until four in the morning again and we only got a couple of hours sleep before we were off again to Zurich. We went directly on stage without a rehearsal or soundcheck. I'm talking about one or two hours sleep in two nights.'

After Zurich The Chieftains launched into their European tour which took them through Venice, Milan, Turin, Florence and Athens.

After just two weeks break they were off again to Canada to play with the Vancouver and Edmonton Symphony Orchestras where the new Galician Overture was performed for the first time. Then the seemingly indefatigable Chieftains left for a three-week tour to Australia, New Zealand and Japan with Sarah McLachlan and Loreena McKennitt.

* * *

At the dawn of 1996 The Chieftains could look back at their most successful year ever as *Long Black Veil* was named album of the year by both *Time* magazine and the *New York Post* and in the top ten list by *The Los Angeles Times*. *Playboy* readers had also voted The Chieftains as the best live act of the year and four years after its release their Christmas album *The Bells of Dublin* had gone gold in America.

In January The Chieftains received three Grammy nominations: 'Best Pop Collaboration with Vocals' for *Have I Told You Lately That I Love You?* with Van Morrison; 'Best Contemporary Folk Album' for *The Long Black Veil*; and, 'Best Children's Album' for the *Winnie the Pooh* film soundtrack.

Paddy Moloney and Derek Bell travelled to Los Angeles for the Grammy's on February 28 but held out little hope of winning. Moloney felt his only chance of a fourth Grammy was for *Winnie the Pooh* as it didn't seem realistic for traditional music to beat the likes of Michael Jackson, Janet Jackson, Boyz II Men or Mariah Carey in the category of Best Pop Collaboration.

'I just wasn't really listening,' says Moloney. 'I never heard them announce that we'd won and suddenly our manager Sam Feldman was shouting "get up, get up." I had to run up and I forgot all about Derek. I had it all planned what I was going to say, "Well guess where's he's from?" And point to Derek's bright green jumper with the harp on.

'I was standing up there alone totally stunned and flummoxed, as they say in Ireland. The only thing I could think to say was, "Well I come from a little island called Ireland. And this is for the Irish." It got a big cheer.'

The next morning the Irish newspaper were ecstatic with headlines like *Chieftains Beat off Jacksons to capture Grammy*, *Irish Music Heroes Grab the Limelight* and *Whack-ho After Beating Jacko*.

'I was totally amazed when we won in the pop section,' Moloney told *The Sunday Independent*. 'I mean beating Michael Jackson and

Mariah Carey . . . that really is something a bit special. It takes The Chieftains to a new level entirely.'

Epilogue

Two months before the 1996 Grammys, Paddy Moloney turned down an invitation to appear on Irish Television's top-rated *Pat Kenny Show* so he could keep a promise to Seán Potts and visit the Piper's Club in Henrietta Street, Dublin. Word had got out that Paddy Moloney would be there and many young up-and-coming uilleann pipers had come down with the intention of pitting their skills against the master.

'I wasn't looking forward to it because some of those young whipper-snappers are geniuses,' says Moloney, who is the only surviving founder member of the club. 'I just wanted to go in and say hello and maybe sound a note and leave.'

But the fiddle-player Paddy Glackin encouraged Moloney to stay so they could play a few tunes together. Moloney agreed and soon found himself in the first real session he'd been in for many years.

'I was put to the test,' he says. 'And it was a horrifying experience until I started to enjoy myself. I'd rather have done three Carnegie Hall concerts I was so nervous.'

After about an hour of playing Moloney developed a cramp in his right hand as he hadn't played at so fast a pace for a long time. He put away his pipes and was drinking a cup of tea when in walked Seán Keane and his wife Marie. The Chieftain fiddler had just come from Ciarán Mac Mathúna's birthday party and on seeing Moloney at the door he shouted, 'Come on Paddy take out those pipes.'

Paddy Moloney obliged and for the next two hours he played with some of the best young pipers in Dublin.

'The cramp in my right hand went away very quickly,' laughs Moloney. 'I started to play harmonies and counter melodies on pipes between two pipers which is something I haven't done for 25 years. This was a great opportunity to get at it again.

'We were playing traditional music at an enormous pace. Incredible. It was my most brilliant night of music for many years. And I proved to myself that I could still do it.'

The Chieftains Discography
(English/Irish)

The Chieftains – 1963
Claddagh CC2

1. Sé Fáth mo Bhuartha, The Lark on the Strand, An Falain Muimhneach, Trim the Velvet
2. An Comhra Donn, Murphy's Hornpipe
3. Cailin na Gruaige Doinne
4. Comb your Hair and Curl it, The Boys of Ballisodare
5. The Musical Priest, The Queen of May
6. The Walls of Liscarrol
7. An Druimfhionn Dhonn Dílis
8. The Connémara Stocking, The Limestone Rock, Dan Breen's
9. Casadh an tSúgáin
10. The Boy in the Gap
11. St Mary's, Church St Polkas, Garrett Barry's, The Battering Ram, Kitty Goes a-milking, Rakish Paddy

The Chieftains 2 – 1969
Claddagh CC7

1. Banish Misfortune, Gillian's Apples
2. Planxty George Brabazon
3. Bean an Fhit Rua
4. Pis Fhliuch (O'Farrel's Welcome to Limerick)
5. An Páistín Fionn, Mrs Crotty's Reel, The Mountain Top
6. The Foxhunt
7. An Mhaighdean Mhara, Tie the Bonnet, O'Rourke's Reel
8. Callaghan's Hornpipe, Byrne's Hornpipe
9. Pigtown, Tie the Ribbons, The Bag of Potatoes
10. The Humours of Whiskey, Hardiman the Fiddler
11. Donall Óg
12. Brian Boru's March
13. Sweeney's, Denis Murphy's, The Scartaglen Polka

The Chieftains 3 – 1971
Claddagh CC10

1. Strike the Gay Harp, Lord Mayo, The Lady on the Island, The Sailor on the Rock
2. Sonny's Mazurka, Tommy Hunt's Jig

3. Eibhli Gheal Chiún ní Chearbhaill, Delahunty's Hornpipe
4. The Hunter's Purse
5. The March of the King of Laois
6. Carolan's Concerto
7. Tom Billy's, The Road to Lisdoonvarna, The Merry Sisters
8. Ghaoth Aneas
9. Lord Inchiquin
10. The Trip to Sligo
11. An Raibh Tú Ag An gCarraig?
12. John Kelly's Slide, Merrily Kiss the Quaker, Denis Murphy's

The Chieftains 4 – 1974
Claddagh CC14

1. Drowsey Maggie
2. Morgan Magan
3. The Tip of the Whistle
4. The Bucks of Oranmore
5. The Battle of Aughrim
6. The Morning Dew
7. Carrickfergus
8. Hewlett
9. Cherish the Ladies
10. Lord Mayo
11. Mná na hÉireann
12. O'Keeffe's Slide, An Suisin Bán, The Star Abe the Garter, The Weavers

The Chieftains 5 – 1975
Claddagh CC16

1. The Timpán Reel
2. Tabhair Dom Do Lámh (Give Me Your Hand)
3. Three Kerry Polkas
4. Ceol Bhriotánach (Breton Music)
5. The Chieftains Knock at the Door
6. The Robber's Glen
7. An Ghéagus an Grá Geal (The Goose and Bright Love)
8. The Humours of Carolan
9. Samhradh, Samhradh (Summertime, Summertime)
10. The Kerry Slides

Barry Lyndon – 1976
Warner Bros. K56189
Music from the film including tracks by The Chieftains

Bonaparte's Retreat – 1976
Claddagh CC20

1. The Chattering Magpie
2. An Chéad Mháirt den Fhomhar (The First Tuesday of Autumn), Green Grow the Rushes
3. Bonaparte's Retreat
4. Away with Ye

5. Caledonia
6. Inion Nic Diarmada (or the Princess Royal), Máire Dhall (Blind Mary), John Drury
7. The Rights of Man
8. Round the House and Mind the Dresser

The Chieftains 7 – 1977
Claddagh CC24

1. Away we Go Again
2. Dochas
3. Hedigan's Fancy
4. John O'Connor, The Ode to Whiskey
5. Friel's Kitchen
6. No. 6 The Coombe
7. O'Sullivan's March
8. The Ace and Deuce of Pipering
9. The Fairies' Lamentation and Dance
10. Oh! The Breeches Full of Stitches

The Chieftains Live – 1977
Claddagh CC21

1. The Morning Dew
2. George Brabazon
3. Kerry Slides
4. Carrickfergus
5. Carolan's Concerto
6. The Foxhunt
7. Round the House and Mind the Dresser
8. Solos: Càitlin Triall, For the Sakes of Old Decency, Carolan's Fairwell to Music, Banish Misfortune, The Tarbolton/The Pinch of Snuff, The Star of Munster/The Flogging Reel
9. Limerick's Lamentation
10. Ril Mór

The Chieftains 8 – 1978
Claddagh CC29

1. The Session
2. Doctor John Hart
3. Seán sa Cheo
4. An tSean Bhean Bhocht, The Fairies' Hornpipe
5. Sea Image
6. If I had Maggie in the Wood
7. An Speic Seoigheach
8. The Dogs Among the Bushes
9. Miss Hamilton
10. The Job of Journeywork
11. The Wind that Shakes the Barley, The Rell with the Beryle

Boil the Breakfast Early – 1979
Claddagh CC30

1. Boil the Breakfast Early
2. Mrs Judge
3. March from Oscar and Malvina
4. When a Man's in Love
5. Bealach an Doirnin
6. Ag taisteal na Blárnán
7. Carolan's Welcome
8. Up Against the Buachalawns
9. Gol na Mban san Ár
10. Chase around the Windmill

The Chieftains 10 – 1981
Claddagh CC33

1. The Christmas Reel
2. Salut à la Compagnie
3. Kiss Me Kate
4. The Custom Gap, The Spindle Shank, My Love is in America
5. Manx Music
6. Master Crowley's Pride
7. The Pride of Pimlico
8. An Faire
9. An Durzhunel
10. Sir Arthur Shaen, Madame Cole
11. Garech's Wedding
12. Cotton-Eyed Joe

The Year of the French – 1982
Claddagh CC36

With the Radio Telefis Éireann Concert Orchestra

1. Killala: The Main Theme
2. The French March
3. The McCarthy Theme
4. Treacy's Barnyard Dance
5. The Irish March: March of the Mayomen, Uilleann Pipes Lament
6. Killala: The Main Theme
7. Cunla, The Yearling Fair Reel
8. Killala: The Opening Theme, Killala: The Coach Ride
9. The Bolero: McCarthy's Arrest
10. The McCarthy Theme/The Wandering
11. The French March/Cooper's Theme
12. The Hanging/Sean Ó Di
13. Killala: The Main Theme

The Grey Fox – 1984
DRG 9515
Soundtrack

The Chieftains Discography

The Chieftains in China – 1985
Claddagh CC42

1. Full of Joy
2. In a Suzhow Garden
3. If I had Maggie in the Wood
4. The Reason for my Sorrow
5. The Chieftains in China
6. Planxty Irwin
7. Off the Great Wall
8. A Tribute to O'Carolan
9. The Wind from the South
10. China to Hong Kong

The Ballad of the Irish Horse – 1986

1. Ballad of the Irish Horse: Main Theme
2. Going to the Fair (Hornpipe)
3. The Birth of the Foals
4. Galway Races
5. Lady Hemphill
6. Horses of Ireland: Part 1
7. Chasing the Fox
8. The Green Pastures (Jig)
9. Sceal na gCapall: The Story of the Horse
10. The Boyne Hunt, Mullingar Races, The Five Mile Chase (Reels)
11. Horses of Ireland: Part 2

Celtic Wedding – 1987

1. Dans Mod Koh a Vaod (Old-fashioned dance)
2. A Breton Carol
3. Dans Tro Fisel (Dance from the Fisel Country)
4. Marches (From the Vannes Country)
5. Dans Bro-Leon (Dance and Song from the Leon Country)
6. Heuliadenn Tonioù Breizh-Izel (A Medley in which each Member of the Band Plays a tune of his Own Choice)
7. Ev Chistr 'Ta, Laou! (Cider Drinking Song)
8. Jabadaw (Dance from Breton Cornwall)
9. Celtic Wedding (A Medley of Song and Dance describing the Famous Ancient Breton Ceremony)

In Ireland – James Galway and The Chieftains – 1987

1. Roches Favourite (Set Dance)
2. Fanny Power, Mabel Kelly, O'Carolan's Concerto
3. Carrickfergus (Air)
4. Down by the Sally Gardens (Air)
5. Give Me Your Hand
6. She Moved Through the Fair (Flute Solo)
7. The Red Admiral Butterfly (Slip Jig)
8. Danny Boy (Air)
9. Crowley's Reel
10. Tristann and Isolde

11. Alleluia
12. When You and I Were Young, Maggie
13. The Humours of Kilfenora, The Independent (Hornpipes)
14. Avondale (Air)
15. Up and About (Kerry Slides)

Irish Heartbeat – Van Morrison & The Chieftains – 1988

1. Star of the County Down
2. Irish Heartbeat
3. Tá Mo Chleamhnas Déanta
4. Raglan Road
5. She Moved Through the Fair
6. I'll Tell Me Ma
7. Carrickfergus
8. Celtic Ray
9. My Langan Love
10. Marie's Wedding

The Tailor of Gloucester – 1988

With Narration by Meryl Streep

A Chieftains Celebration – 1989

1. O'Mahoney's Frolics
2. Galicia
3. Coolin Medley
4. Here's a Health to the Company (Drinking Song)
5. Planxty Brown, The William Davis's, Lady Wrixon
6. Boffyflow and Spike
7. The Strayaway Child
8. The Iron Man
9. The Wexford Carol
10. Gaftaí Baile Buí
11. Millennium Celtic Suite

Over the Sea to Skye – James Galway & The Chieftains – 1990

1. Carolan's Quarrel with the Landlady
2. Three Hornpipes: Eugene Stratton, The Banks, Arthur Seat
3. Over the Sea to Skye
4. A Slip and Double Jig
5. Cath Ch im an Fhia
6. The Rowan Tree
7. Bonny Prince Charlie
8. Lilibulero
9. The Dark Island
10. Skibbereen
11. A Fanfare
12. The Last Rose of Summer
13. Dance in the Morning Early
14. The Three Sea Captains
15. Full of Joy (Chinese Folk Tune)

16. Solo Salutes – Finale

The Bells of Dublin – 1991

1. The Bells of Dublin (Christmas Eve)
2. Past Three O'Clock w/ The Renaissance Singers
3. St. Stephen's Day Murders w/ Elvis Costello
4. Il Est Né/Ca Berger w/ Kate and Anna McGarrigle
5. Don Oiche Ud I mBeithil w/ Burgess Meredith
6. I Saw Three Ships A Sailing w/ Marianne Faithfull
7. A Breton Carol w/ Nolwen Monjarret
8. Carol Medley: O The Holly She Bears a Berry; 9. God Rest Ye Merry Gentlemen; 10. The Boar's Head
11. The Wexford Carol w/ Nanci Griffith
12. The Rebel Jesus w/ Jackson Browne
13. Jackson's Jig
14. O Holy Night w/ Rickie Lee Jones
15–20. Medley: 'The Wren! The Wren!'; The Arrival of the Wren Boys; The Dingle Set-Dance; The Wren in the Furze; A Dance Duet – Reels; Brafferton Village/ Walsh's Hornpipe; The Farewell: The Piper Through the Meadows Strayed; This is the Season to be Merry
21. Medley: Once in Royal David's City
22. Ding Dong Merrily on High
23. O Come All Ye Faithful

Reel Music: The Film Scores – 1991

Treasure Island
1. Opening Theme
2. Loyals March
3. Island Theme
4. Setting Sail
5. French Leave
6. Blind Pew
7. Treasure Cave
8. The Hispanola/Silver and Loyals March

Barry Lyndon
9. Love Theme

Three Wishes For Jamie
10. Love Theme
11. The Matchmaking
12. Mountain Fall/Main Theme

Tristan and Isolde
13. Love Theme
14. March of the King of Cornwall
15. The Falcon
16. Escape and Chase
17. The Departure

The Grey Fox
18. Main Theme

The Year of the French
19. The French March
20. Cooper's Tune/The Bolero
21. Closing Theme & March

Another Country

1. Happy to Meet
2. I Can't Stop Loving You w/ Don Williams
3. Wabash Cannonball – Morning Dew, Wabash Cannonball, Father Kelly's Reels w/ Ricky Skaggs
4. Heartbreak Hotel – Heartbreak Hotel, The Cliffs of Moher Jig w/ Chet Atkins
5. Goodnight Irene w/ Willie Nelson
6. Cúnla – Cúnla, The Friar's Breeches w/ Colin James
7. Nobody's Darlin' But Mine w/ EmmyLou Harris
8. Cotton-Eyed Joe w/ Ricky Skaggs
9. Tahitian Skies w/ Chet Atkins
10. Killybegs w/ The Nitty Gritty Dirt Band
11. Paddy's Green Shamrock Shore
12. Finale – Did You Ever Go A-Courtin', Uncle Joe, Will the Circle Be Unbroken w/ Ricky Skaggs, EmmyLou Harris, Chet Atkins

Best of The Chieftains – 1992

1. Up Against The Buachalawns
2. Boil The Breakfast Early
3. Friel's Kitchen
4. No. 6 The Coombe
5. O'Sullivan's March
6. Sea Image
7. An Speic Seoigheach
8. The Dogs Among The Bushes
9. The Job of Journeywork
10. Oh! The Breeches Full of Stitches
11. Chase Around The Windmill
12. Toss The Feathers
13. Ballinasloe Fair
14. Cailleach An Airgid
15. Cuil Aodha Slide
16. The Pretty Girl
17. The Wind That Shakes The Barley
18. The Reel With The Beryle

An Irish Evening: Live at the Grand Opera House, Belfast with Roger Daltrey and Nanci Griffith – 1992

1. Opening Medley: a) Dóchas; b) King of Laois; c) Paddy's Jig; d) O'Keffe's/ Chattering Magpie's – Reels
2. North Americay
3. Lilly Bolero/The White Cockade

4. Little Love Affairs w/ Nanci Griffith
5. Red is the Rose w/ Nanci Griffith
6. The Mason's Apron
7. The Stone
8. Miscellany: a) Theme from Tristan and Isolde; b) Súisín Ban; c) Good Morning Nightcap; d) The Galway Races; e) The Jolly Tinker
9. Raglan Road w/ Roger Daltrey
10. Behind Blue Eyes w/ Roger Daltrey
11. Medley: a) Ó Murchú's Hornpipe; b) Sliabh Geal gCua na Feile; c) The Wandering Minstrel
12. Damhsa w/ Dean Butler
13. Rachamid a Bhean Bheag w/ Nanci Griffith and Roger Daltrey

The Magic of The Chieftains – 1992
MCTC 048

1. O'Mahoney's Frolic's
2. Coolin Medley
3. The Wexford Carol
4. Marches
5. Boffyflow and Spike w/ Van Morrison
6. Celtic Wedding
7. Here's a Health to the Company
8. The Strayaway Child
9. The Iron Man Medley: a) The Iron Man; b) The Marquis of Tully Baratine; c) The Forfeit; d) O Da Ship
10. Millennium Celtic Suite
11. Dans Tro Fisel
12. Heuliadenn Toniou Breizh-Izel

The Celtic Harp: A Tribute to Edward Bunting – 1993

1. MacAllistum's March – Máirseail Alasdroim
2. Tribute to Bunting
3. The Parting of Friends – Kerry Fling
4. Planxty Bunting
5. Madame Cole
6. The Blackbird
7. Táimse 'im Chodladh
8. Sonny Brogan's Mazurkas
9. The Wild Geese
10. The Green Fields of America
11. Carolan's Concerto
12. The Lament for Limerick

The Long Black Veil – 1994

1. Mo Ghile Mear – (Our Hero) w/ Sting
2. The Long Black Veil w/ Mick Jagger
3. The Foggy Dew w/ Sinéad O'Connor
4. Have I Told You Lately That I Love You w/ Van Morrison
5. Changing Your Demeanour
6. The Lily of the West w/ Mark Knopfler

317

7. Coast of Malabar w/ Ry Cooder
8. Dunmore Lassies w/ Ry Cooder
9. Love is Teasin' w/ Marianne Faithfull
10. She Moved Through the Fair w/ Sinéad O'Connor
11. Ferny Hill
12. Tennessee Waltz/Tennessee Mazurks w/ Tom Jones
13. The Rocky Road to Dublin w/ The Rolling Stones

Film Cuts – 1995

Rob Roy
1. O'Sullivan's March

Circle of Friends
2. Dublin
3. Air – You're the One

Treasure Island
4. Opening Theme
5. Loyals March
6. Island Theme
7. Setting Sail
8. French Leave
9. Blind Pew
10. Treasure Cave
11. The Hispanola/Silver and Loyals March

Barry Lyndon
12. Love Theme

Tristan And Isolde
13. Love Theme
14. The Falcon
15. The Departure

The Grey Fox
16. Main Theme

Far and Away
17. Fighting for Dough

Ireland Moving
18. Train Sequence

Santiago – 1996
BMG Classics

Pilgrimage to Santiago

1. Txalaparta
2. Arku – Dantza/Arin-Arin
3. El Besu (The Kiss)
4. Nao vas ao mar, Toino (Don't go to the sea, Toino)

5. Dum Paterfamilias/Ad Honorem
6. Dueling Chanters
7. Galician Overture
8. Guadalupe
9. Minho Waltz
10. Setting Sail/Muineira De Frexido
11. Maneo
12. Santiago De Cuba
13. Galleguita/Tutankhamen
14. Tears of Stone
15. Dublin in Vigo

Videos

The Year of The French – 1982
The Chieftains In China – 1985
In Ireland with James Galway – 1987
The Late Late Show Tribute to the Chieftains – 1988
The Bells of Dublin – 1991
An Irish Evening – RCA – 1992
Another Country – RCA – 1992
The Making of The Long Black Veil – 1995

Ceoltóirí Cualann

Reacaireacht an Riadaigh – Gael-Linn, CEF–010, 1962

Ó Riada Sa Gaiety – Gael-Linn, CEF–027, 1964
Re-released Gael-Linn, CEF CD 027, 1988

Seán Ó Ríada and Ceoltóirí Cualann – Gael-Linn, CEF–032, 1971, Mono

The Playboy of the Western World – Gael-Linn CEF–012

Ó Riada's Farewell – Seán Ó Riada – 1971
Claddagh 4CC12 (Produced by Paddy Moloney)

Other Recordings Featuring Members of The Chieftains

The Drones and the Chanter – 1971
Claddagh 4CC11 – Featuring solo tracks by Paddy Moloney

The Castle Ceili Band – 1973
Comhaltas Ceoltóirí Éireann CL5 – Featuring Seán Keane and Michael Tubridy

Tin Whistles – 1975
Claddagh 4CC15 – Paddy Moloney and Seán Potts

Ommadawn – 1975
Virgin VL 12043 – Mike Oldfield with contributions from Paddy Moloney

Gusty's Frolics – 1975
Claddagh 4CC17 – Seán Keane

Claddagh's Receipt – 1975
Claddagh 4CC18 – Derek Bell

The Bothy Band – The First Album – 1975

Mulligan LUN002 – The Bothy Band featuring Matt Molloy

Old Hag You Have Killed Me – 1976
Mulligan LUN007 – The Bothy Band featuring Matt Molloy

Watermark – 1976
CBS JC34975 – Art Garfunkel. The Chieftains featured on tracks

Jig It In Style – 1977
Claddagh 4CCF25 – Seán Keane

Out of the Wind Into the Sun – 1977
Mulligan LUN015 – The Bothy Band featuring Matt Molloy

Matt Molloy, Paul Brady and Tommy Peoples – 1978
Mulligan LUN017

Prosperous – 1978
Tara 1001, Tara 2008 – Christy Moore featuring Kevin Conneff

Afterhours – 1979
Mulligan LUN030 – The Bothy Band featuring Matt Molloy

Roll Away The Reel World – 1980
Green Linnet 1026 – James Keane featuring Seán Keane

Carolan's Favourite – 1980
Claddagh 4CC28 – Derek Bell

Seán Keane – 1981
Ogham Records BLB5005

The Best of the Bothy Band – 1981
Mulligan LUN041 – The Bothy Band featuring Matt Molloy

Derek Bell Plays with Himself – 1981
Claddagh CSM51

Rainclouds – 1981
EMI R6054 – Paul McCartney and Stevie Wonder featuring Paddy Moloney

The Heathery Breeze – 1982
Polydor 2904018 – Matt Molloy

Derek Bell's Musical Ireland – 1982
Claddagh 4CC35

Solofria – 1982
CBS S26395 – By Milladoiro featuring Paddy Moloney

Five Miles Out – 1982
Virgin Records V2222 – Mike Oldfield with contributions from Paddy Moloney

I Can't Stand Still – 1982
Asylum Records 52365 – Don Henley (Track 'La Eile' features Paddy Moloney and Derek Bell)

Matt Molloy – 1984
Green Linnet Records GLCD3008 (with Donal Lunny)

From Singing to Swing – 1984
Ogham Records BLB5008 – Derek Bell

Contentment is Wealth – 1985
Green Linnet SIF1058 – Matt Molloy, Seán Keane and Arty McGly

Stony Steps – 1987
Claddagh 4CCF18 – Matt Molloy

Wild Frontier – 1988
10 Records Limited TENT159B – Gary Moore featuring Paddy Moloney

Primitive Cool – 1988
CBS Sony – Mick Jagger. Paddy Moloney guests on 'Party Doll'

The Week Before Easter – 1988
Claddagh 4CCF23 – Kevin Conneff

The Fire Aflame – 1988
Claddagh 4CCF30 – Matt Molloy, Seán Keane and Liam O'Flynn

Spike – 1989
Warner Bros 25848–2 – Elvis Costello. Derek Bell featured on track 'Any King's Shilling'

Ancient Music for the Irish Harp – 1989
Claddagh 4CC59 – Derek Bell

Far And Away – 1991
MCACD 10628 – Soundtrack featuring The Chieftains

Music At Matt Molloy's – 1992
Real World RWMC26

A Celebration: The Music of Pete Townshend and The Who – 1994
Continuum Records CONC1904

Circle of Friends – 1995
Warner Brothers – Soundtrack

Winnie The Pooh – 1995
Walt Disney Records – Soundtrack

Celtic Christmas – 1995
Windham Hill Records – Featuring Paddy Moloney

The Healing Game – 1997
Exile/Polydor – Van Morrison. Featuring Paddy Moloney on the 'Piper At The Gates of Dawn'

Index

Index

Brogan, Sonny, 42–3, 47
Brown, Jerry, 124
Browne, David, 225
Browne, Garech, 45
  background, 24–5
  and *The Chieftains* album, 53–6, 57
  and Chieftains departure from
    Claddagh, 109–10
  and *Chieftains 5* record cover, 111–12
  and Chinese trip, 191, 192
  and Claddagh Records, 33–4, 69, 89
  designing of record covers, 56, 89–90,
    136
  entertaining by, 64, 66, 67–9, 184
  relationship with Moloney, 23, 26–7,
    32–3, 55, 69, 109, 186
  wedding, 172, 173
Browne, Jackson, 97, 121, 186, 237–8,
  299
Browne, Ronan, 88–9
Bunting, Edward, 3
Butler, Cara, 203, 285
Butler, Jean, 203, 229, 243, 273
Byrne, Gay, 220–1

Cambridge Folk Festival, 79–80
Capitol Fourth, A concert, 300–1
Carolan's Concerto, 12, 82
Carolan's Welcome, 169
Carroll, Patrick, 89
Cassidy, Maurice, 154–5, 235
Castle Ceili Band, 51, 63, 64
CBS Records, 140, 151
Celtic Harp, 3–4, 229, 256–7, 264, 283
Celtic Warrior, The, 302, 303
Celtic Wedding, 209–10, 229
Ceoltóirí Cualann, 42–50, 71
  disbanding of, 75, 76
  formation of by O'Riada, 38, 42–4
  invitation-only sessions by, 44–6
  Keane joins, 64
  music for *Playboy of the Western
    World*, 48–9
  naming of group, 46
  public reaction to, 46
  radio performances, 46–8, 61
Chieftains, The
  acting debut, 177
  appointed official musical
    ambassadors to Ireland, 228–9
  articles on, 72, 89, 95–6, 103, 122, 143,
    154

choice of name, 56
contract with CBS Records, 140, 151
criticism of, 142, 293
decision to go fully professional, 105
departure of Tubridy and Potts,
  152–4
discouragement of drinking before
  performing, 266
earnings, 119, 125
effect of fame, 14
first public performance (1964), 65
formation, 53–6
gruelling work schedule, 167, 257–8,
  290, 302
incorporation of dancing on stage
  shows, 202–3
internal problems, 119–20, 138–9,
  142, 143–4, 146
made honorary chiefs of the
  Oklahoma Choctaw Nation, 294
officially honoured by Mayor of
  Dublin, 231
on-stage humour, 205
performing with orchestras, 202
popularity, 66–7, 81, 114
record deal with Island Records, 109,
  110, 111
recording routine, 150–1
relationship between members, 139,
  142–3, 166–8, 206, 214
relationship with fans, 200
routine, 204
rumours of breaking up, 142
signing with BMG, 210
sponsorship deal with Guinness,
  186–7, 188
success, 142, 198, 246
tax situation, 207
three-year contract with Lustig,
  105–6
three-year management deal with
  Mind Over Management, 270–1
21st birthday concert (1984), 198
25th anniversary celebration, 220–1
web site on Internet, 295
Chieftains, The, 53–8
Chieftains 2, 73–5
Chieftains 3, 81–3
Chieftains 4, 93–6
Chieftains 5, 110–12, 114, 122
Chieftains 7, 110, 145–6
Chieftains 8, 149–51

323

Index

concert at Avery Fisher Hall, 294
and *The Long Black Veil*, 88, 204, 277–8
and Moloney, 66, 71, 104, 203–4
Fallon, Davy, 54–5, 65
Famine Symphony, 280, 288–9, 297
Far and Away, 200, 251–3
Fay, Ann, 38, 39
Fay, Martin, 52–3, 54, 143, 145, 165, 232
and Albert Hall concert, 103–4
on going full-time, 105
joins The Chieftains, 42
leaves The Chieftains, 70
love of travelling, 168
meeting with the Pope, 165–6
musical background, 38–40
and Ó'Riada, 40–1, 42
rejoins The Chieftains, 73
Feehan, Fanny, 95
Festival Records, 109
First Annual Chieftains Music Festival
(1991), 242–3
Fitzgerald, Desmond, 90
Flatley, Michael, 202–3, 212, 271
Fleadh Cheoil an Radio (Festival of the
Radio), 61
fleadhanna cheoil, 15, 24
Fleck, Bela, 251
Flynn, Liam, 157, 161
Flynn, Peadar, 12, 13, 15
Folk News, 142
Folk Roots, 230–1
Foxhunt, The, 74
Frame, Roddy, 242
Fuller, Bill, 51–2, 70, 157

Gael Linn Cabaret, 52, 70–1
Galician album *see Santiago*
Galician Overture, 296, 305
Galway, James, 178, 179
first collaboration, 213–14
second collaboration, 231–2
Garcia, Jerry, 96–7, 303
Gardiner, John Joe, 158
Garfunkel, Art, 125–6
Gebler-Davis, Stan, 175
Gibson, Mel, 298
Glackin, Paddy, 307
Golden Folk, The, 37–8, 41
Good Morning America show, 169
Graham, Bill, 96
Grammy awards, 229
(1993), 259, 264–6

(1994), 4, 283
(1996), 305–6
(1997), 303
Grateful Dead, The, 96
Great Music Experience, The (Japan),
281–2, 284–6
Greene, Clara, 62, 63
Grey Fox, The, 197
Griffith, Nanci, 174, 226–7, 243–4, 254
Guinness, Desmond and Mariga, 110,
176
Guinness sponsorship deal, 186–7, 188
Gunderson, Edna, 292

Hagman, Larry, 201
Hall, Jerry, 240, 241
Happy Wanderers, The, 21
Harris, Richard, 229, 288
Henderson, Hamish, 82
Henley, Don, 97, 121–2
wedding, xiv, 297, 299–300
Hibernia, 95
Hickey, James, 243
Hochman, Steve, 255
Hollander, Xaviera, 175
Hollingsworth, Tony, 234–5, 281, 284,
285
Hollywood Bowl, 271
Hong Kong tour, 196
Hot Press, 142, 177, 207, 223
Howard, Ron, 200, 251, 252
Hudson, Garth, 124
Hurt, John, 68–9, 80
Huston, Anjelica, 80, 182, 183, 271
Huston, John, 80, 114, 212
Hyland, Christy, 230

Ibbotson, Jimmy, 247–8, 251
India, 260–3
Ireland Moving, 94
Irish Arts Theater (New York), 83–4
Irish Ballet Company, 146–7, 152
Irish Echo, 212
Irish Evening, An, 243–4, 246
album, 255, 259, 265
concert at Universal Amphitheater,
254–5
Irish Heartbeat, xvii, 217, 218–20, 223,
224, 229
Irish Times, The, 34, 50, 116–17, 119,
148–9, 283–4
Irish traditional music, 4, 14, 25, 52, 83

Index

Pope
  Papal Mass concert at Phoenix Park, 11, 163–5, 169
  private audience with The Chieftains, 165
Potts, Bernie, 139
Potts, John, 18
Potts, Seán, 12, 51, 54, 56, 143–4
  Albert Hall concert, 104
  and Ceoltóirí Cualann, 42, 43
  Chieftains 7 contribution, 145
  decision to leave band, 153, 154
  disappearance of tin whistle, 137–8
  Gael Linn contract, 70–1
  on going full-time, 106
  leaves and rejoins, 70–1, 73
  musical background, 18–19
  plays in Moloney's groups, 27–8, 52
  relationship with Moloney, 19, 138–9
  Tin Whistles, 98
  and United States tours, 124
Potts, Tommy, 88
Pretty, Pat, 100, 142
Pumpkinhead, 97

Radio Éireann, 25, 28–9, 36, 47, 61, 96
Rampling, Charlotte, 101
RCA, 213, 258
Reel Music, 235
Reidy, John *see* Ó Riada, Sean,
Reidy, Julia, 36
reviews *see* albums; concerts; tours
Richards, Keith, 66, 274
Ritz Hotel, 203
Riverdance, 203
Rob Roy, 295
Robinson, Mary, 289
Roche, Kevin, 46–7
Rolling Stone, 122, 170, 225, 239, 292
Rolling Stones, The, 66, 273, 274
  birthday party, 240–1, 272
  open air concert at Slane Castle, 184–6
Ronstadt, Linda, 124
Rosenman, Leonard, 124
Rowsome, Leo, 9, 10, 11, 14, 15, 20, 24, 33, 34, 137
Royal Albert Hall *see* Albert Hall
Royal Festival Hall concert, 123
RTE Symphony Orchestra, 176, 177
Ryan, Richard, 136

Santiago (Galician album), 124, 295–7, 303
Sellars, Peter, 94–5, 170–1
Sgt. Early's Dream, 257
Shannonside Ceili Band, 20
Sharkey, Feargal, 242–3
Sheng, Sun, 195
Skaggs, Ricky, 94, 249–50, 301
Slevin, Mick, 202
Smith, Pete, 149, 234, 235, 236, 259–60, 270
St Patrick Day concerts (New York), 146, 169, 229, 283, 294
St Patrick Day Special (Dublin), 84–5, 87
Steffi (Bell's girlfriend), 163, 166
Stewart, Al, 149
Sting, 176, 286–8
Stivel, Alan, 48
Stokes, Geoffrey, 118
Strauss, Neil, 292–3
Summertime, Summertime, 110–11
Swenson, John, 292

Tahitian Skies, 264
Tailor of Gloucester, The, 224–5
television appearances, xiii–xiv, xv–xvii, 84–5, 169, 220–1, 243–4, 253, 254, 263, 294, 297, 298, 300
Tennessee Waltz, The, 264, 268, 269–70
Texas tour, 173–4
Theodorakis, Mikis, 37
Thompson, Ken, 73
Three Squares, The, 21
Time, 122, 295, 305
Times, The, 75
Tin Whistles, 98
Tindall, Charlie, 20–1
Tom Jones Show, The, 253
Tongue, Alan, 84
Tonight Show with Jay Leno, 254
'Tour de Clare, The', 22–3
tours, 204, 304–5
  Australian, 126–7, 196, 231
  Brittany (1985), 211
  China (1983), 189–96, 207
  European, 221–2, 224, 304
  Hong Kong (1983), 196
  Japanese, 286
  relationship between members on, 139, 166–7, 206, 214
  reviews, 115, 117–18, 170

330

Index

United Kingdom, 112, 115, 137
United States *see* United States
and wives, 139–40
world, 119
Tracey, Larry, 27
Tradition Club, 132–3, 158
Traditional Irish Christmas Show, 178–9,
   211–12
Treasure Island, 232, 233
Trip to Sligo, A, 82
Tristan and Isolde, 169
Tubridy, Michael, 54, 84, 127, 139, 143–4
   Chieftains 7 contribution, 145
   difficulty in early commitment to
     band, 80
   leaves band, 152–3
   in Moloney's early band, 19, 20
   musical background, 17–18
   stage fright, 152
   tour of Clare 22–3
Two if By Sea, 300

Uilleann Piper's Association, 129
uilleann pipes, 10
Ulster Television, 243
Ultravox, 227–8
United States
   Avery Fisher Hall concert, 294
   cancelling of summer tour, 140
   Capitol Fourth concert, 294
   concert in the Capitol Building, 187
   concert at Hollywood Bowl, 271
   first full-scale tour (1975), 115, 116–19
   first major tour (1974), 92, 96–7
   first trip and concert (1972), 82–4
   Hollywood, 200–1
   Irish Evening concert, 255–6
   loyalty of fans, 200
   Northern tour (1979), 153
   Northern tour (1980), 170
   popularity and success in, 119, 124
   second major tour (1976), 123, 124–5

St Patrick Day concerts, 146, 169, 229,
   283, 294
Summer 'Shed' tour with Sarah
   McLachlan, 301–2
television appearances, 169, 254, 294,
   300
Texas tour, 173–4
tour with Galway (1986), 214
tours, 137–8, 155, 166, 204, 229
Traditional Irish Christmas Show,
   178–9, 211–12
Ure, Midge, 227, 228, 243
U2, 143, 259, 268, 289

Van Morrison *see* Morrison, Van
Variety, 118, 214, 255
Vedder, Eddie, 279–80
Village Voice, 118
Vining, Steve, 255, 259, 260, 271, 295
Virgin, Claude, 82

Walsh, Anne, 19, 20, 22
Ward, Jimmy, 23
Watermark, 125–6
Waters, Roger, 234
Watts, Charlie, 185
Week Before Easter, The, 229
Welborn, Tessa, 55–6, 57
Welch, Chris, 113, 123
Wexford festival, 72
Who, The, 279–80
Wilkin, Marijohn, 293
Williams, Don, 250
Williams, John, 252
Winnie the Pooh, xv, 300, 305
Woodtown Music Publications, 75
World Cup, 288

Year of the French, The, 176–7

Zappa, Frank, 255–7, 260, 268–9, 275–6
Zappa, Gail, 256–7, 260, 270, 275, 276

331